D0115953

Structuring an Energy Technology Revolution

Structuring an Energy Technology Revolution

Charles Weiss and William B. Bonvillian

The MIT Press
Cambridge, Massachusetts
London, England

© 2009 Massachusetts Institute of Technology

All rights reserved. No part of this book may be reproduced in any form by any electronic or mechanical means (including photocopying, recording, or information storage and retrieval) without permission in writing from the publisher.

For information about special quantity discounts, please e-mail special_sales@mitpress.mit.edu

This book was set in Sabon by SNP Best-set Typesetter Ltd., Hong Kong. Printed and bound in the United States of America.

Library of Congress Cataloging-in-Publication Data

Weiss, Charles.
Structuring an energy technology revolution / Charles Weiss and William B. Bonvillian.
    p.   cm.
Includes bibliographical references and index.
ISBN 978-0-262-01294-2 (hardcover : alk. paper)
1. Renewable energy sources—Research—Government policy—United States. 2. Energy policy—United States. 3. Federal aid to research—United States. I. Bonvillian, William. II. Title.
TJ807.9.U6W45   2009
333.790973—dc23

                                                    2008043059

10 9 8 7 6 5 4 3 2 1

Contents

Preface

In this book, we argue that a major supply-side program to stimulate innovation in energy technology is needed to complement a demand-side carbon tax or cap-and-trade scheme. Such a program can be launched now while further political support is developing for demand-side measures. It should go well beyond research and development to include measures to encourage prototyping, demonstration, and deployment of a wide range of technology options faster than could be accomplished by market forces alone. It should replace the varied subsidies to specific existing technologies that are anticipated to be the beneficiaries of recent and pending Congressional legislation. This "no lobbyist left behind" approach is likely to cement in currently available technology at precisely the moment when we should be launching ambitious research programs to develop and deploy imaginative new ideas, and laying the policy framework for a more level playing field on which many alternative technologies compete on their merits.

The book formulates an integrated policy framework for advancing new energy technology, building on existing innovation theory. In a new, four-step analytic approach, we first assess numerous promising groups of energy technologies, classifying them according to the likely obstacles to their launch. Second, for each of these launch classes, we develop technology-neutral packages of policies and incentives appropriate for their launch. This analysis leads to the third step, the identification of gaps in the existing U.S. framework for stimulating innovation. In the last step, we propose three institutional innovations to fill these gaps: a new translational research projects agency for energy to identify innovation challenges and nurture the breakthroughs needed to meet them; a government corporation for the financing of demonstration projects, manufacturing scale-up, and conservation investments; and a roadmapping think tank for technology assessment and policy research. All of these fit into a new innovation strategy for energy.

This book is thus different from other approaches to the nation's energy challenges. The authors study and teach in the relatively new field of science, technology, and innovation policy, drawing on their prior career experience working in this area at the World Bank and in the U.S. Senate, respectively. This book aims to bring a new approach to innovation theory to what the authors believe is the most important and complex innovation implementation challenge the United States has ever faced, the challenge of launching new energy technology. We do not promote particular technologies, but instead propose a template for a new energy technology strategy, against which technology proposals can be judged. The 2008 presidential campaign produced proposals for substantial increases in spending on energy technology and innovation, but with limited detail on how that effort was to be carried out. Such implementation mechanisms form the heart of this book. Our aim is to set forth a new integrated framework for the encouragement of innovation in energy technology. We do not pretend to offer definitive solutions but hope to stimulate further evaluations along the lines we set forth because we believe that without a sound policy framework in this area we will not succeed. While the current economic decline will likely stall progress on clean energy technology in the private sector, the agenda proposed here of investment in energy research, demonstration, and implementation could be a Keynesian spur to the economy.

We are indebted to a number of colleagues who have helped facilitate this project. At Georgetown, we have appreciated ongoing policy exchanges with Carl Dahlman and Nate Hultman (now at the University of Maryland). At MIT, we have appreciated policy exchanges over time with Richard Lester, Ernst Moniz, Denny Ellerman, and Henry Jacoby. We are especially indebted for perspectives on particular technologies to MIT faculty and researchers Yet-Ming Chiang, Howard Herzog, Jefferson Tester, Kristala Jones Prather, Gorbrand Cedar, Valdimir Bulovic, Daniel Cohn, and James Katzer, some of whom kindly reviewed particular technology discussions in the book, as we have acknowledged in the notes. We have also appreciated the advice on innovation policy and on energy technology that we have received from the late Vernon Ruttan and from Henry Kelly, respectively. We thank Kent Hughes for sponsoring an early presentation of the ideas in this book at a Woodrow Wilson Center forum, and Susan Cozzens and Georgia Tech for giving us the opportunity to present these ideas to the Atlanta Conference on Science, Technology and Innovation Policy. We also thank our anonymous content reviewers for the general comments they provided. In addition, we thank our research assistants Eric Mooney, Edward Parker, and Argyro Kawado. Finally, we thank Clay Morgan at the MIT Press for his confidence in the value and utility of this work, and Sandra Minkkinen and Elizabeth Judd for their help in editing and preparing the final text.

We have greatly appreciated the support, patience, and understanding of our families during our research and writing.

1

Introduction

The environmental and geopolitical costs of America's addiction to fossil fuels make a federal program to stimulate innovation in energy technology both justifiable and essential. Such a technology supply-side program should be accompanied by policies that ensure long-term, sustained high prices for emission of carbon dioxide into the atmosphere—for example, a carbon tax or a cap-and-trade system, as well as regulatory standards and other measures to foster demand for more efficient overall energy use. But market forces alone cannot provide the pace and scope of innovations required to meet the urgent national need for improved technology for energy supply and efficient end use, and to overcome the huge built-in preferences for existing energy technologies.[1]

Our current technology supply-side efforts consist of underfunded research with an occasional tax incentive or regulatory mandate thrown in. There has been much talk and consensus about the need to introduce new energy technologies but few concrete proposals on how to actually get them into the marketplace at the scale required. Even climate change legislation now before the Congress calls for significant subsidies to existing alternatives to fossil fuels but only small sums for research, development, and deployment of the many new ideas now in active development in commercial and university laboratories.

This book gets inside the "black box" of energy innovation, looking at it as a system, and proposes answers to the problem of encouraging and stimulating the implementation of improved energy technology that has thus far eluded our political system. Given the central role of energy in the economy, a program to stimulate technological innovation in energy will need to approach the dimensions of a major military transformational effort. It must go beyond research and development (R&D) to include all aspects of the innovation process. No single technology or "silver bullet" will suffice; we will need an expanded set of options made possible by a broad range of new technology entrants.

As a working foundation for that program, we propose a new integrated analytic framework, drawing on current innovation theory, as a basis for developing technology policy for energy and comparable complex economic sectors. From that base, we set forth a new, four-step framework for the development of policy to encourage energy innovations. First, we assess energy technologies, not only for their present status and likely future development, but most importantly for the obstacles they are most likely to encounter when they eventually enter the highly competitive marketplace for energy technology. We use these assessments to categorize energy innovations according to the issues they will probably face as they are launched. Second, for each launch path, we define packages of relatively neutral policy measures, from R&D incentives to regulatory measures, designed both to bridge the "valley of death" between research and late-stage development that historically has been the most important barrier to the deployment of civilian technology, and more significantly in our view, to surmount the barriers to the implementation of technology. Third, based on this analysis, we identify several functional gaps in the present system of government institutional support for energy innovation that will hinder our ability to achieve steps 1 and 2. Fourth, we propose public-and private-sector interventions to fill these gaps. This conceptual framework may be applicable to other complex innovation system areas in addition to energy.

Another, equally important problem is the deep politicization of energy policy in the United States. For decades, the environmental wing of American politics, now tied to the political left, has urged subsidies to renewable energy—specifically to sun and wind, with notable neglect of geothermal energy. The right has been no less enthusiastic in its support of subsidies to oil, natural gas, and nuclear energy. The coal and oil industries, moreover, are protected by the congressional delegations in key states where they provide employment. Reflecting these pressures, plus a long regulatory history, the role of the government in the energy sector has long been intense and interventionist. Despite growing geopolitical and climate realities, a balanced, technology-neutral approach to energy policy has not been attempted by either political party. Today, a coherent approach to energy technology policy is still missing from the legislative policy debate in the U.S. Congress; each technology, new and old, seeks its own separate legislative deal for federal backing.

Even in the abstract, to be sure, the idea of technology neutrality has an inescapable limitation, namely, that of the choice of objective. Politics aside, a technology strategy intended to end dependence on oil from foreign sources will differ in important ways from one intended to mitigate global warming by reducing emission of carbon dioxide. To briefly summarize this now highly visible fault line in American politics, both of these approaches will favor renewable domestic sources of energy like wind, solar, and geothermal. But a policy focused exclusively on self-sufficiency in fuels for the transport sector will emphasize domestic sources, carbon-emitting or otherwise. A policy intended to limit emission of carbon dioxide and other forms of environmental damage must stress lowering carbon emissions by all appropriate means, predominantly through new technologies in addition to efficiency and conservation. Fortunately, there remains substantial overlap—the need for new technology—between the two positions.

Since the political system on all sides is now contemplating a major shift on energy policy, are the technologies we need already here? The dominant theme in much of the energy policy literature—especially by analysts inspired by the environmental costs of present patterns of energy use—has been the critical importance of carbon charges in directing the demand for energy and energy technology toward "carbon-free" sources. In response, some industry advocates have argued that carbon charges must be delayed because any major change in energy-use patterns will require breakthroughs in technology that will take time to achieve.

To forestall such criticism, other analysts have pointed to technologies that are at or near the point of readiness for full-scale exploitation and that, taken together, could stabilize atmospheric CO_2 concentrations, so that there is no need to wait for technological breakthroughs for this purpose. In a classic article, Socolow and Pacala have identified fifteen "wedges"—changes in energy use based on technologies said to be either at or near technoeconomic readiness, any seven of which, taken together, would suffice to stabilize CO_2 concentrations by midcentury.[2] Some of these changes are clearly within the range of adoption and timely scale-up. Others—reduced deforestation, a 50 percent reduction in driving by two billion vehicles, or widespread adoption of conservation tillage, for example—would, as the two authors recognize, require major changes in policy and behavior that could take extended periods. Still others, like technology for carbon capture and sequestration, are likely to take years of development and demonstration before they are ready for widespread deployment.

Other policy analyses of climate change and energy security recommend a major effort to effect new technology, although this recommendation often comes almost as an afterthought after a long discussion of carbon charges.[3] (As summarized in chapter 5, the relatively few analyses specifically concerned with energy R&D typically recommend large increases, but most of these reach more specialized audiences.) The Intergovernmental Panel on Climate Change (IPCC), for example, concurs that a portfolio of new technologies can yield CO_2 stabilization, "assuming appropriate and effective incentives are in place for their development, acquisition, deployment and diffusion and addressing related barriers."[4] Beyond this assertion, the processes by which the technologies might be developed, deployed, and diffused have been left largely unstudied.

In sum, technological alternatives to fossil fuels do exist or can be realized.[5] But few are technically or economically ready for deployment on the huge scale needed to make a dent in the demand for fossil fuels. Some are operating on a limited commercial scale, while others now exist only in the laboratory. To cite a few examples of what we can see today, solar photovoltaics are still too expensive, carbon capture and sequestration require prototyping and validation at a huge scale, batteries must realize further materials and cost advances, and fuel cells for transport applications face years of experimentation. Aside from the major research needed to keep rolling out advances for these technologies to cut costs and improve efficiencies, there is a need for ongoing research to seek breakthroughs, especially if we decide we need to go beyond stabilizing the carbon dioxide concentration in the atmosphere at current levels by midcentury. For example, two recent economic evaluations have called for reductions from

1990 levels from 25 percent to 60–80 percent,[6] and the G-8 nations agreed in principle in July 2008 to halve greenhouse gas emissions by midcentury from current levels.[7]

Taken together, these technologies will still require massive investment, involving extensive collaboration between business, government, and universities.[8] What is more, the requirements for the development and deployment of these technologies on a scale sufficient to address the problem of global warming, not to mention the economic and geopolitical costs of dependence on foreign oil, amount to no less than a new *technological/economic/political paradigm* for energy.[9] This new paradigm will involve new technologies backed by policies, regulations, incentives, technology institutions, and public understanding and support. This vast and varied array of new technology will take many decades and many generations of technical innovation to evolve and be adopted on the necessary scale.[10] It would be a serious mistake to concentrate exclusively on short-term technological solutions to the neglect of these more far-reaching approaches.

The problem of climate change is global, so that the new paradigm will need to be global. Even so, technology advance still largely follows a nation-state model.[11] Although multinational corporations are moving the development stage toward international collaboration, other key features of innovation systems, such as research funding, science and technical education, and publicly funded research institutions, remain rooted in national funding and support.[12] The U.S. innovation system has led world technology waves for many decades,[13] and despite the rapid rise of capabilities in other countries, there is no easy substitute for its technology leadership in this arena.[14] There is a trade-off between the need to share technology in order to work together to meet a common danger and to benefit from the exchange of knowledge, on the one hand, and the need to provide incentives to industry to gain competitive advantage through innovation and capacity building, on the other. The United States should keep in mind, too, that the economic advantages of leadership in technology have been the source of its wealth and well-being. Is it really in America's interest to cede leadership of a technological revolution in energy to other countries that now also understand the innovation-based growth model?

Demand-Side Measures by Themselves Will Be Insufficient

Private investment in research on alternatives to fossil fuels is discouraged by the history of wild oscillations in the price of energy. A barrel of oil may cost about $60 as these words are written in the fall of 2008, but it cost more than $140 in the summer of 2008 and less than $20 in 1998.[15] If energy companies were convinced that $100-a-barrel oil were here to stay, some would see the long-term business wisdom of major investments to diversify their raw materials and their technologies, despite their current high profit levels. As things now stand, however, many of them remain opposed, skeptical, or at best ambivalent. Yet there are clear indications that, unlike the price spike induced by the oil embargo of the 1970s, increasing energy prices are predominantly due to a significant rise in world demand from developed and particularly emerging economies.[16]

Here we distinguish between the demand for energy itself, and the demand for improved energy technology. The two are related but are not the same. In the short term, carbon charges or high energy prices will reduce the immediate demand for fossil fuels or energy, respectively. Demand for improved or alternative energy technology, on the other hand, will be created only if these prices are seen as likely to be sustained. We may similarly distinguish between the supply of energy technology and the supply of energy itself; our focus is on the former.

The single policy that would be most effective in stimulating such research, then, would be a sustained policy that stimulates demand for both energy conservation and energy technology. This could come about by ensuring either the high energy prices[17] supported by some focused on energy security, or a high cost of carbon dioxide (and other greenhouse gas) emissions supported by those focused on climate change, or both, for the next few decades[18]—the latter either through a direct carbon tax[19] on CO_2 emissions (known in the literature as a "carbon charge") or equivalently, through a cap-and-trade scheme. The political consensus needed to support at least cap-and-trade policies is stirring and could be reached in the next few years.[20] However, as we will see in later chapters, there is a real possibility of adopting a deeply flawed system because of political pressures from various interest groups.[21]

Even with such energy prices or carbon charges, private capital will not suffice to stimulate technological innovation without major public support.[22] As economist Jeffrey Sachs has noted,

Technology policy lies at the core of the climate change challenge. Even with a cutback in wasteful energy spending, our current technologies cannot support both a decline in carbon dioxide emissions and an expanding global economy. If we try to restrain emissions without a fundamentally new set of technologies, we will end up stifling economic growth, including the development prospects for billions of people. Economists often talk as though putting a price on carbon emissions through tradable permits or a carbon tax will be enough to deliver the needed reductions in those emissions. This is not true. . . . We will need much more than a price on carbon. Consider three potentially transformative low-emissions technologies: carbon capture and sequestration (CCS), plug-in hybrid automobiles and concentrated solar-thermal electricity generation. Each will require a combination of factors to succeed: more applied scientific research, important regulatory changes, appropriate infrastructure, public acceptance and early high-cost investments. A failure on one or more of these points could kill the technologies.[23]

An innovation system must be stimulated by market demand for improved technology, but workable policies to stimulate this demand still presuppose a strong innovation system. What is more, most new energy technologies face a dense network of political traps in the United States because of the huge scale of deployment required, because of the deeply entrenched, price-efficient competitors, and because of the economic interests, policies, and public attitudes that support the old, fossil-fuel-based paradigm.

Ideally, then, economics and technology would develop together. Major supply-side technology development programs would be coupled with policies that create a demand pull for improved energy technology through assured, sustained, high carbon energy prices, incentives for conservation and for the entry of new energy sources, and penalties for wasteful use. This mix would feature public-sector investment leveraging private capital at scale and vice versa.

Presidents since the 1970s have been calling for U.S. energy security, but the record on this issue constitutes one of the greatest public policy failures in our history. Part of this story is the level of investment. Federal support for energy R&D has fallen by more than half since a high point in 1980, and private-sector energy R&D has similarly fallen. These levels of expenditure compare poorly to other major federal R&D efforts that met challenges of similar magnitude: the Manhattan Project, the Apollo Project, the Carter-Reagan defense buildup, and the doubling of the budget of the National Institutes of Health.[24] Advances in energy technology will not occur on the scale required without significantly increased investment by both government and business.

We are optimistic that a public consensus in favor of policies creating a demand for technological innovation will in fact take shape. In the meantime, can we begin to create a new paradigm? If such policies are to elude us for a time, can we at least start down available pathways for R&D and put as many technology supply-oriented policies in place as possible in accordance with a coherent strategy? Regardless of when a technology demand-side program is initially imposed, developing a sound innovation system for energy technology will show industry that the transition to alternative energy technologies is feasible, not the pie in the sky they fear, and in this way will help to defuse political opposition to the sound demand-oriented policies that will also be needed to effect the needed energy transition.

A supply-side technology development strategy for energy would have to be structured quite differently from government-led technology development projects like the Manhattan Project or the Apollo Moon Mission. These projects developed and implemented single-focus technologies in comparatively short-term projects for the government, a single customer with deep pockets. They were managed and executed by unified organizations within the federal government. Energy challenges require a very different development model, in which a complex mix of energy technologies must evolve over decades in the private sector. Given the complexity and unpredictability of this evolution, the resulting innovation system should be technology-neutral to the extent possible.

This is perhaps the most complex technology evolution problem the United States has ever faced. It makes getting to the moon start to look simple by comparison. A coherent strategy will be vital; we aim in this work to begin a discussion of the elements that will be required in such a strategy. Different "front-end" research, development, and demonstration policies, and different sets of "back-end" incentives and, in some cases, regulatory mandates, for implementation and deployment will be needed at different times for different kinds of technology. These policies will depend on the present state of development of the technology, the likely path by which it will be launched into the marketplace, the level of economic competition and political opposition it is likely to stimulate, and the availability of a sound, complementary demand-side pricing system.

Public intervention should spur and support the private sector, with the objective of speeding the development and deployment of a broad range of future energy technology options considerably faster than would be expected from market forces alone. While it is impossible to say which of the many promising energy technologies will come to full fruition, a conservative list would include: fully competitive technology for the production of electricity from wind and sun, plug-in hybrid cars with performance and range comparable to those of contemporary cars but with several times the gas mileage; a "smart grid" that is both far more efficient and can accommodate renewables; reliable and well-characterized technology for enhanced geothermal energy and for carbon capture and sequestration; lighting technologies with twice the efficiency of present-day fluorescent lights; dramatically more efficient buildings, new nuclear technologies if waste storage, safety, diversion, and proliferation issues can be satisfied; and improved manufacturing technologies for a wide variety of energy technologies to lower costs and improve quality.

There will be some who argue from a market economics perspective that a cap-and-trade policy or carbon tax will internalize carbon externalities, while high energy prices will discourage energy use, so that demand pull will be enough to foster new technologies. We believe this fails to fully take into account the realities of the government's extensive intervention underwriting the existing system, and the need to accelerate the pace of technology introduction. An old story about the economics profession is relevant here. A bus is traveling along the California coast packed with neoclassical economists attending a convention. They are accompanied by one reporter. Suddenly, the bus crashes through the guardrail over a 300-foot cliff toward the sea. The reporter starts screaming, but the economists are all silent. The reporter asks the economist seated next to him why he and his colleagues are not screaming since death is imminent. The economist responds, "My friend, there is so much pent-up demand that a parachute will appear."

This book argues that someone should be working on the parachute to feed the pent-up demand. It seeks a strategy for parachute creation and implementation.

2
An Integrated Innovation Policy Model for Energy Technology

Policy support for innovation in energy technology in the United States requires a new approach to the stimulation of innovation that differs in important ways from the traditional American approach to the support of science and technology, and differs even more radically from the pattern of support for energy technology that has dominated U.S. legislation in the past few years. For this reason, the design of government programs to stimulate innovation in energy technology requires a new analytic framework quite different from the one that has historically guided American innovation policy. Without a new analytic innovation framework, our energy technology policies cannot be optimal at a time when we should not risk suboptimal "muddle-through" policies.

First of all, and assuming for the moment that there will eventually be a cap-and-trade or other policy to limit carbon dioxide emissions and encourage energy conservation, innovations in energy technology are likely to be influenced in two fundamental directions. Energy innovations will be both pulled into the market by the new economic and policy environment (*market* or *demand pull*) and pushed by the dynamic of advances in science and technology (*technology push*).[1] Either way, they will face intense competition from well-entrenched legacy technologies based on fossil fuels, whose mature market position will still be reinforced by a formidable array of subsidies backed by powerful political forces and substantial public support. In such a situation, the most important obstacle to innovation—that is, to the widespread adoption of a new energy technology—is at least as likely to come at the moment of market launch as in the space between the research and development stages, which makes energy a different problem for our innovation system than others we have been confronting in recent decades. Policies that encourage such innovation must be designed to overcome these obstacles and to foresee them if possible.

The second difference lies in the fact that there are a multitude of energy technologies that have been neglected in the economic and policy environment of the last twenty years. These should now be given a chance to emerge, but they present a menu of options. No single technology has any special claim on support. This means that our innovation policies need to be as technology neutral as possible so as to create a level playing field. A level playing field should allow technological alternatives to compete on their technoeconomic merits in order to produce an optimum mix of future technological options.

This idea of a level playing field has the added advantage that it will maximize the value of some new energy technologies as enabling technologies—that is, as technologies that stimulate innovation in other areas, much as the revolution in information technology (IT) has revolutionized technology in the service sector, in manufacturing, and in many other fields.[2] It is in sharp contrast to the approach now dominant in Washington, which is to subsidize the deployment of specific technologies at their current state of readiness, in proportion to the strength of their respective lobbies—an approach likely to stifle innovation outside the very specific fields in which technology is being supported.

The third difference lies in the fact that the assumption that the private sector will take up innovative technology quickly may be of questionable validity in the energy sector. This is because, as discussed further below, most new energy technologies do not introduce new functionality at least in their initial stages; in the jargon, they are largely secondary or incremental innovations, as opposed to radical innovations,[3] and must therefore compete on price and quality from the beginning with existing technologies that are efficient, cheap (if environmental and geopolitical externalities are excluded), and deeply rooted in the economic and political structure. Even if they do succeed, these new technologies face the implied, and perhaps the actual threat of predatory competition from long-established, wealthy, and powerful companies.

For these reasons, most new energy technologies face a more difficult challenge than innovations in, say, the IT industry. The latter have typically been radical innovations that introduced new functionality, faced no immediate direct competition, and in most cases could be shaped to fit a relatively straightforward policy framework and regulatory system. These technologies landed in relatively open fields. Energy technologies, in contrast, will parachute into occupied territory, with highly cost-efficient and subsidized legacy technological competitors waiting, ready to open fire. This landscape could be characterized as an "anti-commons."[4] There will be exceptions to this generalization, most notably potentially disruptive energy technologies like solar photovoltaics and lighting LEDs that can withstand such competition by gaining a foothold in specialty market niches and gradually expanding. Some other new technologies, like improved batteries and fuel cells, will gain access to markets in the form of components of standard products or established systems or platforms, with well-established dominant designs.[5] These may well be accepted by the firms that control the platforms or systems that they will serve.

Technologies like biofuels and carbon capture and sequestration are also secondary technologies, components to established energy platforms or systems. However, they face immediate political and nonmarket economic competition from established firms that are not likely to accept them. They will require attention to all stages of the innovative process, from research to development to prototyping to demonstration to incentives for market entry. Their implementation will be unlikely without some form of government regulation or mandate.

In sum, a major government program supporting energy innovation is essential. Private investment is critically important, but will not be able to meet the need in the absence of a large-scale program of support, tailored to the particular circumstances of the energy sector. A full exposition of this argument requires an understanding of the theory of innovation as it has been developed by the economics profession and the emerging field of science and technology policy; it also requires a reworking of this theory for the situation of the energy sector and potentially of other complex sectors.

Three Theories of Innovation

A major purpose of a national science and technology policy is to compensate for the imperfections in the market for technological innovation. The design of such a policy therefore depends, at least in principle, on a clear concept of how technological innovation takes place in response to market forces, and how this process can be influenced by public policy. In this chapter, we briefly explore three such concepts, each of which is the product of a particular historical period.

The first of these concepts is the so-called linear or pipeline model, associated with Vannevar Bush, in which basic research intended to push back the frontiers of knowledge leads to applied research, which in turn leads to invention, to prototyping, to development, and finally to innovation, by which we mean widespread commercialization or deployment. This model was inspired by the World War II–era success of atomic energy, radar, and other technologies derived from advances in fundamental scientific knowledge, and regained prominence in the 1990s from the example of the information revolution and from the promise of similar revolutions in bio- and nanotechnology. In the examples above, the government, and usually the military establishment, played a prominent role in shepherding these technologies through the entire innovation process.

The second of these concepts is the so-called induced innovation theory of the late Vernon Ruttan, in which technology and technological innovation respond to the economic environment. In brief, this theory holds that the technology in use in any economic sector—and, given enough time, the direction of development and research—responds to changes in the market, for example to price signals by minimizing the use of expensive inputs and maximizing the use of inexpensive ones.[6] By extension, the model would predict that technology and technological innovation would also respond to the policy environment, for example by improving worker and product safety and decreasing pollution as policies in these areas are tightened. The induced innovation model was one of a number of models that responded to the realization that nations that were superior in basic research, such as the Great Britain of the 1950s and 1960s, were not necessarily leading innovators, and that a majority of new products used existing technologies to meet new market demand rather than emerging from basic research.

The third of these concepts is not fully articulated in the innovation literature, although it is suggested at a number of points, as discussed below. Innovation in a field like energy requires not only technology supply and a corresponding demand for that technology, but also organizational elements that are properly aligned to link the two. There will need to be concrete innovation institutions, and organizational mechanisms connecting these institutions, to facilitate the evolution of new technologies in response to the forces of technology push and market pull. This third point in our innovation theory framework, that innovation requires organization and organizations to form the new technology and to launch it, is needed to make our theory practical and capable of implementation.

These three theories fit into a historical context. The induced technology model was in part a product of the historical perspective of the 1970s and 1980s, with advances derived from incremental gains in existing technology. In retrospect, this seems to have been a period of relatively leisurely technological change, although in the stiff competition of that period with Japan and Germany it certainly did not seem so at the time. Of course, all along the kind of innovation described by the pipeline model was humming along, bringing out an IT revolution in the 1990s. Underlying both of these developments were organizational issues for our innovation system, only gradually articulated. We will explore each of these three innovation models below.

The First Theory: The "Linear" or "Pipeline" Model
In part as a result of the waves of innovation in IT and biotechnology that have come to fruition in the past two decades, Americans are accustomed to thinking of innovation as resulting from a totally new, world-class technology that makes it possible to do something that has never been done before

(i.e., a radical innovation that creates new functionality), or that makes an old technology vastly cheaper, more powerful, and more convenient (a secondary or significant incremental advance). They expect such innovations to result from new scientific discoveries or engineering inventions that stem from the curiosity of the scientist or the inventiveness of the engineer. This popular conception is in large part due to the fact that these two waves of innovation and the American competitiveness that they underpin, rest on strong, government-funded research institutions that undertake world-class scientific and engineering research.

In this linear or pipeline model, *research* leads to an *invention*, which requires *development* to ready it for *prototyping* and then for *commercialization*. We can now see, as through a rearview mirror, that many of the major technological advances of our time fit this model well: airplanes, computers, nuclear energy, space, and lasers, to name a few. In line with this conception of the innovation process, American science policy, which was formulated by Vannevar Bush following the Second World War,[7] stresses support for basic research, typically in universities or government laboratories, that is intended to push back the frontiers of knowledge of the natural sciences. The original assumption was that industry will seize on the resulting inventions and commercialize them. In many cases, as we will see, government support, particularly from the military, has also been needed as technologies enter the market. This linear or pipeline model stresses the process of technology supply-push, in which new technologies evolve and push themselves into the marketplace, rather than market or demand pull. The technologies spawned by this pipeline model became so central to U.S. economic growth[8] that it became accepted as the standard innovation model underlying most American science policy legislation and the institutions it supports.

As this pipeline model was examined over the last two decades, the policy focus, explored most prominently by Lewis Branscomb and Philip Auerswald, turned to the major obstacle to innovation of this kind, namely the "valley of death," the gap in support and financing between basic research and later-stage development, or in other formulations, between proof of concept and a commercial product.[9] This obstacle is in significant part the result of the institutional gap between performers of basic research (typically in universities or publicly funded research institutes), on the one hand, and the commercially oriented development carried out by private firms, on the other, an institutional disconnect which was designed into our national innovation system as it evolved in the post–World War II era. These authors and others also point out that innovation in the so-called pipeline model doesn't really occur linearly, that the stages are in fact much more interactive, and thus that the term *pipeline* itself is a misnomer. Nonetheless, the term is so widely used that we use it here, recognizing that it does not accurately capture the complexity of the relationship between innovation stages.

This gap between research and commercial development results in a deficiency, articulated by the late Donald Stokes, of research in "Pasteur's quadrant": basic research inspired not by curiosity but by the hope of practical application.[10] Even private venture capitalists accustomed to taking speculative bets on new technology avoid financing the early stages of revolutionary technological advance, deferring investment until a technology is no more than a few years away from production.[11] As a result, the success of many major innovations with wide economic ramifications has typically depended on a strong injection of public money, usually (as Ruttan has illustrated) from the military, enabling them to bridge this valley of death.[12] This is only one of these obstacles that will affect the market launch of energy technologies that are still at the R&D stage today. To understand the other barriers, we need to reach beyond the standard pipeline model and consider the other models.

The Second Theory: The Market-Pull and Induced Innovation Models

Despite the attractiveness and relevance of the pipeline model, particularly to radical innovation, most new products on the market, particularly those reflecting incremental advance, stem from the more mundane process of market or demand pull. In this process, an entrepreneur spots a market opportunity that can be exploited with a new product based on existing technology, develops the product, and launches it onto the market. As the market for the new product develops, competitors appear, and both new and old producers are forced to develop the technology so as to improve the product and lower its cost. Eventually, further improvements may run up against limitations in the understanding of science or technology, requiring an investment in research. The frozen dinner, for example, arose not from new technology, but from the realization that households headed by two working parents or by a single working parent were good customers for meals that needed only to be heated before they could be served. Once the market for the new product was well established, competitive pressures led to the development of new recipes, to the development of better technology, and eventually to scientific research on food biochemistry in the quest for tastier and more varied meals. To be sure, both market pull and technology push are oversimplifications of real-world innovation, a complex and ongoing process in which technical possibilities open up new opportunities and market forces guide the direction in which innovations of all kinds are developed.

Market pull is thus the reverse of the pipeline or linear model of the innovation process. A *market* opportunity gives rise to an *invention*, which eventually creates requirements for *development* and lastly for *research*. Innovations of this kind are more closely tied to the demands of the market than to advances in the underlying science or technology. A change in market conditions—a change in the price of a major input, for example, or a strict code of environmental regulations—will naturally give rise to innovations to meet the changed patterns of demand.

This idea of demand pull leads naturally to the model of technological change by induced innovation. This model, as articulated by Ruttan, deals not only with the process by which completely new products and technologies arise from the demand side, but also with the direction of innovation. It is concerned both with the direction of the evolution of individual technologies, and with the aggregate characteristics of the technologies in use within a given branch of an economy—whether they tend to use more capital in preference to creating more jobs, for instance, or whether their use of energy, transport, materials, or other inputs tends to the profligate or the conservationist.

According to this model, technology in any given branch of the economy may be expected to reflect the price environment, and to respond to any changes in that environment. Major changes in the prices of key inputs or outputs to an industrial process shift the deployment of technology toward those that use less of increasingly expensive inputs. If land is cheap and fertilizer is relatively expensive, for example, farmers will tend to expand their acreage rather than to farm the land that they already own more intensively.[13]

If investors expect that the changed prices are likely to last a long time, investments in R&D—and their eventual output in the form of practical inventions and innovations—will shift in the same direction. This theory also applies to changes in the market and in the policy environment. Changes in income levels and income distribution will lead to innovations that feed either mass markets or specialized, high-end markets. Stricter regulation of environmental pollution or of worker health and safety will lead to changes in technology consistent with the new requirements, in this case in the direction of increased safety and decreased pollution.

This model applies directly to energy technology. If the price/policy environment changes sharply in the direction of more expensive energy, as it did in the 1970s, technologies will respond throughout the economy, at a pace that is likely to depend in significant part on the size and the rate of return of the necessary investment. For our purposes, these shifts may be classified into categories according to the degree of technological change they require. The first such category consists of quick, simple changes in behavior, such as closing the doors of air-conditioned offices when electricity becomes more expensive or driving less when the price of gasoline rises; changes in consumer buying habits, such as eating out less or at cheaper restaurants when the price of food goes up; and simple retrofits, like increasing the insulation on residential housing. In industry, the focus will be on analogous behavior changes and simple engineering retrofits, combined with easily accomplished changes in raw materials and product mixes.

The second category of adaptation to changes in the price/policy environment consists of investments in capital equipment embodying technologies that are already established in specialized niches, much as wind turbines are today, or that can be brought quickly to market in order to take advantage of the new situation. Consumers adjust their buying habits for long-term durables—for example, by buying smaller cars with better gas mileage. The vendors and manufacturers of this equipment expand their operations and improve their technology by learning from experience (what economists call "learning by doing"), by taking advantage of economies of scale resulting from investments in new or expanded production of goods and services whose markets have expanded, and by incorporating into these new investments improved technologies whose implementation had not previously been economically justifiable. All these adjustments arise throughout the economy, at varying rates depending on the degree of learning required, the cost and turnover time of the equipment involved, and many other variables.

The third category of induced technology adaptation consists of technologies that require significant investments in development before they are ready for full-scale implementation and deployment.

The fourth category consists of long-term investments, in both the private and the public sectors, in research leading to new technology and new products and services and (in the case of engineering-intensive technology requiring major initial investments) expensive and time-consuming technoeconomic demonstrations.

Private companies make these long-term investments in research, development, and demonstration when they are convinced that the new environment is here to stay, at least long enough for the resulting technologies to be perfected and come to the market. In any particular company, the response to these changes will be conditioned by its so-called technological trajectory—that is, its product mix, its basic technical capabilities, its history, and its culture. These may lead it to ignore, to undervalue, or even to suppress technologies that threaten its business model or its core capabilities. In such a case, the induced innovation may be brought to market by a different company in the industry, or even by a total newcomer.

In contrast to these private investments, major public investments in research require a political consensus (or at least a technical consensus in the science and engineering community, leading to a strong feeling among government research managers that can convince those members of Congress with a special interest in the particular subject) that new technologies are needed in the public interest. If the previous policy and economic environment is of very long standing, as was the case for energy in the early 1970s, a major change in technology may need to await a turnover in sunk capital, or even a change in the university curriculum to make it suitable for the training of a new generation of engineers.

At any point, these technologies may be overtaken by new enabling or "general-purpose" technologies that undergo explosive development and spawn a continuing stream of innovations throughout the economy, as did IT in the 1990s.[14] These technologies derived from radical innovation, often in accordance with the pipeline model,[15] may require major changes in infrastructure and public policy that may take the better part of a generation to implement, that produce major changes in functionality and productivity throughout the economy, and that are major contributors to—and probably the major engine of—world economic growth. IT, for example, has already had a substantial impact on the energy industry, while developments in biotechnology and nanotechnology are likely to do so in the near future.

To summarize our argument up to this point, new energy technologies will come about using both these innovation models—the pipeline model and the induced technology model. Energy innovation will include both incremental and radical technology advance, and will use both demand pull from market need (assuming that a sound cap-and-trade system or comparable regulatory pressure is introduced) and supply push from government-supported R&D investment in new energy technologies. This application of both technology supply and demand push will be necessary to increase the speed of adaptation if we are to meet the major problem of the energy sector: the scale needed in an energy transformation.[16]

The Third Theory: Innovation Organization

The first two models of innovation address the process by which innovation occurs and the external influences to which it responds, respectively. The third theory addresses the management of innovation and the organizations in which it takes place. In the modern economy, these are key sources for the supply of technology. The role of the innovation organization in innovation theory has its conceptual antecedent in the "evolutionary" approach of economists Richard Nelson and Sidney Winter.[17] They examined the most innovative of the large corporations of the 1970s, such as in the aerospace industry, and found that the key determinants of their success in evolving innovation lay in the effectiveness of their organizational routines for R&D, for management organization, for product commercialization, and for efficient production. Although Nelson and Winter were focused on what was going on inside a company rather than on the larger innovation system, they argued that innovation organization and the routines that connected organizational elements were key to a firm's ability to innovate.

A decade later, Nelson took these considerations to a higher level and looked not simply at firms on the ground, but at national innovation systems. In a 1993 book,[18] he argued that there were national systems of innovation, as well as innovation actors that interacted in those systems. The actors included government agencies that provide support for R&D, government-funded research universities, government laboratories, and educational institutions, as well as strong firms, both small and large, and their R&D laboratories. Nelson saw the firm as the most critical element in this system, but he saw innovation as occurring within a larger institutional system, in which a series of connected and interacting actors influenced the innovation that could and would occur in the firm.

Nelson's focus on the organization of innovation at both the firm and national level, with government, university, and business actors in interactive relationships, allows the valley of death between research and late-stage development discussed earlier in this chapter to be understood within the pipeline model of innovation as an organizational gap between government-supported research and private-sector development. Policymakers attempted to fill this gap with intermediating entities, such as the Small Business Innovation and Research program (SBIR) and the Advanced Technology Program (ATP, now renamed the Technology Innovation Program, TIP).[19]

This gap had an institutional history, as we suggested earlier. World War II was a period of "connected" R&D, in which government support was available at all stages of innovation, and connections and handoffs between research institutions, companies, and the military were comparatively seamless. In the postwar period, under Vannevar Bush's pipeline model, these connections were severed, and the government role was for the most part limited to supporting basic research, largely at the publicly funded research universities that evolved during the war.

As the Cold War heated up and Sputnik created new pressure for technological advance, the military, out of necessity, returned to the connected model of World War II to meet its needs. A key connected organization, the Defense Advanced Research Projects Agency (DARPA), was created in 1957. It emphasized nurturing revolutionary technologies through basic research to solve specific technological challenges. It reconnected basic and applied research, and both of them with development. It was an organizational fix that operated with surprising success to link research advances with private-sector adoption of such technologies as advanced computing, the Internet, and personal computing. The literature around the DARPA model notes its unique role as an innovation organization.[20]

An energy technology transformation will require not only the forces of technology push and demand pull, as described by the pipeline and induced innovation models, but organizational elements as well. New organizational mechanisms will be needed to connect Nelson's innovation actors in order to help bridge the gaps between public and private sectors in developing and implementing new technologies. In addition to connection mechanisms, we will need new institutions to help smooth the interactions between the public, private and academic sectors.

Integrated Innovation in Energy Technology

Energy technology poses multiple challenges to the three models of innovation we have just sketched. First, energy technology is not a single technology but a vast and complex array of technologies that pervade the entire economy on both the supply and the demand side. Many of these technologies are interconnected—for example, plug-in hybrids involve both the electricity sector and the transport fuel sector. Many others have had important environmental and social ramifications. Subsidies for biofuels led indirectly to deforestation in Malaysia and some conclude were one of the factors that led to high food prices and food riots in 2008 in poor countries around the world.

Second, this multitude of technologies is deeply entrenched, having evolved under the influence of a long-standing economic and policy environment that has given rise to huge and politically powerful companies, produced pervasive subsidies, motivated sunk investments in infrastructure, and contributed to a political culture that takes it for granted that fossils fuels are the basis of the economy—the whole underpinned by deeply felt public expectations that cheap and readily available energy is part of the American birthright. Subsidies for fossil fuels and technologies dependent on fossil fuels are everywhere—from federal tax policies to federal highway expenditures. The result is a technological-economic-political paradigm that is resistant to change.

Until the middle of the first decade of the twenty-first century, Americans had enjoyed almost a century of low-cost energy. The temporary price spike in the 1970s produced a flurry of policy measures to encourage the deployment of renewable energy, along with support for research on new technology for energy supply and efficient end use. But the return of cheap energy in the 1980s effectively discouraged any effort at their widespread deployment, except in niche markets. Energy research continued at a relatively low level in both government laboratories and private industry.

This paradoxical combination of a long-standing technological-economic-political paradigm based on cheap energy, a low-level but persistent program of research on alternative energy sources and end-use efficiency, and sporadic efforts to use policy instruments to encourage conservation and renewable energy, has led to a substantial backlog of energy technology at various stages of readiness. Some alternatives, like solar and wind, are established in niche markets and are near (wind) or approaching (solar) competitiveness in larger-scale utility markets. Others, like enhanced geothermal, are approaching the demonstration stage and the possibility of deployment at scale, but still require substantial development and careful demonstration. The same can be said for next-generation nuclear technology, with the added complication that any major expansion of nuclear energy in the United States will have to overcome a legacy of public distrust, as well as critical waste-storage and security issues. Still other technologies, like nanotechnology, are areas of basic research that promise major breakthroughs applicable to a range of energy technologies but are only approaching fruition. Finally, technologies like fusion still require extensive basic research, while others are still at the concept stage.

There are welcome signs that this paradigm may be about to change, and that a cap-and-trade regime may come to pass in the next few years. Such a change in policy is essential in the long run to the encouragement of innovation in the direction of conserving energy and limiting carbon dioxide emissions. According to the theory of induced innovation, it would induce innovation in the direction of low-carbon energy sources and end-use efficiency and would propel many of these backlogged technologies toward technoeconomic competitiveness. Private industry would increase its investments in technologies with these characteristics that are already established in market niches and are poised to expand. Those that are nearly ready for deployment would attract the private technical and financial resources needed to overcome any remaining technical difficulties, reduce costs, and improve quality and reliability, so as to be ready for the competitive marketplace. Private-sector budgets for R&D would grow from their present low levels and give rise in due time to new generations of technology for energy supply and application. So far, so good.

But problems would still remain. These private investments, while essential, will be insufficient, given the urgency of the energy crisis the world now faces, the scale of innovation needed, and the many obstacles to technological change in the energy sector. The aggregate level of such investments will be less than what is needed (in the jargon, will fall short of the social optimum) in the absence of public money. Private investments in induced technological change—beyond, say, the relatively simple retrofits and adaptations and investments in well-tested technology discussed in the preceding paragraph—are unlikely by themselves to take place fast enough or in sufficient quantity to meet the need, even if the recent rise in energy prices proves permanent. The same is true for innovations emerging from technology push. Technology stand-up is gradual; it often takes new technologies four or five decades before they capture the bulk of their markets.[21] We simply do not have that time, given geopolitical and climate exigencies. A major government effort to stimulate innovation is therefore essential. There are several more reasons to expect delay in the emergence of technology. These reasons constitute additional justifications for government intervention.

To begin, there is general agreement among economists that public investments in R&D are an essential complement to private-sector efforts. The arguments here are technical, but the upshot is that private investors cannot expect to realize all of the gains that accrue to society at large from the innovations made possible by their investments in R&D. This disincentive to investment is due to knowledge spillover, or what economists call the "market imperfection of nonappropriability." Much of the benefit (in economics, the value added) from innovation will accrue to the users of the technology. After all, users would not pay for the new technology if they did not benefit from it. Some of the rest of these gains will be siphoned off by imitators, others by employees who leave the firm, taking their knowledge and skills to competitors or to form new businesses of their own, and so on. To be sure, with any luck at all, there will be plenty of profit left for the innovators—but not as much as there would have been had the innovators been able to capture all the social gains for themselves. The result is that in the absence of government subsidies, the aggregate private investment in innovation will be less than would be justified by the overall gains to society.

A second market imperfection resulting in underinvestment in innovation is the valley of death between proof of concept and late-stage development that we discussed earlier. This will be less important for energy technologies that are already near competitiveness, but will delay or obstruct the launch of energy technologies that require long-range research, development, prototyping, and demonstration in order to advance from proof of concept to a commercial product or process.

Over and above these considerations, which apply to all forms of technological innovation, the processes of both technology push and market pull in energy technology are inhibited by the preferences for legacy technologies that are heavily subsidized and deeply embedded in the political and economic systems and in public expectations in all advanced countries. The operators of these technologies are accustomed to the defense of their sources of supply and shipping lanes by the national defense establishment, and to the discharge of their waste products, including carbon dioxide, into the atmosphere without charge (in the jargon, they treat the environment as a free good). These implicit subsidies constitute perverse incentives, in the sense that they encourage activities that harm social assets, specifically the environment and national security.

The beneficiaries of these perverse incentives are likely to fight for loopholes in any new policy environment to enable them to continue. This will give them an advantage over any technological newcomer. What is more, changes in energy technology are unlikely to attract extensive investment by the military except in specific applications to defense, and thus lack the source of financing that has historically been a major impetus to technological change in other sectors in accordance with the pipeline model.

Finally, the design of any plan for government involvement in stimulating innovation must take into account the "routines," to use the Nelson and Winter term noted above, by which both government and the private sector organize their innovation systems. This in turn requires a close examination of innovation organization if such intervention is to result in the establishment of more effective routines for the introduction of innovations into the complex system of energy technology. As will be explored below, these routines will involve government, the private sector, and the links between the two.

We must combine and integrate the induced, organizational, and pipeline innovation models if we are to adequately describe the innovation framework we will require for energy innovation. As we have seen, the induced technology literature has rested primarily on market pull and the role of firms in filling technology needs based on changing market signals. It does not deal directly with the role of government.[22] For its part, the organizational literature on innovation remains limited, reflecting on routines adopted by firms, as well as by government organization through entities like DARPA. Yet both firms and government organizations will be major players in new energy technology. What is more, the predominant literature on technological innovation in recent years remains focused on the strengths and weaknesses of the "pipeline" model, because of the importance of the IT and the biotech innovation waves for which this model provides a good description. This pipeline literature pays insufficient attention to the influence of the overall economic and policy environment as it affects technological innovation in complex networks of both related and unrelated technologies.

In sum, the literature on innovation policy, whether induced, organizational, or pipeline, has not fully confronted this kind of complex technology problem. This is not only an issue regarding energy technology; it applies to other highly complex sectors of the economy where technologies are a factor—for example, health care, transport, physical infrastructure, food and agriculture, and military technology. The complexities associated with the energy sector force a very different analysis from the approaches that dominate the American literature on technological innovation. While each of the three models discussed provides helpful descriptions of aspects of the innovation process relevant to energy technology, only by integrating all three in a unified approach do we move toward a better grasp of the task before us. Indeed, this process has enabled us to draw a new series of policy prescriptions quite different from the approaches that have been articulated to date in other sectors.

The Four-Step Analytic Framework

We expect that the most difficult step in the development and deployment of new energy technology will be the launch of these technologies into the extremely complex and competitive markets for energy technology. This "point of market launch" perspective is the basis for our argument that any program of government support for innovations in energy technology should be organized around the most likely bottleneck to their introduction to the market. This goes beyond the long-standing focus of pipeline theorists on the valley-of-death stage between research and late-stage development. Combined with the principle that public policies to encourage technological innovation should enable alternative technologies to compete on their merits—that is, should be as technology-neutral as possible—this leads us to argue for integrated consideration of the entire innovation process, including research, development, and deployment or implementation, in the design of any program to stimulate innovation in energy technology. This requires drawing on both pipeline and induced innovation models. In addition, there are deep systems issues of organization for innovation that require consideration, because new organizational routines across the public and private sectors will be needed to make possible integrated policies for support to innovation.

These considerations have led us to develop a new innovation policy framework for energy technology. It requires a four-step analysis, which we propose as the basis for innovation policy in this area. We believe that a similar approach is likely to be applicable to technological innovation in sectors of similar complexity.

In the first step, we assess a large number of promising energy technologies, based on the likely bottlenecks in their launch path, and classify these technologies into groups that share the same likely bottlenecks. In the second step, we classify policies for the encouragement of innovation into technology-neutral packages, and match them to the technology classification developed in the first step of the analysis. In the third step, we survey existing mechanisms for the support of energy innovation with the objective of determining what kinds of innovations (as classified by the likely bottlenecks in their launch paths) do not get federal support at critical stages of the innovation process, and what kind of support mechanisms are needed to fill the gaps thus identified. In the fourth step, we recommend new institutions to fill the gaps identified in the third step. These four steps are explored in subsequent chapters.

The first of the above steps draws on pipeline theory, suggesting that support from the government pipeline will be important to standing up and enhancing a range of technology options. But recognizing that these technology streams will need to land in the private sector at huge scale, the second step relies on induced innovation theory. It concentrates on the policy or demand signals that will induce the private sector to take up, modify, and implement the technology advances that originate from the innovation pipeline. Whether these come from a demand pricing system like cap-and-trade, from technology incentives, or from regulatory requirements, they will need to be coordinated and, to the extent possible, will need to be technology-neutral. The third and fourth steps draw on the innovation organization theory advanced here—that the gaps in the innovation system will need to be filled for the handoff to occur between pipeline and induced models, especially at the points where technology supply push meets market demand pull.

This proposed new integrated framework has implications not only for policy theory; it also leads to a different logic for the practical design of legislation. Our discussion of steps 1 and 2 in effect implies that the current legislative process for energy technology innovation is exactly backward. The incentive structure should be legislated first so as to preserve the fundamental technology neutrality needed in this complex technology area, rather than legislating separately for each technology first, with a different incentive structure for each, as has become the standard model for innovation legislation, as for example in the major energy legislation of 2005 and 2007. In contrast, Congress needs to legislate standard packages of incentives and support across common technology launch areas, so that some technology neutrality is preserved and the optimal technology has a chance to prevail. Particular technologies can then qualify for these packages based on their launch requirements. It is important to get away from the current legislative approach of unique policy designs for each technology, often based on the legislative clout behind that technology.

Even if equipped with a new model for energy innovation policy, however, we should not underestimate the complexity of the process for introducing new energy technology at scale. After all, this has eluded us for the last four decades. These difficulties underscore the need for the comprehensive approach outlined in the next chapter.

3

Promoting Development and Adoption of New Energy Technology

The Multiple-Strand Problem in Technology Policy

Advances in energy technology, whether for supply or end use, must occur in a complex system. End-use technologies face a varied and fragmented multisectoral and multiresource landscape, requiring solutions within intricate and closely coupled systems for transport, electricity, and buildings and involving oil, coal, natural gas, nuclear, and renewables. Solutions are needed to address all the varied and controversial issues that justify public intervention to stimulate these technologies—the so-called drivers of political change. These include concerns over energy security, climate, environment, rising economic costs, and potential supply issues with major new users in China, India, and other emerging economies. To add to this complexity, these issues do not necessarily overlap, at least not in the short run. Energy security largely concerns oil and is therefore a problem of the transport sector, while the climate and environmental problems derive from coal-based electric power generation and use, as well as from transport.[1]

Given these complex realities, any strategy for launching new or improved energy technology depends on the structure of the user sector. For example, the fragmented nature of the building sector demands a very different strategy than does the comparatively centralized on-grid electric utility sector. Many strands of technology development will thus be needed on multiple time horizons; there cannot be a single technology focus. Measures will have to be developed to speed innovation in end uses with long turnover times, such as the building sector and the auto fleet. To add to the complexity, the technology-development system will need to consider and retain room for evolving advances over time. Second-, third-, and fourth-generation advances will displace earlier generations. There must be space for both incremental advance and disruptive new technologies; technology lock-in must be avoided.[2] All this will require considerable understanding on the part of policymakers and the public, as part of what we have called a new technological/economic/political paradigm.

This understanding will be greatly facilitated by a major roadmapping exercise that looks at each technology element and its possible and preferred evolution pathways, and then ties each to the right elements of a menu of "front-end" support for research, development, and demonstration; to mechanisms for "back-end" government support for implementation; and to demand-oriented policies providing incentives or regulatory standards to encourage or require adoption. As discussed in more detail below, research for this roadmapping exercise should investigate the "fit" between different innovation types and alternative methods for the promotion of innovation, drawing on a combination of technology expertise and practical engineering and policy experience from inside and outside of government, buttressed by insights from scholarly research on the economics and management of innovation.

This technology roadmapping exercise, although it can be initiated by government and requires its participation, will have to be led by the private-sector entities that ultimately will need to adopt and implement it. Its intellectual framework and findings can then be applied to the problem of choosing among alternative public policies for promoting energy innovation in the critical key domains of technology. This process will have to be an ongoing process open to change, since the evolution of technology is always creating both new opportunities and dead ends. The experience in the semiconductor sector with Sematech, a private-sector consortium that was launched with major federal support, and that still operates both a roadmap and a related collaborative R&D program to keep the industry tied to Moore's law, provides a useful example of a sophisticated roadmapping process.

The Economic Justification for Public Intervention

How can we justify major public investments in "front-end" research and development and "back-end" implementation incentives, as opposed to relying on market forces and private investment? Why should we not assume that the private sector will provide adequate investment in research, or even over-investment and an energy research boom? In the previous chapter, we explained some of the answers to this question as they are given by economic theory, but it is time to confront it empirically and directly. After all, discussions of a cap-and-trade system, coupled with programs that the State of California is adopting, have already been enough to encourage Silicon Valley venture capitalists to pump major money (thought to be in the range of $3.4 billion in 2007[3]) into new energy technology. And there has already been an investment boom in ethanol—and perhaps a bubble—in light of expanded federal subsidies sought by the farm lobby.[4]

Energy security has been an announced U.S. policy for forty years.[5] Yet for decades and until very recently, relatively few private investors have invested in energy research and technology development. Indeed, investment in energy R&D has been sharply declining in both the public and private sectors for the past twenty-five years. There are sound theoretical reasons for concern that this low level could continue, particularly given the mammoth scale of embedded energy infrastructure, valued in the trillions of dollars, which dwarfs the size of all available venture capital. The problem of energy is the problem of scale. Recent venture capital in the energy technology sector typically supports projects that are about to benefit from large public subsidies, or at the very least are expected to yield a handsome profit in preferably three but at most five years.[6] With worldwide energy demand expected to increase over 50 percent by 2030,[7] the scale required if new entrant technologies are to make a difference is huge. Private investment, while critical, has not approached these dimensions and is, for well-known economic reasons explained in the previous chapter, unlikely to make investments commensurate with national or international policy needs, especially in such critical sectors as environment and energy with intergenerational effects.[8]

The practical justifications for federal energy market intervention are well established. In summary, these are:[9] (1) innovation creates public good externalities that cannot be captured by the innovator and so require a government role; (2) because investors in innovation are risk averse, pooling and shifting risk through government policy and support, promotes investment in innovation; (3) potential purchasers of new technologies are averse to the risks of new innovations that have not been fully market tested, an aversion that can be offset by government development and demonstration support and demand incentives; (4) capital markets are focused on short-term returns and are reluctant to take advantage of the longer-term life-cycle cost savings of energy efficiency and new technologies, which can be mitigated by long-term government research, development, and demonstration; and (5) energy incumbents have shifted their environmental and security costs to society (in the jargon, they have "external-ized" these costs), a practice that can be counteracted by government investment and regulation to force them to "inter-nalize" these costs. These are classic economic rationales built around the underlying concept of market failures that can justify and be mitigated by government intervention.

Most important, the dominant energy sources and tech-nologies have erected a network of massive government subsidies for themselves over the decades; these constitute a powerful defense in depth against new entrants. Tax and other subsidies for oil, gas, and coal dwarf any level of support now being contemplated for alternative energy sources or technologies.[10] In other words, there is no level playing field for new entrants. On the contrary, there will likely remain a huge subsidy imbalance against them, which incumbents with their major political power may well be able to maintain. Support for new energy technologies will be required to offset this imbalance.[11] Given the size of the problem and its critical importance to security and the environment, major public support to bolster longer-range technological supply options is essential.

This having been said, government should avoid the tempta-tion of attempting to dictate "industrial policy" in the sense of direct government command and control over the sector, with industry as receiver. Instead, new technology will be located in and integrated into the private sector, with industry as a full collaborator. To resolve these societal environmental energy and security problems, the reality is that government will be imposing government policies through a combination of supply- and demand-side initiatives. Climate change and energy security are now treated as economic externalities by the energy sector; government will be changing these to endog-enous factors, and government policy and mandates affecting the private sector will result in a technology transition driven both by government policy and (when these recur) by high oil prices. However, again, government will not solve these problems; the private sector must do so. In addition, because energy is a trillion-dollar-plus sector, the problem is simply too big for government alone; the level of investment required for transition and infrastructure compels a private-sector market-based investment role.

Defining Terms

We now need to introduce and define several concepts that we will use as the basis for classifying new energy technologies in the first step of our analysis. The first is technology *launch* or *stand-up*, by which we mean the development, introduction, and deployment of new technologies, into larger energy transport and utility systems and as supplements or replacements for those systems. This technology launch is an essential step if an *invention*—a new technological idea, perhaps in the form of a model—is to enter widespread use and thus to become an *innovation*.

Some of the technologies we will examine are still *experimental* and not yet ready for introduction into the energy economy. Others are *potentially disruptive* new technologies that can be launched into *niche* areas apart from established systems where they face limited initial competition, but that may expand to challenge established incumbent or "legacy" technologies.

Other technologies will be secondary and component technologies that must displace established component technologies that perform more or less the same function, but that if prices are made comparable can be accepted by their recipient industries. Hence they are *secondary (or component) technologies facing uncontested launch*. In contrast, other new secondary and component technologies will face initial and continuing political and nonmarket economic opposition from the industrial sectors that must absorb them or from competitors; they are *secondary (or component) technologies facing contested launch.*

We also characterize the range of government support that will be required for launching these new energy technologies. Using the language of the traditional linear pipeline model, we label research and development (R&D) and prototyping and demonstration (P&D) to promote technology creation as *front end support,* and economic incentives and regulatory requirements or mandates to encourage technology implementation and deployment as *back end support.*

Front-end support will also be needed for some *incremental technologies*—that is, technologies that offer relatively small improvements in existing functionality, but that in the aggregate may make a substantial contribution to policy goals. For reasons that will be explained, such incremental improvements are especially important to technologies for *conservation and end-use efficiency* for which existing private-sector and governmental "back-end" incentives are inadequate. Outside the defense sector, the federal government has historically paid relatively little attention to such incremental advance. The innovation pathways for these technologies are discussed in more detail below.

Anticipating the later discussion, both front- and back-end support will also be needed for *scale-up and generic improvements in the manufacturing process.* We will need front-end support for R&D and implementation for *advanced manufacturing processes and technologies* to drive down costs of new energy technologies. Back-end support will also be needed to encourage the scale-up of manufacturing production of new technologies. All of these varied launch pathways will be delineated, with examples, in the next section as well as in chapters 4 and 6.

Step 1: Different Launch Pathways for Different Technologies

In this section, we categorize the many and diverse technologies needed by energy markets according to their varied launch paths, and attach appropriate implementation policies to each category, depending on the foreseeable bottlenecks and obstacles to that launch. We have reviewed a number of promising energy innovations from this point of view and find that they can be grouped into the following classes:

Experimental technologies This category includes experimental technologies requiring extensive long-range research. The deployment of these technologies is sufficiently far off that the details of their launch pathways can be left to the future. Still, researchers developing this kind of technology may face more immediate obstacles. They may lack an appreciation of its importance relative to other possible projects, or may lack a clear vision of the best way to steer their research in order to reach the most fruitful application, so that a potential use can inform the direction of the science. Conversely, these researchers may be unable to raise needed resources for the research because potential sources of finance lack an appreciation of its potential importance, or because they steer it away from its most fruitful application in order to gain short-term advantage.

Undirected, curiosity-driven research provides important science, but there is also a very real need for more directed advance once possibilities can be glimpsed. These problems of connecting the science to potential opportunities for advance have led to a process called *translational research*, where a concept of an area where a breakthrough is needed leads to an emphasis on the advances in fundamental science that are required to get there. In other words, in this experimental stage, there is a need to impose a translational model for a portion of the research portfolio. Finally, technologies emerging from such long-term research are likely to face the classic "valley of death" between the initial technical concept and a viable business; the translational approach can help to cross this barrier as well by providing a more viable direction to the research.

Disruptive technologies These are potentially disruptive technological innovations that can be launched in niche markets and that may expand from this base.[12] Despite their access to these initial niche markets, these technologies must eventually face the obstacles created by the "tilted" (i.e., nonlevel) playing field created by long-embedded subsidies and other cost advantages of established technologies, not to mention the long-standing public acceptance of their overwhelming geopolitical, economic and environmental "external" costs.

Secondary technologies—uncontested launch This group includes secondary (component) innovations that will face market competition immediately on launch but that can be expected to be acceptable to recipient industries. These technologies must face the rigors of the tilted playing field, such as a major cost differential, as recounted for the previous category, without the advantage of an initial niche market. The examples we examine in this category also face specific problems related to the particular technology.

Secondary technologies—contested launch These are secondary (component) innovations that have inherent cost disadvantages, and/or that can be expected to face political or other nonmarket opposition from recipient industries that must be overcome in addition to the obstacles faced by the two preceding categories.

Incremental innovations, focused on conservation and end-use efficiency The implementation of these innovations is limited by the short time horizons of potential buyers and users, who typically refuse to accept extra initial costs unless the payback period is very short (i.e., unless the rate of return from the extra initial expense is much higher than the usual return for similarly secure investments).

Scale-up and generic improvements in the manufacturing process These are improvements for which investment may be inhibited by the reluctance of cautious investors to accept the risk of increasing production capacity and driving down manufacturing costs in the absence of an assured market. We will require advances in both manufacturing processes and technologies relevant to the new energy technologies discussed here to drive down costs and improve quality and quality control, and support to scale up manufacturing to move efficient new products into the market more quickly.

The above categories classify evolving technologies according to their different launch pathways. Categories (5) and (6) are crossover categories and reach not only new technologies but established technologies as well. These six categories are briefly set forth in chart form in table 3.1 and are fleshed out in detail in the next chapter, with specific representative examples selected from the longer list of pending energy technologies.

Step 2: Matching Launch Paths to Policy Packages

In the second step of our analytic framework, we propose that the launch categories be tied to policy packages at the front and back ends, as appropriate to the particular launch path, so as to promote accelerated technology implementation. Because policies individually tailored to each technology could jeopardize optimal technology advance, these policies should be bundled into packages that apply across categories of new technology, so as to create as much technology neutrality as possible. These approaches are also on a political continuum: front-end incentives are the easiest politically, while back-end mandates are the most difficult.

A wide range of mechanisms for promoting energy innovation are in principle available, and are spelled out in more detail in chapter 6. They fall into three general categories:

"Front-end" technology nurturing Technology-nurturing support on the front end is needed for technologies in all six categories of the technology launch pathway. This includes direct government support for R&D,[13] both long and short term; for technology prototyping and demonstrations (P&D); for public-private R&D partnerships; for monetary prizes for individual inventors and innovative companies; and for support for technical education and training.

"Back-end" incentives Incentives (carrots) to encourage technology transition on the "back end" may be needed to encourage technologies in the categories of secondary (component) technologies with both uncontested and contested launch, incremental innovations in technology for conservation and end use, and technologies for manufacturing processes and scale-up. They may also be relevant to disruptive technologies as they transition from niche areas to more general applicability. These incentives include tax credits of various kinds for new energy technology products, loan guarantees, low-cost financing, price guarantees, government procurement programs, new-product buy-down programs, and general and technology-specific intellectual property policies.

"Back-end" regulatory and related mandates Regulatory and related mandates (sticks), also on the back end, may be needed in order to encourage secondary technologies facing contested launch and also some conservation and end-use

technologies. These include standards for particular energy technologies in the building and construction and comparable sectors, regulatory mandates such as renewable portfolio standards and fuel economy standards, and emission taxes. These are by no means exhaustive lists of carrots and sticks.

These approaches are not equally appropriate to all situations. Different policy approaches will be suited to different innovation pathways and conditions. Typically, these policies would be imposed in graduated steps. Technology nurturing through R&D and related support, usually the first stage of government intervention, generally does not create political opposition, since the government's role in supporting R&D is well accepted. The P&D aspect, while part of technology nurturing, is more expensive than R&D and requires collaboration between public and private entities if it is to be well managed, because demonstrations must be designed and carried out so as to lead to commercialization if they are successful. Because major appropriations and a substantial number of jobs are at stake in demonstrations, there is a greater risk that these carrots can be captured by the inefficiencies of the political process. But like R&D support, P&D politically is a carrot. Incentives, the next notch up in the government's role, are more expensive than R&D or P&D and therefore somewhat more difficult politically, but still constitute carrots that are comparative easy for the recipients to swallow.

The third kind of instrument, the "sticks" of regulatory and related mandates, is usually fought hard by the economic actors who stand to lose if they are put in place. The decades of success by the U.S. auto industry in resisting stronger fuel economy standards (until the end of 2007), for example, is the stuff of political legend. In the American political system, sticks are therefore typically policies of the last resort, to be used only when nurturing and carrots will not work. Where new energy technologies are at embryonic and experimental stages, provide new functionality, or can be launched in niche markets, front-end technology nurturing may be all that is needed. Where energy technologies are secondary and component, but acceptable to the recipient energy industries, incentive carrots may be required in addition, particularly to help them to come into price range. Where energy technologies are secondary and component, and will be fought by the incumbent energy technologies in the markets into which they are to be introduced, the "sticks" of regulation and mandates may need to be imposed.

Some of these new energy technologies will compete with each other as well as with established energy sectors. It will therefore be important to maintain as level a playing field as possible among potential competitor technologies, as we have previously discussed, because only time and additional technology evolution will tell us which pathways are optimal. To the extent possible, therefore, there should be common packages for technology nurturing, incentives, and regulatory and related mandates available across comparable and competing technologies to make the technology playing field as level as possible.

Both differentiation and balance will therefore be required in fashioning optimal back-end public policies. As we have previously emphasized, this may require a reversal in our legislative approach to energy technology. Instead of putting each new energy technology in a separate section of a bill that it is considering, and providing it with its own unique support structure based on its lobbying heft, Congress should consider developing packages of incentives, as we have suggested above, and assigning the technologies that share similar launch pathways to the appropriate package. In other words, legislation should create common packages of front- and back-end elements for comparable technologies, and then assign technologies to the relevant packages based on how they will be launched, as delineated in the previous section.

If and when sound demand-side policies are imposed, such as the carbon charges we have previously discussed, many if not all of the back-end supply-side policies may not be needed, in which case they can and should be dropped. However, such macropricing will not work for all sectors. For example, price has little to do with personal transport selections. Consumers buy cars based largely on style and fashion, rather than on price. Therefore, fuel economy standards may need to be imposed or retained to ensure transformation in this sector. For other technologies, such as those for household energy conservation, moreover, consumers tend to insist on such short payback periods that back-end incentives are essential to their adoption.

Table 3.1 ties the multiple energy technology launch categories to the corresponding policy packages delineated above.

The Need for Policy Coherence

As is evident from table 3.1 and its accompanying text, we hesitate to come to definitive general conclusions regarding the wisdom of subsidies and mandates for the implementation of existing technologies that are technically ready but are not quite cost-competitive on their own, such as current generation solar concentrator systems energy today. These policies represent the predominant approach to the encouragement of renewable energy today in the European Union, where they accompany cap-and-trade legislation, and in some U.S. states. Cap-and-trade and carbon tax demand-side programs, if well designed, are inherently more economically efficient than subsidies or regulations but still may need to be supplemented in some sectors. The design and strength of eventual federal cap-

Table 3.1
Policy packages appropriate to the different categories of innovation as classified by their likely pathway of market launch

Technology category	Examples	Government policy packages* needed for:			
		Research and development (R&D)	Prototyping and demonstration (P&D)	Incentives	Regulatory and related mandates
(1) Experimental technologies requiring long-range research	Hydrogen fuel cells, fusion, genetic engineering for energy-related biosystems for storage or CO_2 consumption	Long-term support, translational research	Premature until closer to technology readiness	Premature until closer to technology readiness; need depends on category of technology	Premature until closer to technology readiness; need depends on category of technology
(2) Disruptive technologies launched in niche markets	LED lighting, off-grid solar and wind	Long- and short-term	Government P&D and first market support to bridge "valley of death" could be useful, but private innovation system should dominate	Government incentives support could speed adoption, but private innovation system should dominate. Incentives for conservation, R&D support for precompetitive manufacturing likely required	Instituted on a case-by-case basis

Table 3.1
(continued)

Technology category	Examples	Government policy packages* needed for:			
		Research and development (R&D)	Prototyping and demonstration (P&D)	Incentives	Regulatory and related mandates
(3) Secondary technologies—uncontested launch—facing immediate market competition but acceptable to recipient industry	Improved batteries for plug-in hybrids, enhanced geothermal, on-grid wind and solar	Long- and short-term	Well-monitored engineering and economic P&D may be required	Incentives for users or support for manufacturing scale-up will speed adoption, once technical feasibility is established	Probably not needed
(4) Secondary technologies—contested launch—with built-in extra cost and facing political and/or other opposition	Biofuels, carbon capture and sequestration (CCS), fourth-generation nuclear	Long- and short-term, (including research on environmental, legal, policy, and social science)	Well-monitored engineering and economic P&D will be required to prove technoeconomic feasibility	May be needed to offset increased costs	Regulations, emission taxes, or specific mandates can be deferred until technology is proven, but are essential for adoption thereafter

(5) Incremental innovations for conservation and end-use efficiency	For existing technologies, such as improved internal combustion engines, building technologies, the grid	Long- and short-term	Government precompetitive and "valley of death" support; R&D to show technoeconomic feasibility	Low-cost financing for implementation. These incentives may also be needed for launch technologies in categories 1–4 after introduction	Appliance standards, building codes, and emission limits may be needed to induce adoption of existing technology and the development of new technologies
(6) Scale-up and generic R&D for manufacturing processes	All technology categories	Long- and short-term	Depends on type of technology and established market competition	Low-cost financing for scale-up	Probably not required

* Note: This chart, as it moves horizontally from left to right, assumes a linear timetable of initial support for R&D, then support for demonstration, followed by back-end support. The chart, aside from initial R&D support, also presupposes a gap period on the demand side where interim demand "back-end" measures are needed before an economically sound cap-and-trade or similar macropricing system evolves. The latter could substitute for many but not all of the back-end measures noted here.

and-trade legislation will have a clear effect on the extent to which such back-end support is needed or cut back.

As is evident from the discussion in chapter 4, these policies have succeeded in multiplying the implemented manufacturing and generating capacity for solar and wind technology sever-alfold over what it would have been in their absence. They have made it profitable for companies to expand their manufacturing capacity, reduce their costs, and improve the efficiency of their products. In this way, they go at least part of the distance toward neutralizing the subsidies and other incentives that have long tilted the playing field toward fossil fuels. The subsidies have come and gone in the United States depending on political developments at the state and federal levels, but the technologies themselves have continued to develop, although at a slower pace than if the incentives had been consistent and sustained.

On the other hand, the cases of enhanced geothermal technology and biofuels have shown the difficulties inherent in this approach. The first problem arises from the intermittent and unreliable character of the subsidies that have been enacted, due in part to the varying politics of renewables support. Enhanced geothermal technology, despite initial demonstration tests years ago, has languished, in part because of the risks of exploration and the relatively long time horizon between the drilling of experimental wells and the realization of salable power. In addition to their on-again, off-again timing, these laws sometimes did and sometimes did not define geothermal as a renewable resource. As a result, investors could not be sure that the incentives for geothermal power would still be there when they would be needed. No actual harm has been done, but a technology that may be of value may have been unnecessarily delayed.

The current situation of biofuels, in contrast, is an illustration of the harm that can be done by unwise or premature technology-specific mandates. Subsidies and mandates for corn-based biofuels have resulted in a boom in corn ethanol, a resource that is technologically ready but that offers at most marginal advantages for environment and energy security. These incentives, combined with other coincidental factors in world agricultural markets, may have played a role in a spike in the world prices of corn and other food crops. The risks inherent in using the same resource for both food and energy are only now being seriously examined.[14] Premature support for this specific technology may have locked the country onto an inferior approach and unnecessarily blocked the way to possibly superior cellulosic technologies that may appear in the future.

The geothermal and ethanol biofuel examples illustrate the need for policies for energy technology that are as technology-neutral as possible, that are coherent rather than episodic, and that take full account of technoeconomic and environmental feasibility. These two examples demonstrate the importance of developing a far better launch process than we have managed thus far. The attempt in this chapter to find a more coherent framework to implement energy technologies is not a policy abstraction; we must rethink this process because the consequences of the faulty processes applied to date are significant.

4

Toward a Roadmap for Launching Technological Innovation in Energy

This chapter sets forth a sampling of innovation pathways, citing selected examples of new energy and environmental technologies, and fleshing out the framework described above to suggest in more depth the kinds of government technology policies that will be required for a roadmap to promote energy innovation along different pathways. The discussions of the technologies chosen illustrate the six pathways discussed in the previous chapter; they are not intended to provide an exhaustive exploration of the issues affecting each technology, to cover all pending technologies or to set forth their definitive technical status. Our focus is not on the technologies themselves but on using a group of technologies to define representative launch paths. For each of the selected technologies, we briefly review the current overall status, the development status and prospects, the science and technology breakthroughs possible, the likely launch path, and the potential need for government intervention.

Experimental Technologies Requiring Long-Range Research

Many promising energy technologies are still in the idea stage, but because the solutions to our energy challenges will have to be found over decades, we should increase our support for and pursuit of these possibilities. A robust program of publicly supported, long-term basic research is required in such high-risk and "out of the box" technologies, many of which may never materialize. Because early-stage technology selection is highly speculative, the program should support a broad portfolio of technologies aimed at fostering technology revolutions. These may be radical or incremental, stand-alone, or secondary and component technologies. Given that these technologies are far from commercialization, explicit consideration of specific "back-end" support for dissemination can be deferred until these technologies are closer to market readiness.

A few of the many examples of technologies in need of fostering include fusion and genetically engineered microbes that will consume CO_2. Interesting technologies now being explored at MIT, for example, where one of the coauthors of this book works, involve bubbling power-plant exhaust through a special algae soup so that much of the CO_2 can be recaptured by photosynthesis and later turned into a biodiesel fuel;[1] engineering a virus array to create a small, flexible rechargeable battery;[2] and generating power from the motion of waves and tides more efficiently than is possible with currently available technology. Another highly publicized example is the hydrogen-powered fuel cell for transport, which continues to face so many technical hurdles that it must still be considered an experimental technology.

The Office of Basic Energy Sciences at the Department of Energy has performed important work in recent years by convening workshops of leading researchers in relevant fields to discuss opportunities and challenges in fundamental science related to possible advances in energy technology and to suggest pathways for further scientific advance. Research ideas from these workshops have been compiled and are available to the research community online.[3] While a significant number of new energy technologies are emerging from the drawing tables, some of which are in production, further breakthroughs are needed to turn most of these possibilities into practical reality. Particularly if we are required to go further in carbon and other greenhouse gas reductions than stabilization, further scientific breakthroughs will be needed in new areas where exploration is just starting or where practical results have been barely glimpsed.[4] Vigorous R&D in this experimental category is a policy priority.

We select an example of an experimental technology to highlight the kinds of technology challenges in this area: the hydrogen-powered fuel cell in its transport application, which has received major attention and funding support in the United States and abroad. Despite advances in other types of fuel cells, continuing R&D is required for this type, as discussed below.

Hydrogen Fuel Cells for Transport

Overview Fuel cells, which generate electric power directly from electrochemical reactions, have received a great deal of attention in recent years as the prospective power unit for the hydrogen economy.[5] Fuel cells differ from batteries in that they consume a reactant as power is generated, while batteries store electrical energy for later use in a chemically closed system. Fuel cells are entering the marketplace for distributed power generation but are a considerable distance from entry into the personal and family vehicle transport sector. Because fuel cells could replace internal combustion engines or other power sources in a wide array of areas, they are potentially a disruptive technology that could evolve from niches into the larger transport sector.

While fuel cells can operate with various fuel feedstocks,[6] we focus on hydrogen because of the Bush administration's emphasis on R&D for a "hydrogen economy." These fuel cells feature hydrogen fuel introduced into a flow field on one side (the anode) of a proton-exchange membrane (PEM), where a catalyst splits the hydrogen atoms into protons and electrons. The exchange membrane conducts the protons across the membrane from the anode to the cathode and they combine with oxygen atoms in a flow field on the other side of the fuel cell. The product is electricity (along with water vapor) that could power an electric engine. If efficient and cost-effective, these fuel cells could replace the internal combustion engine and eventually become a disruptive technology.

Technology Status and Prospects   Separate and apart from the question of using hydrogen as a feedstock, fuel cells using various fuels already offer distributed electrical generation for businesses and neighborhoods.[7] As a technology for fixed electricity generation, fuel cells can thus function off-grid and can occupy a market niche with the hope of eventually expanding and becoming a disruptive technology. Fuel cells for transport, on the other hand, must still work through key development steps. A major engineering effort, including both radical and incremental improvements, is required to drive down costs. As discussed below, hydrogen faces a long series of very significant engineering cost challenges if it is to work as an energy carrier in conjunction with fuel cells.

Fuel cells have the advantage that they have many fewer moving parts than an internal combustion engine. Significant progress has been made in reducing the size and weight of the fuel cells themselves; stacks of small fuel cells that will fit inside a car are now achievable. The major technical issues confronting fuel calls for transport applications are size, weight, durability, cost, and speed of charging. As regards durability, the fuel cell's proton-exchange membrane now lasts only about 1,500 to 2,000 hours, less than half the 5,000 hours needed for autos and other commercial vehicles. At least one major U.S. company believes that this 5,000-hour target can be reached by 2010. Even so, catalysts that are cheaper and more active than platinum must be developed if costs are to be reduced from their present level if fuel cells are to compete with the cost of an internal combustion engine. Much work is needed to understand catalytic processes at the molecular level, so that new catalysts can be designed at the nanometer scale for optimal performance.

PEM is another technology on which progress is reported. The current leading PEM is costly and tends to fail in conditions of low humidity, requiring complex castings that draw off some of the fuel-cell power. New manufacturing processes will be needed to make fuel cells competitive. New layer-by-layer assembly technology uses thin, bonded layers of polymers, which are much more flexible and cheaper and are able to operate at 60 percent humidity.[8]

The second set of technical issues concerns hydrogen.[9] Hydrogen as a transportation fuel is not ready. It faces numerous engineering challenges, all of which must be satisfactorily resolved for it to work as a fuel. The complexity of the hydrogen economy leads to low conversion efficiency because current methods for generating hydrogen are inefficient, because storing and transporting hydrogen cost more than other fuels, and because converting hydrogen to usable energy is still very expensive.

In either compressed gas or liquid form, hydrogen offers much less energy density than gasoline. That means that vehicles must be engineered to expand fuel storage to the point where they have a reasonable driving range of 300 miles. If hydrogen is used in its gaseous state, it must be compressed and stored in large high-pressure cylinders. Liquid hydrogen requires less space, but must be cooled to below minus 400 degrees Fahrenheit. Given this complication, auto companies are contemplating using hydrogen as a gas. Hydrogen's flammability also raises safety issues. Although it readily disperses into air and has a higher ignition temperature than gasoline, its flame is not very visible and a wider range of hydrogen concentrations are flammable as compared to natural gas. Safety standards for hydrogen will be required, as well as means to detect it in closed areas like garages.

Hydrogen will also require a massive new infrastructure for production and distribution. A transport and distribution system for gaseous hydrogen will have to be built from scratch with its own pipelines, transport vehicles, and storage and delivery sites. Since such massive infrastructure could be implemented only gradually, it would likely be initiated through regional commercial fleets or other localized networks. Because hydrogen has much less energy density than gasoline, this will need to be a much more expensive delivery system. For example, it will take approximately twenty-two compressed tube tractor trailers to deliver the same energy as is carried by one gasoline tanker, and pumping energy requirements for hydrogen pipelines over long distances may significantly offset the energy available from the delivered fuel.

Potential Breakthroughs through Long-Term Research   Summarizing some of the points made above, the hydrogen fuel cell requires research leading to breakthroughs in a daunting number of technical areas: generation, purification, transport, storage, distribution, utilization, and detection of hydrogen gas, and the integration of the resulting technologies into a nationwide system, plus the development of an economical fuel cell suitable for transport applications.[10]

The production of hydrogen requires cheaper and more efficient catalysts, perhaps resulting from developments in nano- or biotechnology, as well as more energy-efficient processes for generating hydrogen and cheaper and more effective membranes or other methods for separating it from byproducts and other impurities. The transport of hydrogen gas requires new methods to control the embrittlement of steel pipelines, as well as to control the diffusion of the hydrogen molecule (which is tiny even by molecular standards) through pipelines of any composition. Such methods may emerge from a study of the surface reactions of hydrogen with a variety of pipeline materials. The storage of hydrogen gas will require major advances in the fundamental chemistry of easily reversible chemical reactions of hydrogen with other substances, or else cheaper and less energy-intensive means of storing liquid or highly compressed gases at temperatures approaching absolute zero, as well as lighter materials with which to contain them.

For hydrogen to become the fuel of choice for the automobiles of the future will require major advances in fuel cells, as discussed above. The possibility of hydrogen leaks in confined spaces such as pipelines, cars, and garages necessitates considerable research on safety, including a reliable and user-friendly method of detecting dangerously flammable mixtures of hydrogen and air, as noted. Finally, the environmental consequences of the possible introduction of large quantities of hydrogen into the atmosphere need to be thoroughly investigated. All of these diverse requirements depend on fundamental advances in the physics and chemistry of hydrogen, and its interaction with a wide variety of physical and chemical systems. What is more, the widespread use of hydrogen fuel for automobiles and other forms of transport will require a redesign and reconstruction of nationwide and perhaps worldwide systems of fuel distribution. Development of an economical hydrogen fuel cell will thus require advances on multiple, equally daunting fronts. The most promising approach lies in prospective advances in chemical catalysis, which are noted in the section below concerning biofuels.

Likely Launch Path and Potential Government Role   While hydrogen fuel cells for transport are a potentially disruptive technology, the emphasis is still on the term *potentially*; they belong in the experimental category. Government should undertake front-end R&D support for transport hydrogen fuel cells; prototyping and demonstration (P&D) support at scale as well as back-end support can both be deferred until further technology maturity. When hydrogen fuel cells are ready for widespread application, they will probably be launched in such niche applications as nontransport engines before evolving into transport. This is likely to take many years. From an environmental point of view, the value of hydrogen as an energy carrier depends on the source of energy for its production from the ultimate raw material. For example, hydrogen fuel cells will make only a limited contribution to the reduction of CO_2 emissions if the energy for hydrogen production is derived from coal or other fossil fuel.

Disruptive Technologies: Potentially Disruptive Technological Innovations Launched in Niche Markets

Some innovative energy technologies can be launched in niche markets where they do not face serious head-to-head competition. For example, nano-based batteries are already competitive in cordless hand tools, solar photovoltaic cells are competitive for many off-grid applications, and light-emitting diodes (LEDs) are entering niche lighting markets. These technologies can expand from niches without directly threatening incumbent large-scale technologies. The technologies require public support on the front end for long-range research, and perhaps for prototyping and demonstration, but are likely to attract venture and angel capital as soon as they reach marketability. As with all energy technologies, back-end incentives or regulatory mandates could speed their implementation but likely will not be mandatory, and can be applied on a case-by-case basis upon a showing of need. Demand-oriented policies—carbon taxes, cap-and-trade schemes, and the like—and high energy prices will speed adoption of these technologies by helping to overcome the many built-in biases for existing technology and by reducing the price differential for alternative sources of energy, respectively.

Solar

Overview   Since the sun offers ten thousand times more energy than the world consumes, this is a renewable technology bright with potential.[11] Two approaches are dominating the current solar electricity market. The first, photovoltaics, consists of solar cells that convert solar energy from the sun directly into electricity. Solar cells are made of specially prepared semiconducting materials; when sunlight is absorbed by these materials, the solar energy loosens electrons from their atoms, allowing the electrons to flow through the semiconductor material to produce electricity. This process of converting light (photons) to electricity (voltage) is the photovoltaic (PV) effect.

The second approach is concentrating solar power (CSP), which depends on direct sunlight, and couples passive mirrors or lenses that concentrate larger areas of sunlight into a focused beam that heats a working fluid to temperatures from 600 degrees F to over 1500 degrees F, enabling it to run steam generators, turbines, or other conventional technologies for generating electricity. Solar concentrators include the solar parabolic trough, the parabolic dish/engine, and the solar power tower.[12] In our classification, these PV and solar concentrating technological approaches enter off-grid niche markets, or could take the form of on-grid arrays that become secondary, component technologies for centralized, on-grid production of peaking power.

Although solar now supplies less than 0.2 percent of world power generation, annual photovoltaics production grew at around 25 percent a year between 1994 and 2004, and at 45 percent in 2005; growth remained strong in 2006 and 2007 thanks to advances in technology, manufacturing efficiencies, and government subsidies in some nations. Total PV world capacity at the outset of 2007 was 6,500 megawatts (million watts, or MW) at peak, compared to 1,200 MW in 2000. After wind, solar PV has become the renewable technology of choice, with large-scale PV arrays accounting now for 10 percent of the European PV market.[13] Japan and Germany, which have offered substantial government support, dominate photovoltaic manufacturing; the United States is a distant third, with less than a quarter of Japan's production level.[14] However, new energy regulations in California appear to be producing a sizable enough test market to encourage more U.S. production and use.

Because concentrating solar power requires direct sunlight, this technology is most appropriate in areas where direct solar radiation is high; in the United States, Southwestern states are the areas of focus. The first concentrator commercial plants have been in operation in California since the mid-1980s, providing over 350 MW of the world's lowest-cost solar power capacity. The European Union (EU) is moving in this CSP area as well, with a growing list of demonstration projects.[15] The types of systems under development include all three of the concentration devices cited earlier, and also vary in their energy conversion methods, storage options, and other design variables. Concentrating solar is now focused primarily on multimegawatt arrays that are appropriate for the on-grid market, complementing the other major solar technology, PVs, which can be in large arrays but are also appropriate for smaller, off-grid applications.

There is controversy concerning the amount of land that would have to be devoted to the collection of solar energy should this become a major source of electric power. The concern is that land devoted to solar power generation could displace agriculture and contribute to higher food prices. Proponents argue that solar PV farms operating at 12 to 14 percent efficiency would need only about 2 percent of the U.S. land area to supply all U.S. electricity needs, compared to some 40 percent of the U.S. land area now allocated to food production.

Technology Status and Prospects   Photovoltaic electricity produced by current multicrystalline silicon wafer technology costs 18 to 23 cents a kilowatt-hour (kWh), according to a 2006 Energy Department report, given good siting and financing, although costs vary depending on the insolation (the strength of solar radiation) in different areas.[16] In contrast, coal-fired electricity costs in the range of 5 to 6 cents/kWh, natural gas 5 to 7 cents/kWh, and biomass power plants 6 to 9 cents/kWh. This means that solar PV must cross a major cost hurdle to compete, although efforts are underway to bring PV cost down significantly. Concentrating solar, in contrast, is more energy-efficient, around 35 percent-plus efficient in the laboratory, with generally comparable numbers in the field, depending on solar conditions. Correspondingly, CSP is significantly less expensive per kilowatt-hour and is starting to reach the price range of competitor technologies. DOE's 2004 numbers for CSP indicate around 12 cents/kWh, with advances ongoing, and a longer-term technology goal of between 3½ and 6 cents/kWh.[17]

Solar is a rapidly accelerating area, open to new technology advances and new entrants.[18] The most developed markets are Germany, with 2,530 MW of installed capacity, followed by

Japan with 1,708 MW, the United States, with 620 MW, and Spain with 120 MW, as of the end of 2006. German solar companies are planning to invest a total of over 2.6 billion euros by 2010 in these technologies. New markets are evolving, as well. China-based companies are planning to lead the world in PV solar manufacturing, with production rising from 350 MW in 2005 to 1,500 MW in 2007. About three-fourths of solar cell production comes from ten firms, which are accelerating their investment in new manufacturing plants while new European, U.S., Chinese, and Japanese firms are entering the PV field, leading to fluidity in market share.

Three major technology challenges now face photovoltaics: increasing efficiency and reducing production costs; continuing demonstrations at large scale; and pressing for next-generation technology advance. Because solar is a noncontinuous power source (there is night as well as day, and sometimes it is cloudy), storage advances are also critical; some relevant issues will be touched on in the subsection on batteries. CSP (and solar thermal for buildings) have separate cost and efficiency challenges.

Potential Breakthroughs through Long-Term Research   Solar photovoltaic technology is a very active area of research. First-generation solar PV technology—silicon-wafer-based solar cells—includes large-area single-crystal, single-layer diodes made from silicon wafers, an approach that now constitutes over 80 percent of PV production. These solar cells, estimated by the Energy Department in 2006 in the range of 11 to 13 percent efficiency[19] and now pushing 15 percent, are now being made at industrial scale, for example, on long ribbon wafers that will significantly cut production costs.[20] This technology was launched with American venture-capital support largely in Germany, where substantial subsidies are available. Silicon-wafer thickness fell in half from 2003 to 2007, cutting raw material costs and improving efficiency. The second generation of PV materials is called thin film, and is made using thin epitaxial deposits of semiconductors employing a variety of semiconductor materials, from amorphous silicon to cadmium telluride.[21] Major advances have been in thin-film technologies, initially led by space applications, aimed at achieving a complex balance between production costs and efficiency, driving down the former and driving up the latter.

A third generation of PVs, quite different from previous PV semiconductor approaches, is now in the research stage. This includes using such technologies as quantum dots and nanostructures to raise efficiencies and organic or polymer materials to lower production costs.[22] Promising areas of research include organic nanostructured solar cells, bio-inspired solar cells that integrate photosynthetic complexes with solid-state semiconductors, photovoltaic fibers that allow tiny PV cells to be woven into threads, turning clothing, tents, or roof tarpaulins into solar collectors, direct production of solar chemical energy in the form of molecular hydrogen by solar processes analogous to biological photosynthesis, and "quantum-dot" solar, in which dots of nanoscale crystals interact with light and throw off electrons.[23] Several of these approaches benefited from the decade of strong federal R&D investments in nanotechnology.

In parallel, CSP is working to move above 35 percent efficiency—a high level for solar.[24] Further research, development, and demonstration (RD&D) is needed in improving CSP reliability, reducing cost, and demonstrating Stirling engine performance in the field, a supporting technology.[25] One recent CSP large-scale demonstration, funded by a twenty-year power purchase agreement with a major California utility,[26] for example, consists of groups of large 38-foot solar-concentrating dish mirrors connected to Stirling engines, which use the thermal power generated by the focused solar energy to heat hydrogen in a closed-loop system. The expanding hydrogen gas creates a pressure wave on the pistons of the Stirling engines, which spin an electric motor to create electricity with no fuel cost or pollution.

To make both PV and CSP more cost- and energy-efficient, major R&D is required, but the possibilities appear promising. In one example, researchers in an ongoing DARPA-funded project, led by the University of Delaware and including six other universities, five companies, and the DOE's National Renewable Energy Lab (NREL), in July 2007 claimed a record level of 42.8 percent efficiency for a solar cell in standard conditions although field tests remain.[27] Using a new lateral optical concentrating system, the system splits light into three beams, each with light of a different range of wavelengths, that is, a different color. It directs each beam into a cell of appropriate wavelength sensitivity, so as to convert a broader range of the solar spectrum into electrical energy. The system uses optics of less than 1 cm in width, a fraction of previous optic widths, and accepts light from a wide range of angles, limiting the need for tracking devices to move the device to align with the sun. The device is lightweight and portable, so it could readily go on a laptop or a roof. It marks a step in a DARPA project intended to achieve 50 percent energy efficiency in a system as affordable as current solar cells.

Likely Launch Path and Potential Government Role   Solar photovoltaic cells have expanded into a variety of off-grid applications as their costs have come down, a process that continues. Further cost reduction, and hence further expansion, requires a combination of materials research, manufacturing improvements, cuts in installation cost, and economies of scale. This could be accelerated by public support for R&D, "valley of death" support for start-up companies, mandated purchases or quotas analogous to those undertaken by the Carter administration in the 1970s, or other incentives. Expanded application of solar energy would also benefit from improvements in battery storage, a technology that will be discussed later in this chapter.

Solar photovoltaics now benefit from technology-specific, back-end incentives to individual consumers.[28] In 2005, Congress put in place the first federal tax breaks for residential solar since 1985, making temporary credits available for systems installed in 2006 or 2007. Taxpayers are entitled to federal tax credits (after state incentives) of up to $2,000 to cover 30 percent of the cost of a photovoltaic system as well as up to $2,000 to cover 30 percent of the expense of a solar thermal system. As of 2005, some fifteen states offered tax breaks for solar energy, from tax credits to sales tax exemptions, and twelve states offered solar energy rebates.[29] The number of such states has been growing; twenty-five states in 2007 have renewable portfolio standards, and four more have nonbinding goals.[30] For example, California is encouraging a program to install 3 gigawatts (billion watts, or GW) of solar power by 2012, and the other state programs may require 6.7 GW of solar panels by 2025, well in excess of current global production rates.[31] These federal and state tax subsidies and rebates, as well as renewable portfolio standards, need to be evaluated to determine their effectiveness relative to other back-end approaches, including government procurement incentives, technology standards for new construction, loan or price guarantees, and other regulatory mandates.

The European experience is instructive.[32] Despite PV growth there, it is still one of the most expensive emerging technologies. While PV expects to continue driving down the cost curve while it moves toward making a contribution to electricity supply, it may take up to two decades to become cost-competitive unless there are significant technology breakthroughs. In southern Europe, for example, grid-connected PV electricity may be cost-competitive with peak power only by 2015. In Germany, a leader in solar advance, solar PV will account by 2012 for some 20 percent of that country's feed-in tariffs (the tariffs paid by utility companies for decentralized sources of renewable energy that the companies do not themselves own but that they are required to buy at rates set well above market rates), while providing only 5 percent of the electricity produced in the country.

On the other hand, promising breakthroughs continue. For example, Daniel Nocera and Matthew Kanan have discovered a process by which water can be split into hydrogen and oxygen by an electric current, using cheap cobalt and phosphate catalysts and low-cost electrodes instead of the expensive platinum electrodes that have hitherto been needed for this process. Oxygen goes to the surface and hydrogen ions migrate to a second electrode and form into hydrogen molecules for possible use in a fuel cell. This process, which mimics plant photosynthesis, could make it possible to obtain hydrogen directly from solar cells. Storage is the major solar impediment; this might help make solar into around-the-clock energy.[33]

In a second example, a team led by Marc Baldo has found a way to implant inexpensive dyes into glass, absorbing light across a range of wavelengths and gathering and concentrating it at the edges of the glass, thus radically reducing the number of solar cells required for a given power level and increasing the electrical power obtained from each solar cell.[34] No longer would your roof have to be covered with PV cells; your windows might do the job. This could increase solar efficiency and so cut costs, and apparently could be commercialized in a few years. These and comparable breakthroughs could speed up the anticipated timetable for making solar competitive, which might otherwise extend as long as two decades.

LED Lighting

Overview Lighting consumes some 21 percent of all energy used in the commercial and residential sectors and 18 percent of all electricity used in the United States.[35] Thus lighting is a surprisingly significant energy user. Breaking that down, as of 2001, 51 percent of national energy consumption for lighting occurred in the commercial sector, 27 percent in the residential sector, 14 percent in industry, and 8 percent in outdoor stationary lighting.[36] Some 46 percent of electricity used in the commercial sector is for lighting.[37] Some 90 percent of U.S. residences use incandescent lamps, while commercial and industrial sectors predominantly use fluorescent lighting.[38]

Because incandescent lamps are far less efficient than fluorescents, major energy savings are possible from shifting residential lighting away from incandescent bulbs. Lighting efficiency is measured by lumens per watt of electricity (lm/W). A standard 100-watt incandescent lamp lasts approximately 1,000 to 1,500 hours and produces 15 lm/W, while a standard 30-watt fluorescent lamp lasts some 20,000 hours and produces 80 lm/W. Fluorescents are more expensive at up-front purchase, but far cheaper and more efficient over lifetime use. Because the commercial and industrial sectors are sensitive to life-cycle cost efficiency, they use fluorescents, but residential consumers have traded efficiency for lower up-front cost. Consumers have also had concerns about the low buzz of noise and color-rendering issues with older fluorescents.[39] In addition, there are significant environmental concerns over the inadequate disposal process for the mercury contained in current compact fluorescents. U.S. residential consumers have been far slower to shift to fluorescents than their European and Asian counterparts; significant energy savings could result from this shift, and a few retail companies, led by Wal-Mart, are now making promotional efforts.

While there are many small lighting producers, the global market is dominated by three multinational firms, which locked in the global market share early in the last century: Philips (based in the Netherlands), OSRAM (based in Germany), and General Electric (based in the United States). In the United States, the production of lighting (lightbulbs) and lighting fixtures has declined or stabilized since the 1970s, and the value of specialty lighting for such uses as decorative lighting and UV lamps has surpassed that of either of the other two sectors. The downturn in domestic production can be explained by imports, which increased to 50 percent of the U.S. market for lightbulbs by 2004; China accounts for 26 percent of that total. The three dominant lighting firms are increasingly shifting production to lower cost nations. Lighting fixtures have shifted abroad even more intensively, with 86 percent of all U.S. fixture imports coming from China by 2004.[40]

Into this picture of opportunities for efficiency gains from fluorescent penetration into residential markets, and internationalization of production, has come a new disruptive technology: lighting from semiconductors, generally called light-emitting diodes or LEDs. One estimate predicts that widespread use of LEDs would reduce the consumption of electricity for lighting by 50 percent in the United States and would reduce worldwide demand for electricity by 10 percent, the equivalent of about 125 large electricity-generating plants.[41] While the story of the lighting sector in the twentieth century was one of relentless manufacturing efficiency and cost-cutting, the story in the twenty-first century may be one of energy efficiency; for this reason, LEDs appear to be the coming technology.

Technology Status and Prospects LEDs, first made practical by Nick Holonyak of the University of Illinois in 1962,[42] are electroluminescent semiconductor diodes that generate light of a color that depends on the chemical composition of the semi-conductor compounds used. They produce light by allowing electrons to flow in one direction across an electrical junction point, the diode, and drop into a lower-energy state, releasing the difference in energy by emitting light.[43] In contrast to incandescent bulbs, which release 34 units of heat to produce 2 units of light energy, LEDs generate relatively little heat. They last some 100 times longer than an incandescent bulb and convert about 25 to 35 percent of electrical energy into light, as opposed to about 5 percent in an incandescent bulb.[44] They do not require bulky sockets or fixtures and can be embedded in walls or ceilings. LEDs are currently some five times more efficient than incandescents and halogens, but cannot yet compete in white-light markets with fluorescents. They have a ten-year life span, twice that of fluorescents. Because they are semiconductors, they are expected to evolve along the Moore's law curve, and by 2020 are anticipated to be twelve times as energy-efficient as incandescents and twice as efficient as fluorescents. While not yet price-competitive, LEDs are already filling a host of specialty lighting uses and have reached a global market worth over $5 billion (still only a small fraction of established lighting sectors). They hope to flow down a cost curve that could make them half the current cost of fluorescents by 2020.[45]

Because they are semiconductors, LEDs require a complex, many-step manufacturing process very different from the production processes used by the established lighting sectors dominated by the three global producers. While LED R&D is led by the United States and almost half the patents are held in the United States, Asian firms dominate production, with Japan undertaking approximately half of world production, Taiwan a quarter, the United States some 12 percent, and Europe around 9 percent.[46] However, LED quality varies. Lower-performance LEDs face intense price competition and approach commodity status, while high-performance LEDs face significantly less. Overall, LED production patterns to date suggest that competition in the lighting sector overall will grow and become more intense, more diverse, and more international. The three global producers are attempting to cope with this potentially disruptive technology by establishing joint ventures and acquiring smaller firms.

Potential Breakthroughs through Long-Term Research   There are a number of technological problems that must be resolved if LEDs are to displace existing technologies. First, ways must be found to bring production costs down significantly so that they compare with those of fluorescents. Second, the color rendering of LEDs is not yet adequate. LEDs emit light at a particular and precise wavelength that appears different to the eye from natural white light. White light can be created by using several LEDs that emit light of different colors, or phosphors driven by LEDs, but the color spectrum from these processes differs from that of traditional lighting and sunshine, making some colors on objects they illuminate appear dark.[47] Third, LEDs that operate at high ambient temperatures require efficient heat sinks to carry away the heat they generate, even though this heat is much less than that produced by a comparable incandescent or fluorescent. Efforts to resolve these issues are now underway.

New technologies that could reduce costs include organic LEDs (OLEDs), in which the emitting layer of the LED is an organic compound. These may prove significantly less expensive to produce and thus be competitive for use in displays, light sources, and wall decorations.[48] OLEDs emit light over a broader range of wavelengths so that they will also allow a greater range of colors, brightness, and viewing angles, as well as better-quality white light. Kodak pioneered OLEDs and has launched the first digital camera using an OLED display. There are more than seventy display firms, and many are positioning themselves to introduce OLEDs for displays; the first OLED television has been introduced but is still priced above other technologies. The three established global lighting leaders have launched joint ventures to participate in the OLED market, initially for displays. Polymer LEDs, another new technology, have the additional benefit of being flexible.

Likely Launch Path and Potential Government Role LEDs present an interesting glimpse of the pattern that a potential disruptive technology could take in the energy area, since work on LEDs has been ongoing for some time. National-government R&D programs were fundamental in giving rise to the advance of LED technology. A number of nations have built such LED programs, and estimates of current funding levels are cited below.[49] Through its 2005 energy legislation, the United States established a Next Generation Lighting Initiative, with a major initial focus on LEDs and an authorized $42 million per year in six areas: longevity, quantum efficiency, stability and control, packaging, infrastructure, and cost reduction. Japan has a $7.5 million program aimed at developing particular LED technologies and at ensuring follow-on market share. South Korea has a National Semiconductor Lighting Program, combining universities and industries, and funded at an estimated $59 million a year through 2008. Taiwan has a $4 million Next Generation Lighting project. China has launched a five-year, $248 million-per-year manufacturing-oriented program, which includes R&D, five industrial parks, and supporting manufacturing facilities and infrastructure, with industrial collaboration and university participation. The EU is spending some $16 million a year on LEDs as a portion of its Sixth Framework program.

LEDs have followed the pattern suggested at the outset of this section on disruptive technologies, establishing themselves in a series of niche markets that can generate initial revenue and support product refinements and improvements. The pattern has been one of initial government LED research investments, first led by the United States, that have led to three developments: global dispersion of technology development, a growing number of start-ups and smaller firms, and now more substantial government R&D programs as described above (many connected to manufacturing capability), as the promise of the technology has become clearer.

Eventually, if advances in technology continue, LEDs will land in occupied territory—the much larger lighting market— as they attempt to displace long-established incandescent and fluorescent technologies. In anticipation of this stage, the three dominant global lighting producers are attempting to absorb the new technology into their own product portfolios through joint ventures and acquisitions. Whether these established players succeed in capturing and dominating the new technology, assuming remaining cost and technical problems are resolved, or whether a new mix of firms prevails, will be played out in the coming decade. LEDs, then, give us a glimpse of how potentially disruptive technologies could evolve in other energy areas, even though existing technologies now dominate these markets.

Government is playing a major role in this advance[50] in yet another way, namely, through environmental mandates. The lighting sector, in addition to national R&D programs, thus provides a second illustration of the role of government—how its regulatory role can overcome the barriers of price and consumer acceptance for new-entrant energy technologies. In 2007, the U.S. Congress passed major energy legislation dealing with a long series of technologies, including lighting. Subtitle B of that legislation[51] requires a 25 percent efficiency gain for lightbulbs phased in between 2012 and 2014, which effectively bans the current technology for incandescent lighting. By 2020, the bill requires a 200 percent efficiency gain for lighting, which will spur further gains, and, in effect, promote LEDs. The bill also extends the Next Generation Lighting Initiative for R&D through 2013.

The standards enacted by Congress are technology-neutral performance standards. They dictate a level of efficiency but do not specify the technology by which this efficiency is to be achieved. The effect is to encourage the adoption of LED lighting in the next decade or so, without establishing an artificial barrier to yet another new technology that may arise in the future. Tellingly, these new efficiency standards were backed by the Alliance to Save Energy, an industry-led energy conservation group, by incandescent lightbulb manufacturers fearful of chaotic state standard setting, and by electric utilities under pressure to obtain efficiencies, in addition to environmentally oriented conservation groups.

To summarize, LEDs provide an interesting illustration of a series of points about energy technology that we have made in this book. The LED experience illustrates how potentially disruptive energy technologies could evolve in niche markets and then position themselves to land in established energy technology markets, in this case the century-old residential and commercial lighting sector. It suggests the intensity of the global competition for technology leadership that may evolve through technology advance, and ways in which established firms may respond. It illustrates the importance of national-government R&D programs in supporting the evolution of promising technologies. And it illustrates the important role that government regulatory intervention can play in getting new-entrant technologies past cost competition with older technologies and established consumer buying patterns.

Secondary Innovations—Uncontested Launch: Secondary (Component) Technologies That Will Face Immediate Competition on Launch but Are Acceptable to Recipient Industries

The technologies in our next category constitute secondary innovations, typically components in larger systems that must compete on quality and price with existing technologies from the moment of their first introduction. On the other hand, when they do achieve economic competitiveness, they can be expected to be incorporated into existing platforms and systems without significant political confrontations with existing producers. Examples include on-grid solar photovoltaic farms, wind-power generators, and geothermal energy, and in transport, advanced batteries for plug-in hybrid cars. Government support for research would be in order, and support at the prototyping and demonstration stages could speed innovations. On the back end, incentives will be needed, although regulatory mandates may prove unnecessary and can be examined on a case-by-case basis. However, regulatory directives such as fuel economy standards or Public Utility Regulatory Policies Act (PURPA)-like support would speed the adoption of technologies in this category by helping to overcome the bias toward incumbent technologies.

Wind Power

Overview   Windmills date from antiquity, perhaps originating in Persia, and may have come to Europe with returning Crusaders around 1100.[52] A golden age of windmills ensued in Western Europe from 1200 to 1850, which was ended by steam and electric power in the nineteenth century. The golden age of windmills in the United States featured small, wooden, multiblade wind machines on Midwestern and Western farms and ranches from 1850 through the 1930s, until they were brought down by the New Deal's rural electrification. Fast-forwarding to the oil embargo and accompanying energy crisis of 1973, the Carter administration initiated a Large Wind Turbine Program, which was enhanced in 1978 by PURPA, requiring utilities to buy power from small producers at "avoided cost" rates. Led by California, wind power grew in the United States until both the federal and California wind tax credits were allowed to expire in 1985 and 1986. In 1996, in a period of continuing decline in energy prices, Kenetech Windpower, the largest U.S. and world manufacturer, went bankrupt and was acquired by Exxon and then by General Electric. This marked the end of the first recent era of wind power in the United States.

However, while wind power stagnated in the United States, Europe continued to implement the technology.[53] European government support for wind power led to dramatic growth from less than 1,000 MW in 1993 to over 5,000 MW five years later. Both Denmark and Spain were early adopters of feed-in tariffs, by which regional or national utilities are required to buy renewable electricity at above market rates set by the government. The two countries have large renewable sectors as a result, and Denmark now meets half its electricity needs from wind. By the end of 2006, Spain had an 11.6-gigawatt (GW) base in wind-derived electricity, the second largest in the world, edging past the United States. Germany revised its feed-in tariff in 2000, growing its renewables by 12 percent a year since then, and is leading the world with a 20 GW base in wind energy. Interestingly, India has now installed 6.3 GW in wind energy for baseload power. Increased pressure from energy prices, energy security, and climate change has in turn renewed interest in wind in the United States in recent years.

Technology Status and Prospects   Wind power has the advantage of relative technological maturity compared to most other renewable technologies, building on a century of aviation experience with design of rotor blades, two decades of aviation experience with advanced composites, and long industrial experience with generators and gearboxes. As a result, wind power is by far the closest price competitor of all the renewables to fossil-fuel-burning sources of electric power. Wind-energy equipment is now deployed in thirty-six U.S. states and produces about 1 percent of America's electricity.[54] Large-scale deployment is usually the stage where manufacturing efficiency and cost reductions are implemented for a technology, with corresponding technology efficiency and reliability improvements. Wind power has achieved enough deployment at scale to have accomplished many of these improvements.[55]

Wind power is actually a solar technology, since winds result from the uneven heating of the earth's surface by the sun. Only a small portion of wind is near enough to the earth's surface to be accessible and only part of the United States has winds sufficiently strong to be exploited by current technology. Wind also has the defects of variability,[56] both during the day and seasonally, so that wind-derived electric power does not necessarily match demand times and periods. Unfortunately, low-cost storage is not yet available. Were wind to become a major source of energy for the nation, this would lead to problems of systems management, because the present grid is not set up to handle intermittent, decentralized sources of electric power. In addition, optimal wind fields are not necessarily near populous areas in need of electric power, a fact that can lead to significant line loss.[57]

Because wind turbines create no exhaust gases and require no cooling water, they do not face many of the environmental externality problems of other energy technologies.[58] However, they are built with steel, for tower, generator, and turbine, and composites, for blades, and so have secondary externalities through the production processes for these materials. The Federal Non-Nuclear Energy Research and Development Act of 1974 requires that a net energy analysis be performed on any new energy technology involved in the direct production, transmission, or utilization of energy.[59] Estimates indicate that wind turbines have a very short environmental payback compared to many other technologies, of little more than a year,[60] which is to say that the environmental cost of producing the equipment is made up for by the lesser environmental impact involved in the production of wind power compared to other sources of electricity.

Several environmental impacts remain problematic, however. There are serious aesthetic concerns about the visual impact of wind farms in coastal areas and along elevated horizons. While gear and generator machinery noise can be muffled, low-frequency blade noise cannot be. While wind farms can be sited away from migratory-bird flight paths to limit bird-kill problems, it may not be possible to avoid the killing of raptors (eagles and hawks) and of bats. Wind farms are land intensive for the amount of power they generate, but it may be possible to offset some of this problem through dual land use with farms and grazing, and through increasing turbine size.

As of the end of 2006, the wind-power sector consisted of ten turbine manufacturers who supplied 95 percent of all new turbines. Only two of these manufacturers have experience with offshore installation. The total market in 2006 was for 15.0 GW, of which four firms—Vestas, Gamesa, GE Wind, and Enercon—supplied three-quarters. There is a risk that if the manufacturing base and its production capacity does not expand promptly to meet growing market demand, wind-turbine prices, which rose 30 percent between 2004 and

2006, will continue to rise, affecting investor confidence and deployment.[61]

Meanwhile, turbine manufacturers are attempting to improve the power production efficiency of wind-farm sites by building larger turbines,[62] with developments through 2007 summarized below. Vestas, a Danish firm that claims a 23 percent world market share and 35,000 turbines installed, is the largest turbine maker and offers a 3 MW turbine for onshore and offshore installation. Gamesa Eolica of Spain, the second largest manufacturer with over 10,000 turbines installed and 15 percent world market share, produces a 2 MW turbine. Germany's Enercon, the third largest maker with over 11,000 turbines installed, has built 6 MW turbines, the world's largest to date, with precast towers rising to 130 m, for a total height (including blades) of 198 m for onshore installation. GE Wind, with 5,500 installed wind turbines on- and offshore, has expanded its standard 1.5 MW turbine into a 3.6 MW machine, with a blade length of 104 m. All manufacturers are attempting to reduce component weight for greater energy efficiency.

Potential Breakthroughs through Long-Term Research   As noted, wind power is increasingly maturing. Incremental advances being pursued include better power electronics to improve the interface with the grid, improved composite materials for lighter weight and stronger blades, simplified power trains to end the need for gearboxes, which are responsible for 30 percent of costs, and online diagnostics for better monitoring.[63]

Technological challenges remain. Although blade design has taken advantage of long experience with the engineering and design of aircraft propellers, helicopter rotors, and airplane wings, good blade design remains a complex problem, with the design goal of power efficiency offset by the need for blades, gearboxes, and generators that can withstand severe winds and gusts. Blade and gear failure due to fatigue remains a challenge, although operating efficiency in recent years has achieved sustained 95 percent availability in many wind-farms.[64] Longer-term R&D is needed on the generation of power at low wind speeds, so that turbines can be placed in more regions and to improve power-generation availability.[65]

Design work is now underway to try to solve the aesthetics problem by making offshore siting more practical by taking advantage of technologies developed for offshore oil drilling platforms. This would make it possible to locate offshore wind farms further out to sea, out of sight of coastal areas.[66] Current offshore wind farms are built on towers that are fixed into the seafloor. But this will work only in areas 15 m deep or less, and arouses opposition from coastal residents. Paul D. Sclavounos, a mechanical engineering and naval architecture professor with experience in floating structures for offshore oil and gas exploration, has worked with a team, with National Renewable Energy Laboratory (NREL) support, to take wind turbines and place them on floaters that are much cheaper than seabed towers, and could support very large turbines, in the 5 MW range. Thus, they can be located further offshore, out of sight and in reach of stronger and steadier winds. Their design calls for a tension leg platform comparable to that of offshore oil platforms, where long steel cable tethers in depths from 30 to 200 m would connect the corners of the platform to a concrete block or other mooring system on the ocean floor.

Likely Launch Path and Government Role   Wind power is already in the launch stage, although government support for front-end R&D and demonstration of new technologies will continue to be needed to spur technology advance. Government back-end intervention for deployment has been critical for the expansion of wind power to date, and although this technology is increasingly cost-competitive, this intervention will continue to be essential for stimulating further expansion. This intervention can take a number of forms, including regulatory requirements such as goals for reduction of CO_2 emissions, goals for use of renewables in overall energy consumption, and mandates for utilities to meet a floor amount of electricity generation from renewable sources. Other possibilities include incentive systems, such as feed-in tariffs and tax breaks, to make renewable sources of energy more economically viable.[67] Wind will be an early beneficiary of any carbon charge that may be adopted because it is now the most cost-competitive of all of the renewables. As an intermittent source, it will also benefit from improvements in battery storage.

Europe has led the way in implementing these regulatory and incentive steps; the EU has offered a 20 percent binding target for renewables. Feed-in tariffs have been the most effective approach to date. They are a more direct intervention than a market-based system and have produced strong and relatively prompt results, particularly in Germany, Denmark, and Spain, as noted above. Germany's feed-in tariffs have been estimated to amount to 4.3 billion euros by 2012; overall, its feed-in tariff for renewables was three times as high as wholesale European power rates.[68] As a result, it leads the world in wind-power energy and is creating a new manufacturing sector as well. In the United States, while wind power benefits from renewable portfolio standards in a growing number of states, such a standard has not yet been employed at the federal level, and was dropped from the 2007 energy technology legislation[69] because of the opposition of the Bush administration.

Because of the large scale of wind farms, with large sites attempting to serve up to 200,000 consumers, and the cost of the increasingly sizable units that are now as tall as thirty-story buildings, wind power appears likely to remain predominantly a source of power for larger electric utility systems, rather than an off-grid option for the niche market of individual consumers. Therefore, back-end technology incentives and regulatory requirements appear to be needed in the United States to move this technology toward more widespread deployment.[70] There may also be a requirement for support for R&D leading to generic improvements in manufacturing technology, as well as low-cost financing (or government purchase) to encourage manufacturing scale-up beyond the assured demand of the private market.

Batteries for Plug-in Hybrids

Overview   Energy storage is a key to a series of major energy opportunities, from transport to renewables. Transportation now accounts for approximately 70 percent of U.S. oil consumption and 33 percent of CO_2 emissions. Electrical storage on cars and trucks can open the way for less dependence on oil-based liquid fuels. This discussion will focus on the use of batteries for hybrid and plug-in hybrid electric vehicles (HEVs and PHEVs), in which an electrical motor assists and boosts a small internal combustion engine, and in the case of a plug-in, the battery is recharged at an electrical outlet. The concept faces a cost challenge. While the IC engine is smaller in a hybrid of either kind, new power components must be added to the car—batteries, an electric motor, and power electronics —to effectively coordinate the two power systems.[71]

Technology Status and Prospects   After a century and a half of relative stagnation, a number of battery advances now appear within reach. Modern materials science, including nanotechnology, chemistry, and advanced modeling and design, are combining to give rise to improved electrode materials. Continuing major advances are needed in energy density, power rate, cost (including materials costs), and durability (battery lifetime) to make these opportunities real.

Existing HEV battery technology is based on long-established nickel metal hydride technology. These batteries are expensive, heavy, and large. They are made largely in Japan, and were a reliable choice for the first generation of hybrid cars. Rechargeable lithium ion batteries, coupled with advances in nanotechnology, create new possibilities for high-power batteries. A more stable, safer, and more powerful battery along these lines is emerging using nano particles of lithium iron phosphate modified with trace metals.[72] The higher power rate of such a battery could substantially increase fuel economy and increase performance if, for example, it could be made to capture braking energy more fully so as to be powerful enough to start and drive in largely an electric-only mode. The rate of energy storage inherent in braking a ton-and-a-half car from 40 to 0 mph in ten seconds amounts to a charge rate of 24 kW, which could be sufficient to charge a battery in 2.5 minutes.

Next-generation HEV and PHEV batteries are likely to be based on lithium ion technology, and will offer significantly higher energy density, smaller size, and higher power at less cost and improved safety and stability. These new technologies are already evolving, and lithium safety issues are being addressed. Researchers are also using computational modeling to design crystal structures at the nanoscale that can move lithium ions and electrons quickly through their structures. While an internal combustion engine reaches high power at high RPM, an electric motor has high torque, and reaches full power quickly at low RPM. In other words, a hybrid can offer considerably better auto performance. A standard compact hybrid car operating on its electric engine could reach 0 to 60 mph in four seconds, for example. To be sure, HEV technology does not necessarily promote energy savings because hybrid capability can still be coupled with a large internal combustion engine that limits energy savings. In other words, energy efficiency gains will have to be designed in as an explicit choice.

In a larger sense, however, battery technology can create new synergies because in some forms it can provide storage for a range of intermittent energy sources, such as wind and solar, and also can be a power buffer for other vehicle energy sources: internal combustion gasoline, diesel, or biofuel engines, or fuel cells. Plug-in HEVs (PHEVs) are the next stage, assuming that battery prices continue to come down, and new lithium ion nano-enabled batteries may enable the PHEV stage to evolve quickly. Fuel efficiency in the range of 150 mpg or more for a PHEV compact car appears possible on a commuter route, depending on its length as detailed below, compared to around 45 mpg for current HEVs, depending on the model. A major benefit of the PHEV is that it can bring direct competition and corresponding arbitrage between liquid fuels (whether petroleum-based or biofuel) and electricity.[73]

Potential Breakthroughs through Long-Range Research Batteries may seem simple to the user, but their operation depends on complicated chemical and physical phenomena. These involve chemical structures and processes on the scale of nanometers and on time scales ranging from seconds to a few femtoseconds—a few quadrillionths [10^{-15}] of a second, or about the time it takes light to pass the width of a human hair. For this reason, until now the design of batteries and other means of energy storage has largely been based on Edisonian methods of cut-and-try, rather than on a fundamental understanding of the relevant physics and chemistry.

Major advances in technique have now made it possible to study directly the fine details of the nanoscale structure of battery electrodes, as well as those of their interface with the electrolytes, the solutions that carry current between them. Powerful new methods are also available with which to study the details of the charge transfer processes by which electrical charge is transferred between electrode and electrolyte, as well as the changes in their physical and chemical structure with time that affect the useful life of the battery and its ability to charge and discharge rapidly and repeatedly. Once these processes are well understood, it should be possible to use the new understanding of nanoscale structures to design and build new chemical and physical structures for electrodes and electrolytes, so as to produce revolutionary improvements in battery cost, lifetime, weight, storage capacity, speed of charge and discharge, and the ability to sustain repeated cycles of charge and discharge—in short, all of the parameters critical to energy storage in a plug-in hybrid car.

Research needs to continue, then, in critical areas, including (1) fundamental understanding at the nanoscale, using new processes such as nanoscale self-assembly and new tools to understand the interfaces and (2) nanoscience-enabled high-energy lithium battery materials (including the potential of nanomaterials to make full use of the reversible capacity of high-energy positive electrode materials).[74] More immediately, materials costs need to come down.

Large-scale, inexpensive storage is needed to make intermittent renewables, including wind and solar, more viable. Sodium-sulfur and redox flow cells are two large-scale stationary battery technologies now being evaluated by utilities. These technologies are not suitable for transportation, in the first example because of high operating temperature, and in the second because of low energy density, but they are scalable to large total size.

Likely Launch Path and Potential Government Role   Battery breakthroughs are on the way and moving quickly. Power tools are now powered by new lithium ion batteries, in which nanotechnology engineering makes possible much more rapid charging and discharging. While lithium batteries evolved in Asia for electronics, the power-tool sector functioned in the United States as a niche in which new lithium ion battery advances could be tested and initially implemented. Comparable batteries will soon shift into the auto sector for HEVs and particularly for PHEVs. New batteries are thus potentially powerful enablers of energy-saving progress in the transport sector.

A highly publicized initial model is General Motor's "Volt," a form of PHEV expected to enter the market with limited production in 2010.[75] It will run purely on electricity from onboard lithium ion batteries for up to 40 miles (64 km)—far enough that it will cover the average daily American commute of 33 miles (53 km). Since fewer than 25 percent of Americans commute more than 40 miles, this means most commuter travel will require no gasoline. After the batteries are drawn down, the vehicle will use a small internal combustion engine that drives a generator to resupply the batteries, so that the range of the vehicle is extended to some 640 highway miles (1,030 km) with fuel consumption of 50 mpg overall for this full range. Recharge (the "plug-in") is expected to occur from a standard electrical outlet, preferably at night from utility baseload power (or during the workday if outlets are available, using possibly more expensive peaking power), and take some six hours. Unlike GM's previous two-seater electrical vehicle, the "EV-1," the Volt will be a four-door and carry four or five passengers. Its internal combustion engine will have no mechanical linkage to the wheels (unlike current hybrid vehicles), so that the engine can run at constant speed, with corresponding optimal efficiency and mechanical simplicity. For this reason, GM has discarded the term *hybrid*, calling it an electrical vehicle with a "range extender"—the small IC engine—or "E-REV," although it has both electric and IC engines and plugs in, so that it satisfies the definition of a PHEV.

Separating the electric drive train from the booster IC engine used to charge the batteries makes possible flexibility in the type of engine to be employed. Initial GM plans call for a turbocharged 1-liter engine with three cylinders that would be flex-fueled, that is, would be capable of running on gasoline or E85 (85 percent ethanol, 15 percent gasoline), with a 12-gallon tank (45 liters). Although fuel cells are still too high in cost as compared to newer lithium ion batteries, the Volt could also be fuel-cell powered. Cost remains a major question, and tax credits for PHEVs will be important to bring prices within consumer range. The cost of new batteries remains high; further manufacturing process experience will help drive it down, but the industry indicates that materials are still the predominant battery cost factor and are a priority R&D challenge requiring further attention.[76] GM faces competition from comparable electric vehicles announced by Toyota, Nissan, and others as well as possible new vehicles from start-ups.

New batteries will be components in established transport platforms, not separate systems. Because they will make possible better performing cars and trucks, HEVs and follow-on PHEVs are likely to be accepted on launch as components of evolving systems, based on their cost and performance, without nonmarket opposition from existing technologies. Government has already invested substantially in hybrid-technology R&D through the 1990s Partnership for a New Generation of Vehicles program, which stimulated the evolution of a great deal of technology. Government has also funded the nanotechnology R&D program; the National Nanotechnology Initiative, which started in the late 1990s, continues through the present, and has yielded new battery breakthroughs. Lithium ion battery R&D has received specific support from DOE and

DOD. Government front-end support for R&D on manufacturing process and lower-cost components for batteries is still required, as noted above, in addition to the other research tasks enumerated above.

Back-end incentives for technology implementation in the past have provided significant impetus to hybrid evolution, particularly California's low- and zero-emission vehicle standards and federal tax credits for HEV purchases. New federal fuel economy standards passed in 2007 will assist.[77] Expanded back-end incentives, including extension and expansion of federal tax credits for purchase of PHEVs, would encourage improvements and scale-up of manufacturing technology and accelerate PHEV penetration into the lower-cost segments of the automobile market. This would be desirable, given that turnover in the automobile fleet normally takes over fifteen years.

Geothermal

Overview   Geothermal energy may be entering a new day.[78] New advances in geothermal reservoir creation and stimulation may make it cost-competitive with existing electricity generation technology, and if so could provide electric utilities with substantial additional generating capacity. While U.S. electricity generation has increased some 40 percent in the last ten years, this has been achieved largely by bringing online combined cycle generation plants fired by natural gas. Given rising natural gas prices and demand, geothermal could be adopted as a growing component of the existing generating network in a nonconfrontational launch. This contrasts with previous projections of the Energy Information Agency, which assumed that growing electricity needs will be met through natural gas (increasingly from foreign sources) and from coal.

Technology Status and Prospects   Three geothermal technologies are well established: electricity from natural hydrothermal resources, geothermal or ground-source heat pumps, and direct use of geothermal energy for heating buildings and processes.[79] A fourth technology, engineered deep geothermal systems, also known as enhanced geothermal systems (EGS) or hot dry rock, promises to provide a major advance in the scale of geothermal energy. A 2007 evaluation published by MIT and supported by NREL concludes that technology advances in deep well drilling techniques and reservoir characterization and stimulation, along with numerous successes at field demonstration sites around the globe— for example, at the Soutz site in Europe and at Cooper Basin in Australia—have reinforced the potential of deep geothermal for becoming a significant provider of baseload electricity.[80]

EGS consists of drilling into a high-temperature rock formation and hydraulically fracturing (or "stimulating") it to create large reservoirs of hot, permeable rock and to connect them to a second well, known as a production well. Water is then heated by pumping it through these deep reservoirs and back to the surface via the production well. It is then used to produce power through any of a number of energy-conversion technologies, ranging from turbines to heat exchangers to cogeneration, with only a small visual footprint and therefore limited impairment to landscapes. The water is then recycled back into the reservoirs in a closed system, so that pollution and excessive water use are limited.

Unlike established geothermal technologies, which are usable only in areas where geothermal resources are comparatively near the surface, new EGS technology has made geothermal potentially accessible in most areas of the United States, assuming continuing technology advances and efforts to drive down costs. EGS plants can be modular, and therefore readily deployable throughout the United States. The 2007 study estimates that the geothermal resource base in the United States exceeds 14 million exajoules (EJ), compared to total world energy consumption in 2002 of 400 EJ and U.S. consumption of 100 EJ.[81] In other words, geothermal energy constitutes a truly massive, renewable resource in the sense that it would be barely touched even if ways were found to derive all the world's power needs from it. Because drilling costs increase nonlinearly with depth, only some of this source is now accessible in the United States at reasonable cost, largely in the Western states, but even this would constitute a huge new renewable resource. Unlike other renewables that rely on diurnal patterns of the sun or ever-changing weather, geothermal heat is consistently available twenty-four hours a day, and so could provide baseload power. These characteristics make geothermal an attractive resource.

Three sets of incremental technological innovations have made this new option possible. First, incremental advances in drilling technology over the last thirty years, including robust drill bits, innovative drilling casings, better sensors and electronics, and new methods for rock penetration, have made possible deeper penetration to sources of hotter resources 4 to 6 km below ground level. Over time, geothermal could be available nationwide if cost efficiencies are introduced to make drilling at 10 km more cost-effective. Second, there have been advances in power conversion, particularly in the production of electricity from lower-temperature working fluids using Rankine cycle turbines.[82] Third, larger reservoirs can now be formed, thanks to evolving hydraulic rock-fracturing and reservoir-imaging techniques, creating the possibility of increased production flow rates with improved lifetimes at higher temperatures.[83] With continuing advances in reservoir production and reductions in drilling costs, much of the nation could exploit EGS economically.[84]

Potential Breakthroughs through Long-Range Research   Because EGS borrows heavily from advances in petroleum recovery, many elements of EGS technology for the capture and extraction of geothermal energy are already in place. A key remaining issue is to develop the ability to better engineer the deep reservoirs into which water will be pumped and from which it will be recycled. This means more work on hydraulic stimulation in order to make possible commercial production rates and lifetimes.

Exploration for geothermal resources uses seismic techniques derived from petroleum exploration. However, geothermal exploration requires higher spatial resolution, which can best be achieved by the use of measuring instruments that can be introduced into the hot environment in the exploration hole. The present market does not justify the investment that would be required to develop such robust equipment, a chicken-and-egg situation that could be resolved by suitable incentives. Overall, there is also a strong need for better cost data, based on realistic experiments and demonstrations.

Likely Launch Paths and Potential Government Role   EGS will be on-grid and so is a secondary technology that must compete from its initial market launch with established technologies for generating electricity. Large-scale demonstrations would be useful to show the technoeconomic feasibility of new geothermal technology. The federal role with EGS would include front-end research, development, and technology demonstrations. A series of sites of different types should be selected for testing engineering for optimal reservoir creation. An RD&D competition could be held to stimulate consortia of industry, academic, and laboratory teams to research, explore, and field-test a range of sites for optimal reservoir creation. The expectation of the 2007 study group is that these development tests could foster private-sector investment and make this technology cost-competitive in the electricity sector, although some back-end federal support may still be required.

The 2007 study concluded that a relatively modest federal investment in RD&D (at least compared to existing federal energy technology subsidies) over the next fifteen years would demonstrate EGS technology at a commercial scale, cut risks for private investment, and make possible the development of 100,000 MW of production by 2050. It proposes a combined public-private investment in the range of $750 million to $1 billion (averaging from $40 to $80 million per year) for demonstration and deployment and associated research and development, with the federal government providing most of the funding in the initial years and the private sector picking up more in the later period. Many of the report's recommendations on geothermal advance were adopted in the 2007 Energy Act.[85] Depending on the evolving cost structure, government back-end incentives may be needed, particularly to spread EGS beyond the Western states. It is important that any incentive regime take into account the relatively long time horizon (two or three years) between the initial exploration of a potential geothermal site, and the sinking of wells for the production of electric power. An investor must be sure that any promised incentive will still be there when production begins.

Secondary Innovations—Contested Launch: Secondary (Component) Technologies with an Inherent Cost Disadvantage, Facing Political and/or Nonmarket Economic Opposition

The technologies discussed in this section are secondary; they may be components in established systems or substitutes for existing resources to be utilized in larger energy-use systems. However, they will be contested economically and/or politically by powerful incumbents or other forces. Two examples in this category are biofuels and carbon capture and sequestration (CCS) technologies, which face a direct conflict with existing major oil producers and coal-based electric utilities, respectively. These forces will oppose their launch and implementation, politically and through other means. Moreover, these technologies face major cost challenges. Although one major foreign-based oil producer is looking closely at adoption of biofuels, their launch will likely result in confrontation with other firms.

Both incentives and regulatory mandates from the government will have to be designed for this category to facilitate the transition. The large mandates for the production of ethanol from biofuels that have already been obtained as a result of pressure from the powerful agriculture lobby suggest that still further mandates are possible for this technology. Since CCS adds cost to coal-fired utilities without providing any compensating commercial advantage, only a mandate will compel its adoption in the absence of macropricing of CO_2 emissions— that is, a carbon charge. Given that government will in any case have to finance adequate technology demonstrations, regulatory mandates may be deferred until problems connected with purely technical feasibility have been resolved.

Aside from regulatory mandates, both these technologies require public support—for R&D, in the case of biofuels, and for demonstrations, in the case of CCS. Nuclear power is also included in this discussion because the secondary and incremental technology advances that would be incorporated into a new generation of U.S. nuclear power plants will face a heavily contested launch, not from industry but from citizens' groups concerned with environmental safety and proliferation issues, which can be overcome only by government regulatory mandates, the adoption of which will face serious political opposition.

Biofuels

Overview   Biofuels could provide a liquid fuel for the transport sector, competing directly with gasoline.[86] Corn-derived ethanol, the most readily available biofuel, is already mandated by law as a component in U.S. gasoline. In the 2005 Energy Act, Congress required refiners to use 7.5 billion gallons of ethanol per year by 2012, over and above the 51 cents-per-gallon tax credit compared to gasoline. These two factors have led to an ethanol boom. The industry is expected to have the capacity to make more than 11 billion gallons of ethanol by 2009.[87] There are more than a hundred ethanol factories clustered largely in the top six corn-growing states, with some 74 facilities under construction as of early 2008. Title II of the 2007 Energy Act raises the renewable fuel standard to 9 billion gallons in 2008, with increases in progressive steps to 36 billion gallons by 2022; of that total, cellulose-based advanced biofuels are required to make up 21 billion gallons by 2022.[88]

Although U.S. oil firms are starting to move, British Petroleum (BP) has taken leadership, beginning a $500 million multiyear biofuel R&D initiative, and the Department of Energy's Office of Science has launched its own effort, establishing three multiyear R&D centers at $25 million a year each. Brazil provides a model. It has already shifted off reliance on oil, placing its transport system on E80, an 80 percent ethanol blend derived from its plentiful sugar cane crop, building on its long-standing policy of support for fuel ethanol derived from sugar cane.

There is a deeper, long-recognized problem with using corn for ethanol. While corn-based ethanol is the biofuel far ahead ·in market entry, it is very energy-intensive to produce, conferring at best only marginal greenhouse gas environmental benefits. A 2007 study concludes that this margin depends on many inputs and that its energy balance can be positive or negative depending on the underlying assumptions.[89] Concerns also abound about the soil-depletion effects of greatly expanded corn cultivation, and about the consumer price and supply problems associated with diverting a major world food crop to massive biofuel production.[90] A 2008 World Bank staff study suggests that as much as three-quarters of the run-up in food prices in 2002–2008 may derive from increases in the subsidized production of biofuels in the United States and the EU.[91] Recent Midwestern flooding has emphasized potential problems from crop damage due to natural disasters when production of food or feed crops like corn are displaced by energy uses, adding further strains on the availability of food and feed crops.

In sum, corn can be only a transition crop. Politically, however, the transition to other biofuels will be difficult. Corn growers constitute a powerful political lobby, one of the most powerful in U.S. agriculture. Having driven corn prices quite high through ethanol production, they are unlikely to embrace a shift from corn-based to biofuels not derived from corn; there is no switchgrass growers' lobby. The United States is finding itself in a situation where it is not only addicted to oil, it is also addicted to corn. On the other hand, the environmental benefits of large-scale production of ethanol or more optimal biofuels from plant material such as agricultural waste and switchgrass seem clearer—although they still require a thorough evaluation and face cost issues.

If biofuels were to supply 10 percent of world energy needs by 2100 (some 120 EJ), some experts estimate that 2 billion acres of land would have to be dedicated to biofuels, assuming a 40 percent energy efficiency in biomass conversion. This is five times the cropland of the United States, the world's most productive agricultural producer per acre.[92] This acreage total could be altered by use of land not now regarded as arable, by larger-scale use of agricultural waste, improved crop performance, and increased energy conversion rates. A related problem is the availability of water supplies, particularly in drier regions, for this level of production. One possible answer to the political and environmental problems with corn-based ethanol is to explore corn stover, the unused part of the corn plant, such as stalks, now largely discarded as agricultural waste. If corn stover becomes a sound biofuel source (and there are serious technical and cost issues as well as questions of energy efficiency that must be resolved, as will be discussed below), it could offer a politically workable way to transition corn producers off of corn-based ethanol, and because it is a waste product and not a new crop, lessen the adverse environmental effects of biofuels.

Technology Status and Prospects   Is the biofuels buzz justified? Since Congress continues to mandate ever-higher ethanol content in gasoline,[93] will ethanol continue to fit with the current gasoline distribution system, and with existing auto engines? For better or for worse, the growing capacity for ethanol production will soon hit the so-called blend wall. Auto fuel that contains more than 10 percent ethanol is too corrosive for the existing gasoline distribution system. As produced in standard industrial processes, ethanol contains about 5 percent water. This acts as a corrosive. If the blend wall is passed, the nation will need new networks of ethanol pipelines, storage tanks, and station pumps. In other words, shifting above the 10 percent level means building an extremely expensive parallel distribution system.

Potential Breakthroughs through Long-Range Research   The requirement for large-scale industrial production of biofuels gives rise to a great variety of promising areas of research.[94] On the agricultural side, we may foresee the development of new energy crops and crop varieties, especially those suited to growing on land not now suitable for food-crop production, through both traditional breeding and gene modification.[95] (Ideally, such crops would grow better on poor soils than on good soils, so that farmers would have no incentive to displace food crops.) Such research would be complemented by research on techniques of sustainable agriculture, including agronomy and pest control. Oil-forming algae are still another possible source of biofuel. These, too, require research to develop fast-growing species that can resist disease and contamination by other microbial species.

Unlike sources of biofuel like sugar cane and cornstarch, which produce sugars or sugar polymers (such as starch) that have been fermented for millennia, trees and many of the more promising newer "cellulosic" energy crops, such as switch-grass, produce lignocellulose, a complex chemical structure that is resistant to traditional techniques of fermentation. Cheap and efficient technology for conversion of lignocellulose to biofuel would therefore open up major possibilities for biofuel production on land not now used for food crops, as well as from corn stover and other lignocellulosic agricultural waste.[96] These technologies will require demonstrations at industrial scale once they have been proven in pilot plants.

Powerful new tools for the understanding of the intimate mechanisms and dynamics of chemical catalysis promise major long-run advances in these and other catalytic processes.[97] It is now possible to observe catalytic processes at the molecular level at femtosecond (10^{-15} second) or even attosecond (10^{-18} second) speeds, and to use this knowledge to design and synthesize more effective and efficient catalysts that will speed reactions, increase their yields, and allow them to take place at lower temperatures.

It will also be important to develop techniques to monitor the environmental impact of biofuel production, especially on soils, water use, and greenhouse gas production, as well as its effect on land use, both in the United States and abroad, so as to guide the development of policy. These impacts may be direct—as when biofuels are planted on land previously devoted to food crops—or indirect, as when forests are cut down to grow crops that are newly profitable because of the increase in the price of agricultural commodities.[98] Research is also needed on measures to encourage the uptake of carbon dioxide by soils, and conversely, to minimize the loss of carbon dioxide when land is converted to biofuel production.

Research is also needed on improved methods of thermochemical conversion of feedstock into fuel, including gasification of biomass to produce diesel fuel. Finally, improved technology is needed for biomass combustion. Promising technologies in this area include circulating fluidized bed boilers and techniques for firing biomass together with coal in order to run steam turbines.

To summarize some of the key technology-related research needs in more technical terms, each of the four critical stages of biofuel development requires significant R&D, including both bioengineering and chemical engineering, if optimal fuel properties are to be achieved:[99]

Biomass production requires crop optimization to increase biomass yields so as to reduce the amount of farmable land needed for biofuel feedstocks. Plant genomics, genetic engineering, and traditional agricultural research methods are all needed to develop optimal crops and crop varieties with traits that will enable them to be grown on land that is now considered nonarable wasteland, while minimizing the level of intervention needed to sustain production.

Biomass preparation and treatment will require work at the first stage of biorefining, in which plant material is separated into its cellulose, hemicellulose, and lignin components. This is a multistage process that needs to be simplified and stream-lined through chemical engineering and through bioengineering related to the properties of the new types of cellulosic biomass that will be utilized as feedstocks.

Conversion of biomass sugars into a biofuel by microbial fermentation, the next biorefining stage, requires bioengineering to create new microbes that can carry out this sugar conversion with improvements on two fronts. First, microbes can be created to produce new molecules with better fuel properties than ethanol. Butanol is one such possibility, and alternatives with even better characteristics appear promising.[100] Second, these microbes must be able to operate in a manner that is less inhibited by toxic compounds that now affect and limit the process.

Separation of biofuels from fermentation broths will require the development of novel methods to reduce the energy costs of traditional distillation. Improvements in production leading to higher product concentrations will lead to a decrease in separation costs. Alternative fuels developed from biomass that have higher energy density and are more hydrophobic than ethanol may also make possible new options for biofuel separations that improve recovery and reduce costs.

Likely Launch Path and Potential Government Role   The government is already playing a major role on the front end at the R&D stages, for both cellulosic ethanol and biomass alternatives with better fuel and corrosion characteristics, and will need to continue to do so. Support for technology demonstrations will also likely be required, including on distribution systems. On the back end, the government has already intervened with major regulatory mandates. Despite this, given that important parts of the oil sector may still not welcome non-petroleum competitors, a package of government tax and production incentives, as well as continuing mandates geared to better types of biofuels, is likely to be required to ensure a technology transition.

The oil industry, in general, remains concerned about the shift to biofuels. Ethanol, in particular, requires huge new infrastructure investments because its corrosive characteristics are incompatible with existing fuel infrastructure. The farm lobby, with its massive direct and indirect employment base, major backing from agribusiness interests, national geographic presence, and long-standing political organization, has thus far proven a more potent political force than even the oil lobby. If the oil industry faces continuing political pressure from the farm sector, it may find biofuels more adaptable than other fuel competitors to its type of distribution networks, since they are liquid fuels with properties more akin to gasoline than other options. BP is one oil company that appears to be thinking ahead about this political contest, and its research in significant part is focused on finding biofuel options—it is now focused on butanol—that would be more compatible than ethanol with pipeline, transport, and pumping infrastructure, and would thus enable a less costly shift. Butanol can also be blended into gasoline at higher concentrations than ethanol without altering auto engines.[101] Make no mistake, this will be a contested transition, but the farm sector may be able to use its political muscle to force the oil industry at least to hedge its fuel options, making more room for biofuels. The problem is that this lobby may now be locked in to corn ethanol, and a shift to cellulosic ethanols or other biofuel types may prove very difficult.

One lesson of the corn ethanol experience is that environmental studies of the possible consequences of biofuel production at large scale must be performed in parallel to the research stage before the outset of the commercial transition period, so as to ensure that as biofuels are scaled up, they can be produced in an environmentally sound manner.[102] Indeed, if sounder environmental pathways for biofuels are not developed, biofuels could be a costly dead end with potentially major adverse consequences. This transition period for R&D, the needed environmental studies, and as discussed below, potential changes in distribution infrastructure and engine modifications in the auto fleet, could take a decade or more.

The current truck distribution system for ethanol is not energy-efficient and so should be only an interim solution. Going above the blend wall also means modifications to auto engines, significant enough so that they will have to work their way through the fifteen-year life of the auto fleet. Congress has already begun to require a percentage of "flex-fuel" vehicles (autos that can be ethanol or gasoline powered) in total auto production, but because of fleet turnover and the additional distribution system, ethanol is not a short-term fix. The "blend wall" will create a gap where ethanol distribution systems and auto engines will have to catch up to expected levels of agricultural production. This gap period could provide time to shift from corn-based ethanol to cellulosic ethanol or, if they can be bioengineered, to other related biomass-based fuels that are more environmentally sound, pack higher fuel density, are less corrosive, and require less of a shift in infrastructure.

Carbon Capture and Sequestration

Overview   Electricity consumed by residential, commercial, and industry users accounts for 42 percent of U.S. CO_2 emissions. More than half of that electricity and some 85 percent of emissions from the generation of electricity come from coal-fired plants; overall, coal accounts for 37 percent of U.S. CO_2 emissions.[103] Like China and India, the United States[104] is home to one of the world's largest coal reserves.[105] While technologies to clean up traditional coal pollutants (NOx,

SOx, mercury, and particulates) are available at reasonable cost, climate change and CO_2 emissions present a much larger challenge to coal, which in the United States has a carbon content, depending on the type of coal, ranging from 35 percent (for lignites) to 87 percent (for anthracites).[106]

Because the United States, like the world in general, is overwhelmingly dependent on coal for electricity, coal cannot be replaced any time soon as an energy source. Even with the entry of alternatives, growing electricity demand dictates that U.S. coal consumption will grow by midcentury. China is now building the equivalent of two 500 MW coal power plants a week; this pace is quickening.[107] These and other non-CCS plants will be expensive or impossible to retrofit should CCS become practical in the future. With sixty-year life spans, new coal-generating facilities worldwide over the next thirty years are expected to introduce into the atmosphere almost as much CO_2 as has been released by all the coal that has been burned since the onset of the industrial revolution.

Technology Status and Prospects   CCS is the leading mechanism offering the prospect of allowing continued use of coal while resolving coal's profound CO_2 emission problem. But is CCS technically feasible? Experts argue that the major components of CCS are already available because they have been developed for and are being used in other industrial processes. CO_2 is already being stored in deep onshore or offshore geological formations, including depleted oil and gas fields and salt formations, through techniques developed by the oil and natural gas industry. Both the United States and China have extensive networks of saline aquifers that will work for storage, generally without requiring pipeline transport from coal plant to storage beyond a range of 50–75 miles.[108] In other words, there may not have to be pipelines everywhere because these pipeline networks will be regional rather than national in scope like natural gas pipelines. Thus, NIMBY ("not in my backyard") problems may be at a manageable scale.

However, CCS is very expensive compared to today's generation mix, and transforms coal into a much more expensive fuel. It will raise the price of electricity generated by coal by some 50 percent at the power plant and by some 25 percent for the consumer.[109] However, compared to a future mix of low carbon sources, CCS may prove cost competitive. Several major sequestration projects at large scale (a million tons per year) are now in operation—Sleipner in the North Sea, Weyburn in Saskatchewan, and In-Salah in Algeria.[110] Thus, the sequestration technology is already at the large-scale demonstration stage. However, none of these storage demonstration projects is tracked by sensors or monitors sufficient to provide an adequate level of assurance concerning the ability to store very large quantities of CO_2 over the long term without significant risk of escape, especially given the scale of storage required: a 500 MW power plant over its lifetime will generate a billion barrels of liquefied CO_2, a huge volume that must be sequestered indefinitely.[111] In addition, these demonstrations are sequestration projects, not power projects, and therefore do not have large capture costs and can be only partial models for operations that integrate capture, transport, and sequestration.

A viable CCS technology would consist of three stages: separating the CO_2 from utility and industrial sources, transporting it to a storage site, and isolating it from the atmosphere for hundreds of years until replacement alternatives evolve. A recent major report on the future of coal from MIT identified four major challenges facing CCS: (1) cutting the costs of CO_2 capture, (2) establishing scientific certainty regarding the security of extremely long-term storage of CO_2 in geological formations at the very large scale required, (3) developing the best practices for operating CO_2 storage fields long term, and (4) developing a regulatory structure that would permit the introduction of CCS.[112] R&D will be needed to meet the first challenge of cutting the costs of CO_2 capture, which is the most expensive stage in CCS technology. While Integrated Gasification Combined Cycle (IGCC) with CO_2 capture appears to offer the most economical capture technology at this time, it is not suited for all types of coal, and needs to be supplemented with R&D on a range of other technologies for this purpose.

Although most geologists are confident that long-term storage is possible without significant leakage, full scientific testing, monitoring, and evaluation of storage approaches will be required to provide assurances that CO_2 storage can indeed be made secure. In addition, operating a CO_2 storage field will require development of effective operating practices, analogous to the sound operating practices required for oil fields. Best and most cost-effective practices will also have to be developed for integrating capture, transport, and sequestration stages. Major sequestration demonstration projects are needed, and should be designed so as to develop these practices in different kinds of geological sites.

Potential Breakthroughs through Long-Term Research   Major scientific challenges are involved in ensuring that the extraordinarily large quantities of carbon dioxide that would have to be injected into the earth will in fact stay there for the time needed to mitigate the effects of global warming. This is because significant advances in the geosciences are required to achieve a satisfactory understanding of the fate of carbon dioxide once it is injected in huge quantities into complex subterranean structures.[113]

Research is required to describe, model, predict, and monitor the path of injected CO_2 in various geological formations, and the hydromechanical, chemical, and biogeochemical processes that take place as it interacts with the many kinds of mineral structures, fluids, and microorganisms that are found beneath the surface of the earth, with special emphasis on the interfaces (boundary layers) between them. (As an aside, biological processes may be important here, because a high percentage of the biomass of the planet is thought to be lodged in subsurface microorganisms.)

This research presents multiple difficulties. First, the site of these phenomena is relatively inaccessible. Second, the research requires integrated modeling of phenomena that involve many different kinds of fluids and mineral structures and that take place on wildly different spatial scales—from nanometers to tens of kilometers. Third, it requires models of phenomena that will not take place for hundreds or thousands of years and hence cannot be verified by empirical observation.

At the more immediate level, the biggest potential for long-term breakthroughs in CCS technology lie in improved techniques for the capture of carbon dioxide from exhaust stack gases that do not rely on solvents, and changes in power-plant design to minimize carbon dioxide emission even as they produce cheap power.[114] Additional areas for process research will no doubt emerge from the demonstration projects now being planned in Europe for the decade beginning in 2011.

Likely Launch Path and Potential Government Role   The federal government will be required to play a central role in the process R&D and in the scientifically monitored demonstration projects required. The *Future of Coal* (2007) report from MIT makes a strong case for putting in place three to five large scale demonstration projects (over a million metric tons of CO_2 storage a year each) to provide working, integrated models for industry to resolve operating and cost questions. The timetable for establishing such demonstrations, however, has been pushed back by the Department of Energy's cancellation of "FutureGen," its major CCS demonstration, which was established with industry collaboration. Citing escalating project costs, DOE announced that it would instead support multiple smaller CCS projects, planned to be operational by 2015.[115] Assuming that a workable demonstration program and schedule can be reestablished, the government, in parallel, will also have to establish a proper legal framework for CCS, and to coordinate this with evolving international legal frameworks, so as to create a regulatory regime that will control CCS systems and ensure their long-term storage viability and maintenance.

Since the coal and electric utility sectors are unlikely to greet the huge cost imposition of CCS with enthusiasm, CCS as a potential component of coal-fired energy generation will be a contested launch, with industry reluctant to accept it and holding out for an extended demonstration period. Therefore, back-end incentives and, likely, mandates for CCS implementation will be required. Indeed, until a sound regulatory regime is thought through for CCS, it is unlikely to gain political acceptance. As Howard Herzog, a leading expert, has defined the problem,

The regulatory scheme must resolve issues associated with the definition of property rights, site licensing and monitoring, ownership, liability, compensation arrangements and other institutional considerations. Regulatory protocols need to be defined for sequestration projects, including site selection, injection operation, and eventual transfer of custody to public authorities after a period of successful operation. . . . Attention must be paid to the question of what accompanying market-based incentive structure would optimize implementation of CCS and the accompanying regulatory system. Finally, another key policy area is "credits" under a "cap-and-trade" regime for climate, and how CCS would fit within such a national and international climate policy framework . . . [and] how to account for sequestered carbon and potential leakage. These are important regulatory issues and . . . need to be addressed with far more urgency than is evidenced today.[116]

CCS is not only a national problem. A sound international control regime, workable in developing as well as developed nations, is essential if CCS is to succeed in making coal an environmentally acceptable fuel in the future.

Nuclear Power

Overview Along with hydropower, nuclear is the major source of carbon-free energy, supplying one sixth of the world's energy.[117] With the exception of two dramatic and high-profile accidents, Chernobyl and Three Mile Island, nuclear power has been reliable and safe. The problem of global warming has given rise to a reexamination of the role of nuclear power. Although no new nuclear power plant has been built in the United States in thirty years, more than 20 GW of nuclear capacity has been built in the world since 2000. There are 441 nuclear power reactors operating in 31 countries worldwide, and another 32 reactors are under construction abroad.[118]

The U.S. experience with nuclear power contrasts most sharply with that of France. France has 59 nuclear reactors operated by Electricité de France (EDF), which supply 78 percent of the total power generated in France.[119] Over the last decade France has exported 60–70 billion kWh net each year, making it the world's largest exporter of electricity, gaining France 3 billion euros in exports each year. France's emphasis on nuclear power dates from a French government decision in 1974, taken just after the first oil shock, to expand the country's nuclear power capacity rapidly. France faced a situation where it had substantial nuclear engineering expertise and limited energy resources. Nuclear energy, in which the fuel cost is but a relatively small part of the overall cost, made policy sense for the purpose of cutting imports and achieving greater energy security. In contrast with American practice, the French nuclear program has built many standard plants, enabling it to standardize construction and management practices and in this way to achieve advantages in cost, reliability, and safety. France now claims a substantial level of energy independence and is close to having the lowest-cost electricity in Europe. Over 90 percent of its electricity is from nuclear or hydro sources. Just as Brazil has pointed to the possibilities of large-scale development of biofuels, France has done so for nuclear power. Could the United States place a new emphasis on nuclear?

Technology Status and Prospects   The production of electricity by nuclear technology has been steadily and incrementally improving, with third-generation reactors offering better fuel technology and passive safety so that the reactor shuts down without operator intervention in case of an accident. Fourth-generation reactors such as new high temperature gas reactors, including pebble bed reactors and lead-cooled fast reactors, as discussed below, are now being researched and are expected to offer further improvements and efficiencies. Nuclear technology also needs to cut costs (although carbon pricing for its competitors, coal and gas, would make it very cost-competitive). In addition, it has to solve its decommissioning and waste-storage problems, and, internationally, to find ways to resolve the threats of diversion, proliferation, and vulnerability to terrorist attack, and to ensure universal adherence to the strict construction standards needed to ensure safe operation. The problem of diversion and terrorist attack will be particularly difficult if a worldwide expansion of nuclear power is accompanied by widespread reprocessing of nuclear fuel, in which case there would be a large number of vulnerable fuel shipments. DOE is attempting to manage these issues through its Global Nuclear Energy Partnership (GNEP) program, although this program faces a number of concerns.[120]

Potential Breakthroughs through Long-Term Research The Department of Energy has developed a technology roadmap for U.S. Generation IV reactor priorities, and five of the six technology concepts identified in it are being pursued at different levels of support, depending on the state of each technology and its ability to meet program goals noted below. DOE has summarized these six as follows.[121] Two are thermal neutron spectrum systems, the Very-High-Temperature Reactor (VHTR) and the Supercritical-Water-Cooled Reactor, with coolants and temperatures that make possible hydrogen or electricity production with high efficiency. Three are fast neutron spectrum systems (the Gas-Cooled, the Lead-Cooled, and the Sodium-Cooled fast reactors) that aim to enable more effective management of actinides through recycling of most components in the discharged fuel. DOE is not currently researching the sixth concept, the molten salt reactor. Of these efforts, DOE has given priority to VHTR, a system compatible with electricity and hydrogen generation. This effort is part of the Next Generation Nuclear Plant (NGNP) program authorized in the Energy Policy Act of 2005.

Most of these designs are generally not expected to be available for commercial construction before 2030, with the exception of the version of the VHTR pursued through NGNP, which DOE has aimed to complete by 2021. The goals of the Generation IV program are to improve nuclear safety, to improve proliferation resistance, to minimize waste and natural resource utilization, and to decrease the cost to build and operate these plants. Concern has been expressed in congressional hearings about whether the technical challenges for this program will disrupt the technology implementation schedule.[122]

Underlying these DOE programs are a series of longer-term basic research challenges to attempt to ameliorate some of the major problems associated with nuclear power, in particular the safety and proliferation problems associated with nuclear fuel, and the volume of highly radioactive waste produced by a nuclear power reactor. One approach to easing the problem of nuclear waste disposal has been to reduce the lifetime of radioactivity of this waste by separating out the recyclable nuclear fuel, and then transmuting longer-lived radioactive isotopes into elements that have shorter half-lives and hence need to be stored for shorter periods—say, centuries instead of millennia. Here a scientific problem is the lack of fundamental understanding of the materials and chemical properties of transuranium elements (elements with atomic numbers higher than that of uranium), which are toxic and radioactive and some of which are available only in minute quantities. In particular, it is important to understand how these elements can be efficiently separated from each other, the best way to transmute them into shorter-lived isotopes, and how they behave under the conditions of high temperatures and intense irradiation that prevail inside a reactor. Such research could also lead to better fabrication techniques and more efficient nuclear fuel cycles, and perhaps to fuel cycles that do not use or produce materials that can be made into nuclear weapons.

A better understanding of how the waste products of nuclear fission migrate within the fuel element as the reactor continues to produce power could lead to a lower volume of nuclear waste and ease the problem of waste storage.[123] Even with the lower volume of waste that may be made available by these techniques when they are developed, more work is required to understand the fate over long time periods of the containers for nuclear waste and of the chemical species that are found in these wastes. Here there is a need for many of the same kinds of research that are required in order to understand the fate of carbon dioxide injected into the earth as a result of a future program of carbon sequestration, with an added emphasis on the study of possible radiochemical interactions with subterranean structures, and of the path of fluids that could dissolve or entrain radioactive or toxic materials.[124] To be sure, decisions as to whether to expand nuclear power in the next decade are unlikely to be able to await the results of this long-term basic research.

Likely Launch Paths and Potential for Government Intervention
Expansion of nuclear power in the United States will need to be accompanied by a series of secondary and incremental technology advances for safer and more efficient fourth-generation power plants, as noted above. This development is already heavily supported by government incentives. However, further nuclear development in the United States, although not opposed by industry, will continue to be heavily contested and will require a continuing, concerted but politically controversial government effort to ensure and streamline the availability of new power-plant sites, to manage waste storage, and to deal with environmental and security problems. Energy legislation passed in 2005 takes major steps in this direction, as well as providing loan guarantees sought by industry to lower the cost of financing for new nuclear plants. Another form of support, in the form of limitations on liability suits that in effect transfer the risk of accidents from utility companies to the government, has been in place for decades. Further government mandates and incentives will be required to overcome what will be a politically contested technology launch.

Worldwide, as noted above, major problems need to be overcome if nuclear power is to expand to a level that makes a significant contribution to the global warming problem. Worldwide construction, safety, environmental, and security standards for nuclear plants need to be developed, adopted, and enforced. The regime to prevent diversion of nuclear materials will need to be reexamined to enable it to accommodate much larger volumes of nuclear material. There is thus a crucial need for effective national and international regimes, of which the GNEP proposal noted above is an aspect, to address the profound policy problems that would be created by a major expansion of nuclear power.[125] Even if the technical as well as the domestic and international political problems related to the expansion of nuclear power can be overcome, opposition from citizens' groups concerned with environmental safety and nuclear proliferation will continue. These may continue to prevent or seriously delay construction and increase construction costs in the United States. In sum, nuclear power has already obtained substantial government R&D support for gains in efficiency and other incremental improvements and for accompanying government incentives and mandates, but faces major domestic as well as international policy challenges if it is to expand on a scale sufficient to make an impact on U.S. and global CO_2 emissions and energy security.

Incremental Innovations for Conservation and End-Use Efficiency

Conservation is an end-use issue, not a resource issue, and for the most part involves incremental improvements to existing as well as new technology. It includes efficiency in the end use of existing energy technologies, such as in the building sector, and incremental advance for other technologies, such as efficiency in the grid and the internal combustion engine. Support for research may be required, particularly for these efficiency and incremental gains; R&D and demonstration support appear to be required for both changes in technology and gains in efficiency.[126] Low-cost financing may be required to encourage investments that do not meet the requirements for quick payoff that consumers and businesses have come to require for investments in conservation and end-use efficiency.

Aside from carbon prices, which are critical signals for nearly all energy innovations, the important issue here is back-end policies specific to each end-use sector. In this area, these policies will generally take the form of regulatory and related mandates—especially standards, such as new building codes, appliance standards, lighting standards, or enhanced CAFE standards for the internal combustion engine. These need to be put in place promptly, because there is plenty of technology already available, and still more that could be readily put in place by incremental advances that are likely to emerge from public and private initiative. Government front-end support for RD&D, as noted, may also be required, particularly for efficiency gains.

The IC engine and building technologies provide examples of the need for ongoing conservation and end-use efficiency through incremental technology gains. A mix of front-end R&D and back-end incentives, as well as regulatory mandates, such as standards and codes, will be required, tailored to the needs of particular technology pathways.

Internal Combustion Engine Improvements

Overview The United States consumes around 7 billion barrels of oil each year, primarily to burn in internal combustion (IC) engines.[127] These costs approach three-quarters of a trillion dollars a year in direct expenditures, with oil at about $100 a barrel as we just experienced in the summer of 2008. Petroleum combustion accounts for some 42 percent of U.S. CO_2 emissions.[128] A 4 percent improvement (around a mile per gallon) in engine efficiency would translate into a savings, with oil in this price range, of around $22 billion a year, or around 600,000 barrels of oil a day, since vehicle use accounts for 14 to 15 million barrels a day.[129] We pay many prices for our IC engines. Aside from climate, geopolitical, and energy security effects, they are the major source of air pollution in most urban areas and diesel particulates appear to be correlated with urban mortality rates.

The manufacture of the IC engine, together with the fuel and petrochemical industries, are major components of the U.S. economy, but the economic role of engine manufacture in the United States has been declining due to global competition. New efficiencies in IC engines and their fuel consumption are thus a key medium-term (15–25 years) energy economic opportunity area. An improved IC engine could also help restore the dwindling competitiveness of the U.S. automobile industry. From an environmental perspective, if incremental IC improvements were to be adopted more rapidly than plug-in hybrids or other fundamental technology changes, they might make possible faster overall savings in emissions. For example, a fundamental technology shift that offers a 50 percent fuel savings but is adopted in only in 2 percent of the nation's vehicles would have one one-hundredth the impact of an incremental IC engine advance that provides a 20 percent fuel savings in half the nation's vehicles. Of course, the reality is such that both incremental and fundamental approaches are in order. We should not neglect opportunities from incremental advances in efficiency.

A report from a team led by automotive engineering expert John Heywood supports these findings.[130] Low rates of fleet turnover and the history of gradual implementation of new engine technologies in the auto sector mean that the rates of fuel consumption and emissions of vehicles using mainstream IC technologies will dominate this sector for a long time to come. Europe, which has long faced higher fuel costs, has experimented with low-emission diesels and smaller and lower-weight vehicles, and these technologies are now well understood. More aggressive adoption in the United States of these kinds of mainstream vehicle technologies, which may well require regulatory interventions if high fuel costs do not continue, could lead in the mid-term to substantially greater savings in fuel consumption and hence in emissions than breakthrough technologies such as PHEVs. The latter may, however, predominate in the longer term.

Technology Status and Potential In addition to the mainstream approaches noted above, a number of IC advances are under consideration, including, for example, Homogeneous Charge Compression Ignition technologies to substantially improve IC efficiency and reduce pollution. Another example is a new approach announced by researchers Daniel Cohn, Lesley Bromberg, and John Heywood at MIT's Plasma Fusion and Sloan Automotive labs. It takes several established automotive technologies, including the turbocharger and direct fuel injection, and combines them with the use of a small amount of ethanol to prevent engine knock on acceleration, making it possible for a significantly smaller engine with significantly lower fuel consumption to provide a power output comparable to that of today's IC engines.[131] This approach could provide an efficiency gain comparable to that provided by the hybrid or diesel at notably lower incremental cost, resulting in a fuel savings payback time of between two and three years. This could make possible more rapid mass-market adoption of engine technology with higher fuel efficiency. The new design is being tested by Ford with cost-share funding from the Energy Department. The research team believes that this "ethanol-boosted gasoline engine" concept could be ready for use in production vehicles by 2012.

Likely Launch Pathways and Possible Government Intervention Incremental advances in the IC engine that do not require major retooling offer medium-term reduction in CO_2

emissions pending introduction of longer-term alternatives, such as PHEVs and later, fuel cells. In the longer term, the technology could be extended to provide the IC component in hybrid engines. Incentives likely are not needed if gasoline prices remain high because the advance is incremental. However, to ensure something resembling a level playing field, it may be advisable to extend to advances in incremental efficiency some aspects of the incentives being offered for more fundamental advances, in order to reduce the payback period for savings, since significant gains are possible from both. Regulatory mandates may also be in order. The new CAFE standards or expanded fuel economy standards may speed the introduction of this technology.

Building Technologies

Overview Almost 40 percent of greenhouse gas emissions come from residential and commercial buildings.[132] Because buildings have a lifespan of fifty to a hundred years, retrofitting is key—deploying new efficiency technologies solely in new construction is too slow a process. It has been estimated that the United States will need to reduce building energy intensity by a factor of 1/2 to 2/3 from current standard practice by midcentury to meet energy and environmental goals. This will require a reduction in energy intensity in new buildings by a factor of 2/3 to 3/4 from current practice, and a factor of 1/2 from building renovations.[133]

Technology Status and Potential Although reductions on this scale are a dramatic challenge, the energy conservation opportunities are legion: more energy-efficient appliances (whose manufacture and use would be encouraged by the publication of efficiency standards and ratings), and compact fluorescent lights that last ten times longer and use one-quarter of the energy are just two examples. Significant savings can be achieved using technologies already available on the market, including high-efficiency bulbs and ballasts for fluorescent fixtures, compact fluorescent bulbs, daylighting and actively controlled window shading, highly insulated windows (low emissivity, argon filled), pigments for roofing and walls with high reflectivity and emissivity to minimize heat gain, highly efficient heating, cooling, and hot-water systems, and many others.[134]

Newer approaches for passive systems where further R&D is justified include:

• Light-emitting diodes (LEDs), as discussed previously, that are even more efficient and longer lasting than fluorescents
• Windows with controllable optical and thermal properties that can optimize daylighting and heating/cooling
• New materials for building shells that have superior structural and insulating properties
• Sophisticated networks of wireless sensors and controls to continuously adjust lighting, ventilation, heating, and cooling to occupant requirements
• Thermal storage units that allow active heating or cooling equipment to operate when temperature conditions make them most efficient and when utility costs are lowest
• Advanced control systems that can continuously optimize thermal and lighting conditions and can be integrated with electric utility dispatch signals to optimize systemwide generation and use networks
• A variety of strategies that can minimize the myriad small energy demands that collectively exceed lighting in most homes today (power supplies for computers, televisions, door openers, and so on)
• Low-cost distributed generation units such as small, efficient fuel cells that could provide both electricity and waste heat
• Renewable energy technologies that can be integrated with buildings, including "geothermal" heating and cooling that

couple a building to the constant temperature of the subsurface, and photovoltaic electric units incorporated into roofs and awnings.[135]

While many of these technologies can be used in both new and existing buildings (e.g., advanced appliances and lighting), major retrofits of the building shell can be expensive. Short of this, many low-cost steps can be taken with existing buildings without a major renovation, such as sealing and new insulation for energy savings of 20 to 30 percent. Window replacements, externally applied insulation and other measures could lead to greater savings. Much of what needs to be learned, however, concerns how to combine these and related new technologies optimally into workable and affordable overall systems.

Although further advances will be important, it is possible to reduce building energy consumption by a factor of 1/2 to 2/3 even with existing technology. Passive and advanced residential and commercial buildings in the United States and Canada have already demonstrated reductions in heating energy use of 75 to 90 percent, for example.

Likely Launch Pathways and Possible Government Intervention The building sector is notoriously slow to adopt innovations, while both builders and purchasers of real estate, residential as well as commercial, are notorious for preferring low initial costs to minimum life-cycle costs, and thus for insisting on short payback periods (i.e., high rates of return) on investments in conservation that raise initial prices but save money in the long run. For these reasons, new codes and standards that promote new and established efficiency technologies for both new construction and renovation are needed. A mass of service firms with trained professionals capable of implementing the new building technologies on a large scale will also need to be promoted. The fact that significant energy cost savings may be achievable within five to seven years after renovation or construction may enable broader implementation of an economic model in which the energy savings finance the initial efficiency investment. Demonstrations of energy-saving technology at scale may assist in educating the market, both builders and consumers.

While energy service firms are now an expanding sector, creating incentives for utilities to promote energy savings, as some states have done, instead of simply rewarding them for expanded energy consumption, could promote their introduction. New appliance and lighting standards that fit technology advances in these areas also require implementation. Aside from back-end regulatory mandates through standards and codes, front-end R&D should be expanded, and financing incentives on the back end, at both federal and state levels, could also assist earlier adoption. Adoption of standards and codes through construction that is federally financed and assisted could spur technology transition.

Manufacturing Production Scale-Up and Generic Process Improvements

As we have seen, secondary and incremental innovations are required in processes for manufacturing the equipment that embodies most of the technological options we have discussed. There is a substantial role for government-supported R&D to facilitate these improvements in manufacturing processes, which are needed over and above the improvements in design that are discussed for each technology in the previous sections of this chapter. Energy storage for plug-in hybrids and intermittent renewables (wind and solar), geothermal, and building improvements are major examples.

There are also generic ("precompetitive") manufacturing problems that cut across energy technology sectors and that would yield major public benefits. These justify public intervention through front-end R&D, analogous to that carried out by the Sematech project, a government-supported industrial consortium in the semiconductor manufacturing sector in the 1980s and early 1990s.

There is also a need for government support for the scale-up of manufacturing capacity, to encourage expansion of production capacity beyond what private investors might carry out based on conservative assumptions of the assured market. In essence, the public would be accepting some of the risk associated with these investments in order to encourage a more rapid expansion of production capacity, lower costs due to economies of scale and resulting technological improvements, and faster market penetration of a socially desirable technology.

Plug-in hybrid (PHEV) automobile technology is perhaps the most important example of this requirement. Widespread adoption of this technology now appears possible in a relatively short term, given ongoing battery advances. However, since PHEVs would likely be introduced in the U.S. auto industry only in costly models and hence only by the tens of thousands of vehicles, and a complete turnover of the U.S. auto fleet takes over fifteen years, it will take decades for PHEVs to reach a level of production that makes a major difference in U.S. oil consumption levels. This is an area where low-cost financing to scale up early production in cooperation with industry could make a major difference. The resulting expansion could be phased in so that bugs can be worked out of design and manufacturing processes in time to prevent them from being reproduced on a large scale. Institutional mechanisms through which to organize this effort, particularly the industry consortium model, are discussed below.

Finally, in the case of some innovations, there may well be serious problems in creating the infrastructure necessary for major expansion. Biofuels present a noteworthy example. Because, as previously discussed, ethanol, including cellulosic ethanol, is too corrosive to move through existing pipelines and pumps, separate systems will have to be built if these biofuels are to grow enough to provide a significant share of U.S. transport energy. If cellulosic biofuels are launched by the existing petroleum industry, so that oil companies provide the financing for this infrastructure, government financing may not be needed. If the further expansion of biofuels leads to a broad confrontation with the oil industry, however, government capital support for a new distribution system may be required. This would involve a major capital expense. Less serious but still significant problems of systems improvement and management would be associated with any possible future major expansion of the supply of intermittent sources of electric power, such as solar or wind, to the electrical grid.

In summary, this chapter has explored concrete technology examples that fit each of the six basic patterns we previously identified for technology launch. We have found that each of these categories will require its own appropriate set of front- and back-end support. Table 3.1 sets out information on the particular technologies identified in this chapter, tying them to the launch pathways and to the applicable policies cited above, as well as to new institutional needs identified in chapter 6.

To repeat, the underlying purpose of this chapter is not to present a review of the state of selected technologies for its own sake, although we hope that our readers will find this useful, but to use a range of technologies to show how a system could be organized to support a menu of technologies, some of them ready or nearly ready for implementation and some still in the research stage. In Thomas Friedman's words, "[Our] favorite renewable energy is an ecosystem for energy innovation."[136] The issue we explore next is the approximate level of support for technology implementation that will be required and how it can be funded.

5

Energy R&D and Implementation: What Is the Right Level of Funding and Where Will the Money Come From?

What Are the Right Energy R&D and Implementation Numbers?

What scale of research, development, and implementation effort will be required to reduce dependence on petroleum on some reasonable timetable and to achieve stabilization or a reduction in carbon dioxide (and GHGs) by midcentury? To gain support for strengthened federal energy R&D and for implementation, it will be important to have at least a broad estimate of the range of funding required. We will deal first with R&D levels.

This question is particularly important because we have been moving in the wrong direction on the funding of energy R&D. As we have previously noted, both federal and private-sector spending on energy R&D have been in a long-term decline for a quarter of a century. Federal energy R&D funding in the period 1980 to 1995 fell by 58 percent, and has stagnated since then.[1] In real dollars, federal energy R&D is half its level of 1980,[2] the last time the government made a major attempt to spur new energy technology. U.S. private-sector energy R&D funding has shown a long-term decline as well, falling 50 percent from 1991 to 2003, and also stagnating since then.[3] While defining the exact forms of spending that constitute R&D in the diverse energy field is not simple, one study for the year 2007 estimates private-sector energy R&D in the United States at approximately $1.6 billion (in 2003) and public-sector R&D at about $3.4 billion (in 2006 dollars), including the categories of fossil fuels, nuclear, photovoltaic solar, wind, end-use efficiency, and energy-related basic science.[4] Declining energy R&D in the United States has been accompanied by a corresponding decline in patenting levels, a measure of reduced innovation.[5] While venture capital funding started to flow in 2006–07 to energy technologies,[6] this is commercialization funding, not true R&D, and still only represents a small fraction of the implementation need.

Among OECD countries, the government R&D story is similar. From 1980 to 1995, public spending on energy-sector R&D fell in every major OECD country except Japan and Switzerland.[7] The International Energy Agency (IEA), in a 2008 report, estimates total public-sector R&D in OECD nations, including the United States, at $10 billion, and private-sector R&D in OECD countries at $40 to $60 billion.[8]

Why has U.S. private-sector energy R&D declined in this period? There appear to be four reasons.[9] First, a significant part of the energy sector has been deregulated; the end of government economic regulation tends to increase competition, decrease profit margins, and exert corresponding pressure to cut back on R&D. Second, 1980–2000 was a period of low energy prices that discouraged investment in energy-efficient technologies and in the R&D behind them. Third, no new nuclear power plants have been constructed in the United States since the Three Mile Island accident in 1979, which has discouraged R&D in that field, historically a major area of federally sponsored R&D. Fourth, energy has been a mature, economically efficient, and cost-competitive sector, a fact that has also discouraged companies that might have used technological innovation as a means of entry into the sector. In turn, low energy prices and a political failure to confront the issues of climate and energy security have been a disincentive to federal energy R&D support. This is not only a U.S. phenomenon; other OECD nations have similar explanations for the parallel declines in their support for energy R&D.[10]

Clearly, more R&D will be needed to transform the sector, but the proper level of expenditures is ultimately unknowable. There are no reliable models from which the "right level" can be derived. Even so, we can make some comparisons by looking at other areas of the U.S. economy that are intensively adopting new technologies in a manner roughly comparable to the technology transition that will be required in energy.

The information technology and biopharmaceutical sectors have been undergoing innovation waves in recent years and typically spend between 10 and 20 percent of their revenues on R&D.[11] The biotechnology industry, in part because it includes numerous new companies still living off of venture capital, spent approximately 40 percent of its revenue on R&D in 2005,[12] while the pharmaceutical industry estimates that it invests 18 percent of sales revenue in R&D.[13] Biopharmaceuticals—bios and pharmas—estimate they spent $58.8 billion on R&D in 2007.[14] While much of that expenditure is for is development and likely extends into aspects of commercialization, it nonetheless indicates the scale of that industry's efforts. The IT sector typically spends between 10 and 15 percent of its revenues on R&D. U.S. semiconductor firms alone spent $18.4 billion on R&D, or 16 percent of their sales revenues.[15] These are technologically expanding sectors, well above the R&D intensity (percent of annual R&D of revenue) average of 2.6% for U.S. industry as a whole.

In contrast, the energy sector is underinvesting in R&D, compared not only to other sectors that are actively implementing new advances in technology, but compared to industry rates overall. U.S. private-sector energy R&D intensity is about 0.23 percent, less than one-tenth the average for U.S. industry as a whole.[16] In the early 1980s, energy firms invested more in R&D than drug companies did. Then biotechnology took off and at the same time energy R&D dropped, so that drug companies now invest many times more than energy companies.[17] In the same 1980–2006 period, the percentage of total U.S. R&D spending, both public and private, on energy fell from 10 to 2 percent.[18] Even combining public and private expenditures, energy R&D is less than 1 percent of the annual revenues of the energy sector. These data from other technology-intensive sectors suggest that energy R&D, public and private, should be multiplied at least several times to get to the range of technology development and adoption that will be needed.

Furthermore, private-sector R&D spending lies predominantly in mature sectors concerned with incremental advance, rather than in areas that might lead to major advances. This means there is a need for a larger share of public as opposed to private expenditure on R&D than in other fields, in order to spur new technologies that are unlikely be picked up by existing incumbents.

Numerous studies have concluded that we need to be spending from two to ten times current energy R&D levels; it simply is not clear what the right multiplier is. The President's Council of Advisors on Science and Technology (PCAST) study of 1997 recommended roughly doubling applied R&D at the Energy Department over five years.[19] The *Stern Review* of 2006[20] and the National Commission on Energy Policy's (NCEP) *Ending the Energy Stalemate* report of 2004 similarly recommended a doubling of energy R&D spending.[21]

Still other studies have recommended increasing funding to much higher levels. Davis and Owens, using a real option pricing technique to estimate the value of renewable technologies in the face of uncertain fossil-fuel prices, argue that an options value approach to energy R&D justifies multiplying current R&D levels by four.[22] Schock and colleagues at the national energy laboratories valued energy R&D by estimating the insurance levels needed to protect against oil price shocks, electricity disruption, pollution, and climate change. By comparing these costs with the probabilities that energy R&D might resolve them, they concluded that a quadrupling of R&D would mitigate the risks.[23] The IPCC *Special Report on Emissions Scenarios* in 2000[24] recommended six to nine times the current R&D levels in order to meet its projections for acceptable emission levels. Nemet and Kammen in 2007 proposed five to ten times the current levels of energy R&D, noting precedents in major federal R&D programs such as the Manhattan Project, the Apollo Program, and the Carter-Reagan buildup in national defense.[25]

Turning to the level of spending on implementation, in the most extensive study to date along these lines, the IEA in its 2008 report for OECD nations, estimated a combined overall energy R&D *and* implementation funding need for two scenarios: (1) stabilization at 2005 CO_2 levels by 2050, and (2) a reduction of 50 percent from 2005 CO_2 levels by 2050.[26] IEA estimated that the first scenario can be achieved by technologies now evolving that require ongoing incremental advances; IEA estimated the cost of this scenario—R&D plus implementation investment—at $17 trillion by midcentury, or $400 billion per year, or 0.4 percent of global GDP. IEA estimated that the second scenario would require not simply incremental advances but a series of technological breakthroughs[27] costing about $45 trillion, or $1.1 trillion (1.1 percent of global GDP) per year. Of course, the implementation phase is far more expensive than the R&D phase. IEA placed the technological "learning" share of the two deployment scenarios at $2.8 trillion and $7.0 trillion by midcentury, respectively, although this term does not translate directly into

R&D levels.[28] The IEA estimates that these expenditures would be offset by fuel cost savings and economic gains.[29]

IEA's assumptions about the need for incremental advances in the first scenario should not, however, be taken literally. It does not make sense, after all, to halt a search for radical advances in technology through R&D and focus solely on incremental advances, even if such incremental gains might get us to stabilization. In addition to any such incremental advances, it would still be highly advantageous to have breakthroughs, radical innovations that could cut costs and improve efficiency still further.

In short, there is no need to make a choice between incremental or radical innovations. We will need to undertake both in order to achieve either the stabilization or the reduction scenario. In any case, the IEA concurs that the industry comparison data make it clear that, given the magnitude of the scientific and technical problems, we will not reach either stabilization or reduction by midcentury with existing levels of investment.

There is every reason to believe that increased R&D in energy will provide direct economic benefits over and above the social goods of improved energy security and reduced emissions, especially if the policies that promote them are technology neutral, as we have here advocated. After all, each of the major technology projects we have discussed as precedents—the Manhattan Project, the Apollo Project, and even the recent defense buildup—has yielded at least several times its cost in further innovation and in business and employment growth.[30] It is well established that there is a high social return to R&D, many times the private return, including in the energy field.[31] Here there is no question of crowding out other desirable innovations. Studies of major federal increases in R&D have found that the supply of scientists and engineers is not fixed and there is flexibility in deploying talent when a variety of fields come to bear on a new initiative. In addition, the increase in technical learning resulting from R&D has led to technical advances in other areas and stimulated a corresponding growth in R&D in the private sector.[32] R&D investment in one field tends to have a snowball effect across related fields.

Another way to estimate the proper level of expenditure on R&D would be to evaluate each energy area in which scientific and technological advances are needed over an extended period, tallying area by area, technology by technology, and adding up the levels of R&D funding needed to get to the total. But it is very hard to predict breakthroughs that can change the level and focus of R&D in either direction: by reducing the need for R&D in a given area if a breakthrough creates a lower-cost solution, or by raising it if it signals a promising new area of inquiry that will have to be sustained over an extended period. In other words, these estimates would have to be changed all the time to account for new technology advances and opportunities. This kind of area-by-area evaluation will need to be made, preferably through the kind of technology roadmapping exercise discussed later in this book. But that effort will have to be an ongoing annual process subject to constant revision. While a five- to seven-year technology roadmapping effort can be undertaken (subject to frequent ongoing revisions), a fifteen- or twenty-year look at this level of detail for an R&D funding estimate would inevitably be misleading, more guesstimate than estimate.

Regardless of how the estimation is carried out, then, it is clear from the foregoing that energy R&D spending should be increased at least severalfold. It should start with modest increases because, as discussed in later sections, the institutions of the innovation system face gaps and are not fully ready to manage significant new funding. However, as the institutional gaps are filled, R&D funding should be ramped up over time.

Similarly, the "right" level of public investment in the implementation of innovative energy technology, which is a much more costly stage in the innovation process than R&D, is hard to estimate since it depends in part on the hard-to-predict results from investments in R&D. While deployment costs of current technologies can be estimated over the short term, it is harder to gauge the long-term costs and/or savings that will ensue from the eventual deployment of advances in technology that are still in the R&D stage. After reviewing a range of possibilities for innovation in technology, the IEA estimated the proper level of investments in the implementation of technology, both private and public worldwide, and came up with multipliers over current spending of between 6 and 18, depending on the scenario it was using for CO_2 stabilization or reduction.

Energy technology and infrastructure is on so huge a scale that the public sector must assume a disproportionate role in providing funding support at the demonstration and initial deployment stages of its implementation. One expert has informally calculated that it will take some $165 billion in public-sector support over the next decade to demonstrate and deploy 50 GW of new energy technologies (wind, solar, enhanced geothermal, cellulosic biofuels, CCS, smart grid, nuclear, efficiency improvements, and so on), in order to create sufficient economic and technical momentum for these technologies to be scaled up in subsequent decades with private sector leadership.[33] Public funding for the implementation of energy technology will also require a ramp-up period, regardless of the multiplier, because of the same institutional gaps as those that limit the expansion of energy R&D.

Cap and Trade as a Potential Source of Funding for R&D and Implementation?

If we need to multiply our investment in energy R&D and implementation, where will we find the financial resources at a time of growing deficits and constraints on federal spending because of entitlement commitments[34] and the political difficulties connected with raising taxes? Cap-and-trade legislation aimed at emission reductions is a major potential source of revenue for energy R&D.

Briefly, for the benefit of the general reader and using a framework from an economic analysis by the Pew Center, a cap-and-trade economic system for climate change would work essentially as follows.[35] The system sets a "cap" on emissions that applies either economywide, or to specified high-emitting economic sectors (utilities, transport, large industries, fuel suppliers, and so on). The cap is set by imposing quantitative limits on the total emissions of CO_2 and other greenhouse gases (GHGs) per year (or other compliance period). These limits would presumably be based on some estimate of the tolerable increase in their atmospheric concentration, hopefully derived from a reasonable compromise among the scientifically sound, the environmentally desirable, the technically achievable, and the politically agreeable.

The system then allocates, sells, or auctions (or, over time, all three) tradable "allowances," which provide the right to emit a certain number of tons of GHGs in the time period, to the sources of the emissions covered by the program. The total number of allowances is equal to the cap. In a "downstream" cap-and-trade program, emitters of GHG emissions must acquire and "spend" allowances equal to their emissions. In an "upstream" program, fuel suppliers must acquire and spend allowances equivalent to the carbon content of fossil fuels they distribute.

The purpose of a cap-and-trade system is to require companies creating GHGs to pay for the right to do so, and in this way to force them to include the environmental costs of their emissions in their calculations of the cost of doing business. At the same time, the system minimizes the overall cost of reducing GHG emissions throughout the economy. If a company can reduce its emissions early and cheaply, it can sell its allowances to another company that can do so only at greater expense. The advantages of this scheme are twofold. First, the potential gains from these transactions encourage early reductions in emissions. Second, the reduction in emissions will be the same but the cost will be less than if each company had been required to reduce its emissions by a specified amount. At operation here is straightforward economic theory that imposing a price on the right to emit will drive firms over time to new technologies that provide lower-priced, competitive solutions that result in lower levels of emissions.

The primary focus of a cap-and-trade program must be on sources of emissions that can be both measured and monitored with reasonable accuracy and at acceptable cost; these include most sources of carbon dioxide (CO_2) emissions from fossil-fuel combustion as well as many sources of other GHG emissions. Having accuracy and transparency in the system of measuring emissions is key to the fairness and integrity of the program. Sources that are not easily measured (small-scale emitters) and that are therefore not easily regulated through a cap-and-trade program, could "opt in" to the system, could be covered through supplemental regulations, or could simply be left out of the system.

Cap-and-trade systems can vary widely in their economic and environmental impact depending on these design features and on the level of emission reductions sought over a given period. There are a series of major practical design issues in every cap-and-trade system:

How is the cap set?   How ambitious are the targets, to what extent are they based on sound data and evidence, and is the compromise that they represent between the technically achievable, the economically affordable, the environmentally desirable, and the politically achievable a viable one, given the need to deal with global warming?

How flexible is the system?   What option do firms have to meet reduction mandates obligations by purchasing allowances, by sequestering carbon so as to reduce their emissions, by controlling GHGs other than CO_2, by "banking" allowances to use them later, or by "borrowing" allowances from later allocations?

Does the program reach downstream or upstream or both, and to what sectors does it apply?   Does the system put controls on firms that emit GHGs ("downstream") or does it control their fuel suppliers ("upstream")? Does it apply broadly across emitting sectors (economywide) or does it reach only major emitters in some sectors?

How are allowances allocated?   Does the system allocate some or all of its allowances free to emitting firms reached by the program, does it auction them to the highest bidder, or does it use a combination of approaches that changes over time? If free allowances are distributed, what allocation formula is used? Which sectors and which firms receive the allowances, what is the allocation rationale, and, underlying these questions, how well can the emissions on which allocation is based be measured? An initial allocation of free allowances to existing emitters would constitute a windfall to firms that have not put much effort into energy conservation, but, as a practical matter, some level of initial free allocation may be felt to be politically necessary if industry is to support a cap-and-trade scheme. If allowances are auctioned, for what purposes are the revenues used? How might the allocation process change over time—for example, allocations may be free in opening years, then shift to a growing percentage of auction-based distribution.

Is there a cost cap?   Does the system incorporate a "safety valve" when a sector's costs rise to a certain level, in which case additional allowances are made available at a preset price? In other words, is there "cost containment" or an "exit ramp" from compliance when prices (for example, the price per ton of coal) reach a certain level?

Is it international in scope? Can firms meet reduction requirements by purchasing allowances abroad, or by sequestering or reducing carbon emissions abroad? If so, what proportion of their allowances can be met abroad, and to what extent must they be obtained in nations also imposing a comparable climate control regime? How will the system handle imports from noncomplying nations that gain lower costs and market entry from noncompliance? Will there be some mechanism for trade adjustments, for example, by imposing a carbon tax on imports from countries that do not impose a carbon charge? Will emissions allowances be purchasable from so-called carbon sinks, as, for example, from newly planted forests that sequester carbon dioxide as they grow, or from standing forests that would release carbon dioxide if they were to be cut down? If so, to whom will the purchase price be paid: to governments, to logging concessionaires, or to the people who plant the forests or who depend on them for their livelihoods?

This cap-and-trade (or "marketable permits") approach was initially tested and found workable in a highly successful attempt to control acid rain under the Clean Air Act Amendments of 1990.[36] That successful effort was made possible by the availability of technologies for the control of the sulfur dioxide (SO_2) that causes acid rain, paving the way for a prompt shift in technology and consequent reduction in emissions. Overall, the acid rain cap-and-trade system marked a dramatic departure for the environmental movement from command-and-control regulation toward more flexible, economically efficient market-based controls. The acid rain cap-and-trade system was well understood at the time by its advocates working on the Clean Air Act Amendments to be a stalking horse and test case for an analogous means for the subsequent control of GHG emissions. On the other hand, the administration of a cap-and-trade regime for GHG emissions would be on a vastly larger scale and would be more complicated and difficult than for the more straightforward problem of acid rain, especially if it were made international in scope.

Cap-and-trade legislation will generate major revenues over time through permits and auctions. Proponents of this legislation[37] have generally agreed that much of this revenue will be needed to promote R&D and implementation of new energy technology, lest the economic pressure from the cap-and-trade system build up without the means available to make a shift to lower-emitting technology. In other words, proponents in the political system have, in effect, wanted the assurance that technology will be available to meet the demand created by the policy pull caused by a cap-and-trade strategy; they have sought a combined technology-push supply-side strategy and a technology-pull demand-side strategy.

It is, however, by no means guaranteed that the revenue stream from a cap-and-trade regime will in fact be devoted to the stimulation of technological innovation. In fact, to judge from the recent legislative history in the U.S. Congress, the opposite could well prove to be the case. The leading Senate legislation in 2008, the Lieberman-Warner bill,[38] will generate major revenue over the forty-year period it covers, some $7 trillion according to the estimates of the Senate Environment and Public Works Committee. In a period when political forces make tax increases unavailable, this legislation, although its fate and final form are not yet clear, has become the only major new federal revenue source available in the immediate future. If a major increase in new energy technology R&D and implementation of new energy technology are in fact to be funded, cap-and-trade legislation may well need to be a key funding source. It is the only likely new revenue train leaving the congressional station. While this legislation did not pass in 2008 and likely will change significantly before eventual passage, we present below a detailed review of the technology support provisions of this legislation because they illustrate the political issues that must be faced if adequate funding is to be found for new energy R&D and implementation.

The Lieberman-Warner bill was the first cap-and-trade bill to be approved by a major congressional committee. Its legislative history illustrates the issues. As the bill moved through the Environment Committee process in December 2007 and to the Senate floor in June 2008, the legislative sausage-making process had begun. By the time Environment Committee Chair Senator Barbara Boxer (D-CA) helped round up the votes to get the ever-changing bill through committee and into floor consideration, the bill had allocated all of the $7 trillion in potential revenues from allowances and auctions.

The specifics of this process are both illuminating and discouraging. Half the $7 trillion was returned to industry in the form of free allowances. For the $3.3 trillion remaining, the legislation proposed a number of programs and funds, many of them financed by a percentage of the revenues from the sales of carbon emission allowances and others given a percentage of the allowances directly. The committee estimated the cash value of the allowances on the cap-and-trade market, and explained the distribution of these funding estimates in its written explanation of the bill to the Senate. Because other constituencies had to be taken care of in the bill, only 9 percent of the revenue from the auction of carbon permits in the bill's start-up year of 2012 was allocated to technology R&D and implementation. Under the terms of the bill, this percentage would change only slightly over time.

Support for new technology was a major loser in this process. Of the 9 percent allocated to technology overall, incumbent industries seeking subsidies to the implementation of existing technologies were the major winners. The amount to be spent on R&D was minimal. As table 5.1 indicates, the utility sector received some $92 billion in awards for low-carbon electricity production, the utility and coal sectors received some $14 billion for demonstration and implementation of carbon capture and sequestration technology, the agriculture sector received $26 billion for cellulosic biofuels, and the auto industry received $4 billion to offset purchaser costs of hybrid medium and heavy trucks, plus $68 billion to retool production lines for hybrid, plug-in hybrid, and electric auto production. Funding to industries for deployment of presently available and evolving technology totaled some $191 billion. Funding for a program for "International Clean Technology Development" was listed, but no funding was specifically allocated. Energy R&D funding over the next four decades was to be only $17 billion, or approximately $425 million a year, a small fraction of current federal energy R&D funding levels and a tiny amount compared to payoffs to the constituencies listed above. A comparable House cap-and-trade bill later circulated by the Energy committee contained zero R&D funding.

Far from encouraging new technology by multiplying funding for R&D, then, the Senate and House in these bills were effectively ensuring that energy R&D may never multiply and only short-run innovation would gain support. As we will see below, this emphasis on innovations that could be on the market in a relatively short time, as opposed to more fundamental innovation that might take somewhat longer, is in part an unintended consequence of the well-intentioned argument that GHG emission goals can be achieved with technologies that are within reach.

The positive news was that technology implementation funding was included, even if R&D was not. However, almost as problematic as low R&D, these funding streams were not in the form of fixed dollar allocations over a limited initial

Table 5.1
Summary of the provisions of the technology program of S. 3036, the Boxer-Lieberman-Warner Cap-and-Trade bill

Program/fund name	Estimated funding/ value of allowances	Administered by
"Transformation acceleration" fund	$17 billion through 2050	ARPA-E
Low- and Zero-Carbon Electricity Technology Fund	$92 billion through 2050	Climate Change Technology Board*
Carbon Capture and Sequestration Technology Fund	$14–$15.7 billion through 2050	Climate Change Technology Board*
Bonus Allowance Account	No total provided	EPA
Clean Medium- and Heavy-Duty Hybrid Fleets Program	$4 billion from 2012 to 2017	DOE
Climate Change Transportation Technology Fund	$68 billion	EPA
Program to encourage cellulosic biofuels	$26 billion from 2012 to 2030	EPA
Low-carbon fuel standard	N/A	N/A
Clean Development Technology Deployment Fund (International)	None provided	International Clean Development Technology Board**

* Established in bill. Five-person bipartisan board appointed by the President, with members serving five-year terms. Congress has veto power over its spending for thirty days.
** Established in bill. Consists of the Secretaries of State (chair), the Treasury, Energy, and Commerce, the Administrator of the EPA, the Administrator of the U.S. Agency for International Development, the U.S. Trade Representative, and other officials.
(Data for chart compiled by Edward Parker, MIT Washington Office.)

Description

R&D: Advanced research projects

Technology implementation: Awards money for the production of electricity through low-carbon means such as nuclear and solar power

Technology implementation: Kick-starts demonstration and deployment of ten CCS projects

Technology implementation: Distributes emission allowances in the long term to entities that perform CCS

Technology implementation: Awards allowances to entities that buy advanced medium- and heavy-duty hybrid trucks to kick-start fleet conversion

Technology implementation: Helps auto manufacturers retool their facilities to make hybrids, plug-ins, fuel-cell cars, advanced diesel cars, electric cars, etc.

Technology implementation: Distributes allowances to entities producing cellulosic biofuels

Technology implementation: Sets up a market for deductions in the carbon content of fuel through biofuels, plug-in vehicles, and hydrogen. Integrated with current Renewable Fuel Standard, which will be revised

Technology implementation: Helps other countries reduce their greenhouse gas emissions

period but of percentages of allowance revenues, generally for the full duration of the bill. In other words, the dollar figures above were only estimates, while the percentages were fixed in the language of the bill. These specific percentages for industrial sectors will sharply limit flexibility in technology evolution as new technology solutions arrive. This could lock in technology for decades and make it much more difficult for these technologies to be displaced by alternatives in the future.

Furthermore, much of the implementation of technology could be financed with loan guarantees or low-cost, longer-term loans; it does not necessarily need to be paid for by grants to private industry. In other words, even though the cost of technology implementation is by nature significantly higher than the R&D stage, and therefore funding is likely to be needed for the implementation of major technology if the required reductions in emissions are to be reached, much of this implementation can be financed by loans rather than by outright grants, so that the cost to the government will be lower. By contrast, because R&D is by nature high-risk, it cannot be financed by loans or cost-sharing arrangements and will be much more dependent on direct government grants.

The Lieberman-Warner bill did not pass the Senate. It reached a total of fifty-four votes on a cloture motion, when the forty-eight votes cast on the Senate floor are combined with commitments from six absentee senators (including the three leading presidential candidates at the time), who pledged in writing to support the bill. Sixty votes are needed for cloture (to cut off filibuster debate and move to pass the legislation), and ten of the fifty-four senators who supported cloture later stated they wanted further changes to the final bill, noting that a vote for cloture is not the same as a vote on final passage. Nonetheless, this legislation and this vote constituted the high-water mark for climate legislation to date and a major advance for the bill's proponents. The fact that the bill failed to include the funding for the R&D needed for the nation to develop the technologies it must have to reach GHG stabilization or reduction is a critical gap that must be addressed in the next version of the legislation.

It is difficult to predict the political forces that will ultimately dictate the outcome of this issue. Since numerous industries have a stake in obtaining new and improved technologies so that they do not face prohibitive costs that they fear could be imposed through the cap-and-trade system, it may be possible to form political alliances to alter this legislation and redress the R&D funding problem. Otherwise we simply will not get there. Another potential problem is that antitax sentiment in Congress may keep the bill "revenue neutral"—in other words, that the government will not touch or retain for governmental purposes any of the funding stream from cap and trade,[39] even for R&D on new technology. Since numerous industries have a stake in obtaining at least the funding for implementation, they may assist in staving off this threat.

Aside from cap and trade, another possible source of funding for energy R&D could be from canceling the federal tax subsidies to incumbent high-emitting energy industries, principally the oil industry, which were provided most recently in the Energy Policy Act of 2005.[40] While a majority in Congress tried in 2007 to alter this act to cut these subsidies and use the recouped revenue to offset the $21 billion cost of incentives for implementing new energy technologies called for in the 2007 Energy Act,[41] they were blocked from doing so by the Bush administration, which termed the cancellation of these industry tax subsidies at a time of record energy profits an unacceptable tax increase. A new administration may take a different view. In any case, while this recouped tax funding could be an initial funding step, it will not generate the volume of funding that will be needed for R&D and implementation over time. The cap-and-trade bill appears to be the only bill on the current legislative horizon that could provide over time the funding levels needed to achieve an energy transformation.

There is, of course, another alternative. It would be possible simply to ramp up our funding for energy R&D in the ordinary budget requests of the Department of Energy, so that the extra funding would come from existing tax revenues or (more likely) by an increase in the deficit. This would be modest compared to the subsidies to fossil fuels cited in the previous paragraph. In fact, through its passage of the America Competes Act of 2007,[42] Congress is already committed to doubling the basic research programs sponsored by the DOE's Office of Science over a decade, although obtaining appropriations funding for fiscal years 2008 and 2009 has been frustrated by political battling between Congress and the administration concerning overall federal budget levels. In the Energy Act of 2007, Congress further authorized major increases for a series of new energy technology R&D programs.[43]

These two laws, America Competes and the 2007 Energy Act, indicate that the bipartisan majority in Congress has already shown a strong disposition toward major increases in energy R&D. It is certainly possible to contemplate that as political pressure around energy issues grows and as energy security and climate needs become more apparent, a major increase in the modest amount we now spend on federal energy R&D could be politically obtainable. After all, the National Institutes of Health doubled their spending from 1998 to 2003 on the strength of a politically less pressing argument. While it would be foolish to forgo the opportunity to create a stable, long-term funding base available for several decades for energy R&D from cap-and-trade revenues, it is not the only option. If there are continuing delays in the passage of climate change legislation, the 2007 energy and innovation legislation cited above indicates that there is a political consensus around funding for energy technology to start ramping up R&D now, given presidential support.

This baseline budget spending has two other advantages over cap-and-trade funds. First, it is baseline and once in place, would be more likely to withstand fluctuating trends in funding than a cap-and-trade regime that would be dependent on inherently less stable annual auctions and allowance trading. Second, a cap-and-trade bill will likely be back-end loaded. In other words, political and practical compromise will delay the effective start-up date for a cap-and-trade bill, while critical data on emissions is collected and administrative and regulatory institutions are formed. In addition, affected industries are likely to use the political process, through free allocation of a portion of initial allowances and limited auctions, to avoid major revenue flow to R&D in the opening years.

For these reasons, revenues for R&D and implementation are likely to be delayed if cap-and-trade is to be their only source. Since R&D and implementation should be ramped up over time as institutional innovation gaps are filled, it is not all bad that this back-end loading should occur. But it will be important to accelerate baseline funding from regular agency budget processes in the interim. It should be emphasized, however, that given the size of the likely needs for R&D and implementation funding, taken together with the pressures on federal agency budgets, cap-and-trade funding will certainly be needed over time for both R&D and implementation. One could envision a practical evolution here, where baseline appropriations start to ramp up federal energy R&D in opening years as new R&D efforts are being organized and implemented, after which cap-and-trade revenue starts to flow to build up to the level of support to R&D and implementation that will be required.

The debate between environmental and industrial advocates has inadvertently created a political problem that could impede adequate funding for innovation. Many industry sectors have been arguing that passage of cap-and-trade legislation must await progress on energy technologies that would enable them to meet cap-and-trade targets, so let's just hold off for a decade. On the other side, some environmentalists supporting prompt passage of cap-and-trade have been taking the opposite perspective. They argue that while additional research might well be useful, we have all the technology we will need to meet cap-and-trade requirements already in or ready for production. Pacala and Socolow's "wedges" article provided a basis for this position:

We agree that fundamental research is vital to develop the revolutionary mitigation strategies needed in the second half of this century and beyond. But it is important not to become beguiled by the possibility of revolutionary technology. Humanity can solve the carbon and climate problem in the first half of this century simply by scaling up what we already know how to do.[44]

They describe, as previously noted, fifteen major energy initiatives, seven of which could bring emissions down during the next fifty years to an acceptable level, which they estimate as avoiding about a third of the total CO_2 emissions that would otherwise be released. Of course, Socolow and Pacala were not trying to win a political debate by arguing that energy R&D should be defunded; their point was that we should begin to meet the challenge by using our available technological capabilities, not that R&D should stagnate.

In sum, all the reports cited above indicate that major R&D investments are required even if we somehow end up four decades from now relying only on the technologies currently on our drawing boards. Four decades in science is a long time. To wait four decades to provide adequate support for research would be a highly unfortunate abandonment of scientific and technological opportunity, akin to having committed ourselves in 1920 to continuing to fly biplanes across the Atlantic for the ensuing half century. Why make it hard on ourselves? We should want to get all the savings and gains from existing and new technologies we can, and well-funded R&D is essential to this task.

In reality, we have plenty of R&D work to do on the technologies that are now within range of implementation, as our discussions in chapter 4 of many of these technologies have made clear. This will be expensive. The IEA 2008 report mentioned above, for example, indicated that $17 trillion will be needed for combined implementation and R&D just for improvements to known technologies if GHGs are to be stabilized at 2005 levels by 2050.[45] OECD nations are not even close to this spending level. There are enormous benefits and savings to be obtained from further improvements, as just the technology advances of the last two decades have shown. Increased R&D funds are needed despite the current financial crisis, and could actually help us grow out of it.

To underfund R&D is to ignore the risk that our efforts to mitigate global warming with existing technologies may not be sufficient, despite the optimistic forecasts we have cited. The risks will be even larger if we must achieve reductions instead of stabilization.[46] Both industry and environmental advocates have every interest in strong funding for R&D in the quest for both incremental and radical advances; it would be unfortunate for both if they double-dared the political system into failing to fund R&D.

6

Institutional Gaps in the Mechanisms of Support for Different Stages of Innovation

In the first step of our analysis (in chapters 3 and 4), we classified many of the most promising new energy technologies according to the most likely obstacles to their market launch once they are technoeconomically ready to compete with "legacy" technologies that are already on the market. In the second step (also in chapters 3 and 4), we discussed technology-neutral packages of policies to facilitate the launch of each of these categories of innovation.

This chapter now completes the final two steps of our analysis of a way to structure an energy technology revolution. In step three, we review the system by which the federal government now supports research, development, and to a lesser extent deployment of innovative energy technology, and identify the institutional gaps between them. In step four, we recommend institutions and supporting policies with which to fill these gaps to facilitate the revolution in energy technology we must achieve.

Step 3: Identifying the Institutional Gaps

The major federal efforts in energy research and development are located in the Departments of Energy and Defense. We shall find that they leave serious gaps in the system for promoting technological innovation in energy.

Three major institutional elements in the Department of Energy (DOE) have roles in technological innovation in energy. The DOE Office of Science sponsors primarily fundamental research. It has performed excellent and important work in recent years, including the hosting of workshops around the nation to define key areas of basic research related to energy, but its role has not been to deal with the transition from research to practical technology. The Office of Energy Efficiency and Renewable Energy (EERE) funds and manages primarily later-stage applied research and development, as well as technology demonstrations.[1] It has a limited history with successful demonstrations; its staff lacks depth in financing and in the management of commercial project engineering.

The DOE also hosts seventeen national laboratories of widely varying size. These laboratories employ probably the largest collection of PhD scientists in the world working for a single agency, approximately 12,400.[2] Of these seventeen, the largest three (Lawrence Livermore, Sandia, and Los Alamos) have historically focused primarily on the design and development of nuclear weapons, whose sole customer is the federal government. These three defense-oriented laboratories are the historic flagships of DOE's laboratory fleet, and are funded jointly by the Departments of Defense and Energy. They have an appropriate legacy of secrecy given their primary mission, and high overhead costs because of the importance and depth of attention required for this mission. For these reasons, they have a limited history of successful transfer of commercial products into the private sector. There are outstandingly talented individuals and excellent programs within these entities, but they do not perform many of the broad range of both front- and back-end energy missions that are now required.[3]

As Victor Reis, a senior advisor to the Secretary of Energy and former Director of DARPA, has pointed out, the deployment of this large army of scientists raises important questions regarding the strategic focus of the DOE research. Roughly 5,000 of these scientists work at the three weapons laboratories, despite the fact that the size of the U.S. weapons arsenal is decreasing, compared to the considerably smaller number that are working at laboratories where new energy technologies are the focus, although energy technology research is likely to increase.[4] For example, the National Renewable Energy Laboratory (NREL) in Golden, Colorado—the DOE lab specifically assigned to that field—employs only about 350 PhD scientists.

The Department of Defense (DOD) also carries out research on energy technology, focusing on ways to reduce its energy logistic "tail."[5] Its budget for energy related research is a fraction of DOE's, and it is focused on niche areas with operational relevance to the military.[6] More modest programs relevant to energy R&D are located at the National Science Foundation (NSF), Department of Agriculture, and the National Institutes of Health (NIH).

We may identify six separate institutional and programmatic gaps in these arrangements. On the front end, there is, first, no strong DOE program explicitly devoted to "translational" research—breakthrough research tied to needed energy technologies, whether they are radical or incremental, disruptive or component, and then translating the technologies that derive from the breakthroughs through to the prototype stage, in a connected and integrated fashion and with commercialization in mind.[7] A second front-end gap concerns commercial demonstrations at scale, with careful monitoring to ascertain technical feasibility and economic costs. A third gap concerns improved manufacturing technology and processes, especially cost-cutting and production scale-up and related financing. Underlying these three gaps is a fourth, the need to encourage and facilitate technological collaboration between government and industry across the board, and to carry out ongoing technology roadmapping exercises in collaboration with the private sector.

On the back end, the current menu of incentives for the implementation of technology is often dysfunctional, with subsidies tilted toward technologies, especially oil and other fossil fuels, that contradict our new national needs. Coherence needs to be brought to our current subsidies, and a package of new incentives and disincentives (regulations and mandates) assembled to match our needs. A system of carbon charges, such as cap-and-trade, could resolve much of this problem, at least as it concerns carbon dioxide emissions and global warming. However, a workable and sound program along these lines may still be some time away, so we will need to consider interim measures. The lack of a coherent approach to designing and enacting these incentives and financing policies constitutes a fifth gap. A sixth concerns bringing new talent into the energy field and incentivizing it through technology prizes.

Each of these six innovation institutional gaps corresponds to a critical innovation bottleneck for one or another of the classes of innovation discussed in chapters 3 and 4. The limitations of this combined federal effort have thus become critical in view of the national energy crisis, and need to be remedied, regardless of whether a carbon charge or other demand pricing system for energy is imposed.

Step 4: Filling the Gaps

Because energy technology solutions must be developed and deployed in the private sector, private-sector leadership in the innovation system is important. Industrial policy imposed by government fiat will not work here; we do not need a new alphabet soup of interventionist New Deal–like government agencies. Nor do we need a government-controlled Manhattan-

or Apollo-type project because the government will not be the customer here. The private sector will be the customer, and needs to be fully involved from the beginning.

We do need a targeted approach that calls for two new entities: a translational R&D entity and a government corporation for financing, each of which fills one of the gaps in the innovation institutions that we identified in the previous chapter. Both should be closely allied to and partnered with the private sector. We also need a third element, a technology roadmapping effort—collaborative between government, industry, and the academy—to think through together the new technologies required and the ways to develop them and ensure their deployment.

Table 6.1 summarizes and integrates the results of the four-step analysis that forms the main argument of this book. The table shows how our policy packages and institutional recommendations for the promotion of innovation in energy technology derive from our examination of the obstacles and bottlenecks in the launch paths of the technologies we examined in each of the six categories of innovation that we have identified. Reading across the table for any one technology or category of technology shows the logic by which the recommendations are derived from the obstacles that were identified. Some of these obstacles, as noted, apply to all six categories of innovation; others apply only to the specific categories or to specific technologies.

This table should help the reader place steps 3 and 4, the process of identifying and then filling gaps in innovation institutions, into the logic of the first two steps in our analysis. This chapter now explores in detail step 4 in this analysis, the conclusions of which are briefly summarized in the final column of the table. Each section corresponds to one of the six functional gaps identified in the preceding section of this chapter.

Table 6.1
Policy and institutional recommendations for categories of innovation, derived from likely obstacles to product or process launch

Category of innovation	Example	Bottlenecks and obstacles
All categories of innovation	*All categories of innovation*	Overall: Lack of macropolicies or carbon charge; established technologies do not pay for externalities; limited support for R&D; lack of policy overview; tilted playing field
(1) Experimental technologies	*All experimental technologies* (example: hydrogen fuel cells for transport)	Valley of death; lack of support for basic science related to energy; lack of contact (or too much contact) with eventual users
(2) Disruptive technologies launched in niche markets	*All disruptive technologies launched in niche markets* (examples: off-grid solar, LEDs)	Tilted playing field; intermittent pattern of past subsidies
(3) Secondary innovations with uncontested launch	*All secondary innovations with uncontested launch*	Tilted playing field

Policy recommendations	Institutional recommendations
Macropolicies and carbon charges; **Front-end** technology nurturing (including support for R&D, translational research; Prototyping and Development (P&D), education and training; prizes); roadmapping **Back-end** support: incentives and/or regulations, depending on launch pathway	Translational research in ARPA-E; roadmapping in public-private think tank; —financing through energy corporation, depending on launch pathway
Front-end technology nurturing: roadmapping (P&D and back-end support not yet needed)	Translational research by ARPA-E; roadmapping via public-private think tank
Front-end nurturing: roadmapping; front-end nurturing, including support for R&D on precompetitive manufacturing technology **Back-end** support: incentives for manufacturers to bridge valley of death; conservation incentives for users to speed adoption; financing to speed manufacturing scale-up; regulation/mandates on case-by-case basis	Translational research by ARPA-E; roadmapping via public-private think tank; support for precompetitive manufacturing technology via industrial consortia supported by ARPA-E
Front-end nurturing: front-end support for R&D on precompetitive manufacturing technology **Back-end** support: incentives for manufacturers to speed capacity scale-up; conservation incentives for users to speed adoption; financing to speed manufacturing scale-up	Translational research by ARPA-E; roadmapping via public-private think tank; support for precompetitive manufacturing technology via industrial consortia supported by ARPA-E; manufacturing financing by energy corporation

Table 6.1
(continued)

Category of innovation	Example	Bottlenecks and obstacles
	Wind	Environmental issues; scale-up issues
	Batteries for plug-in hybrid autos	Long turnover times in auto fleet
	Enhanced geothermal	Intermittent incentives; exploration risk; need for engineering-economic demonstrations
(4) Secondary innovations with contested launch	*All Secondary innovations with contested launch*	Tilted playing field; political and non-market economic opposition expected; need for research on technology, policy, and social and environmental impact
	Biofuels	Competition with food crops; review of land-use limits on scale-up; infrastructure requirements of scale-up; likely opposition from incumbents
	Carbon capture and sequestration	Extra cost; need for carefully monitored technoeconomic demonstrations
	Nuclear	Public distrust; environmental, safety and security (proliferation) issues

Policy recommendations	Institutional recommendations
Front-end R&D on energy systems management and off-shore design	Possibly low-cost financing for manufacturing scale-up via energy corporation
Investor fear of premature scale-up	Low-cost financing for manufacturing scale-up via energy corporation
Front-end funding for carefully monitored engineering-economic demonstrations **Back-end** sustained incentives	Energy corporation to finance demonstrations
Front-end nurturing, including support for R&D on precompetitive manufacturing technology **Back-end:** incentives for manufacturers to speed capacity scale-up; conservation incentives for users to speed adoption; financing to speed manufacturing scale-up	Translational research by ARPA-E; roadmapping via public-private think tank; support for precompetitive manufacturing technology via industrial consortia supported by ARPA-E; low-cost financing for demonstration and scale-up via energy corporation
Front-end support for research on new cellulosic crops, and on environmental, economic, and land-use consequences of scale-up, including effect on food prices	Funds for infrastructure via energy corporation if private financing is unavailable
Front-end support for demonstration projects; back-end mandates once technology is technically proven	Support for demonstration projects via energy corporation
Policies and research to address issues cited in text	Review whether financing is required above 2005 energy act provisions

Table 6.1
(continued)

Category of innovation	Example	Bottlenecks and obstacles
(5) Incremental gains in conservation and end-use efficiency	Internal combustion engines	Oscillating gasoline prices; consumer preference for power over economy; need for prototyping and demonstration (P&D)
	Building technologies	Buyer preference for low initial cost unless payoff is very fast; lack of mandate for energy efficiency
(6) Manufacturing technologies	Scale-up	Investor reluctance to scale up unless market is assured
	Generic (precompetitive)	Antitrust laws; industry reluctance to collaborate

Policy recommendations	Institutional recommendations
Front-end cost sharing for P&D; equitable treatment with other technologies offering comparable efficiency	Translational research by ARPA-E; roadmapping via public-private think tank; possibly: financing from energy corporation for manufacturing scale-up
Back-end mandates: appliance standards; conservation requirements in building codes	Translational research by ARPA-E; roadmapping via public-private think tank; low-cost financing from energy corporation for residential and small commercial efficiency improvements
Back-end low-cost financing	Low-cost financing via energy corporation
Front-end support for precompetitive manufacturing process and technology research through industrial consortia	Government-sponsored industrial consortia and support for precompetitive research, supported by ARPA-E; translational research by ARPA-E; roadmapping via public-private think tank

(1)   Filling the Gap in Translational R&D: A DARPA for Energy

The Defense Department's Defense Advanced Research Projects Agency (DARPA) is generally considered the nation's most successful public entity for the promotion of research leading to technological innovation.[8] A proposal for a similar agency for energy, generally referred to as "ARPA-E," passed Congress in 2007 but has not been funded or implemented.[9]

However, there are profound challenges involved in making a DARPA model work at DOE. This model requires very careful legislation and executive-branch directives, and even more importantly, the insistence of senior agency leadership on the recruitment of outstanding and energetic talent. Experience with HSARPA, the DARPA analog authorized by Congress for the new Department of Homeland Security but never effectively implemented, shows that legislative language can promote, but in the end cannot dictate, an innovation culture.[10] This entity never received support from the Department's leadership, languished under the direction of competitive interests in the agency, and was never given authority to budget and run its own R&D portfolio.

The history of DARPA also provides important lessons.[11] While DARPA has played many roles over the years, and has departed from its groundbreaking model in important ways in recent years,[12] its most important role is sometimes described as working "right-left." DARPA represented a break from the "basic science only" model of most U.S. research agencies.[13] As suggested in chapter 2, it has aimed for a "connected" model that crosses the "valley of death" between R&D, and reaches beyond these to late-stage technology development all the way up to the prototyping stage—precisely those stages in the U.S. R&D pipeline that have traditionally been institutionally separate.

This practice has put DARPA's work on science and technology on a continuum. DARPA staff decide up front on a breakthrough technology that must be achieved on the "right side" of the innovation pipeline, and then reach back to the "left side" of the pipeline for the breakthroughs in science that must be found and nurtured in order to get there. In so doing, DARPA has spawned important revolutionary science as well as technology. DARPA prides itself on addressing only the most difficult "DARPA-hard" problems, the "grand challenges" in technology, by nurturing the science needed to meet them. The DARPA model has also been called a "translational" model, in that it aims to translate science breakthroughs into technology development for technologies that tend to be radical and revolutionary rather than incremental.

A key to DARPA's success has been the creation of hybrid collaborative teams that create the capability for more readily crossing the "valley of death." These teams combine the best university researchers with outstanding firms (usually, but not exclusively, recent start-ups, small or mid-sized firms hungry for technology advance) on the development side. DARPA has also had authority to offer technology prizes to inventors and firms as incentives and to reward important advances. An ARPA-E should have this power as well.

DARPA has not been perfect. It has had good days[14] and bad,[15] but it does present an interesting and, in the U.S innovation system, a unique model for the translational problems we face in energy. A DARPA-like "connected" role for scientific and connected technological development does not exist at DOE. Given the need for breakthrough energy technologies, such a role should be the central mission of an ARPA-E.[16] An ARPA-E would focus on components, but components at the device scale, not the overall energy systems or platforms themselves.

Where should such an ARPA-E be located? An ARPA-E located in DOE risks being captured or blocked in its role by competing DOE entities with similar missions. These have powerful ties to Congress and energy interests, and will be jealous of ARPA-E's prerogatives and potential funding. For this reason, a direct tie to the Secretary is essential, as the new statute provides, if an ARPA-E within DOE is to have the creative authority within the Department needed to enable it to pursue the required outside-the-box research and is not to become a tool of the established bureaucracy's projects and agenda, as illustrated by the problems at HSARPA at the Department of Homeland Security.

Alternatively, ARPA-E could be a wholly owned government corporation entirely outside of DOE,[17] although at the cost of losing its roots back at DOE and, through the cabinet, to the president. This is a serious problem and potentially limits the entity's political protection and support available through a supportive Secretary, although the problem could be mitigated to some extent by naming the Secretary of Energy as chair of its board. Locating ARPA-E in a government corporation would ensure more hiring flexibility and competitive salary structures more comparable to those of the private sector, than if it were to be a DOE entity. It would also guarantee that the entity would have full freedom from overly restrictive and slow-moving government procurement requirements.[18] The 2007 authorizing statute placing ARPA-E under the DOE Secretary, recognizing these issues, attempted to extend to it the flexible personnel and contracting powers acquired over the years by DARPA.[19]

Whether inside or outside of DOE, an ARPA-E should follow an "island-bridge" model,[20] isolated on a creative island from bureaucratic harassment and second-guessing and with its own protected budget, but with a strong bridge back to the political protection and clout of a cabinet agency to ensure that its ideas will be pushed forward. These features are important to fostering the culture of innovation and translation that has been critical to DARPA's past success and will have to be replicated if an ARPA-E is to work. Technology breakthroughs on an ongoing basis over the coming decades will be vital if energy security and environmental challenges are to be met, and filling the translational research institutional gap could make an important contribution.

(2)   Filling the Demonstration Gap: Organization for Engineering Demonstrations

In addition to translational R&D, there is a need for demonstrations of engineering-intensive technologies that the commercial sector has no strong incentive to carry out on its own.[21] Government cost sharing can be appropriate for the demonstration of new process technologies that worked well at laboratory and pilot scales but that require expensive and risky demonstrations at full scale, costing $100 million or more if they are to succeed in the market. Cost sharing for such demonstration projects can help ensure private-sector discipline and a private-sector stake in the demonstration. They should be set on a sliding scale, depending on the market's willingness to invest in a new technology. The small, light, flexible DARPA model, staffed by technology gurus with inevitably limited expertise in large-scale project engineering, project management, and financing, is not the model required to implement large commercial demonstration projects with major industries. But what should the institutional model be?

John Deutch, former Undersecretary of Energy, Deputy Secretary of Defense, and Director of the CIA, argues that the government corporation provides an organizational structure that can be used effectively for engineering demonstrations.[22] To be sure, the record of government-funded and government-run large-scale energy demonstration projects has been mediocre. Projects such as the Clinch River Breeder Reactor, the Barstow Solar Power Tower, and two DOE-run synthetic fuel plants faced large cost overruns due to collapsing oil prices two decades ago, and conveyed only limited technology information to the private sector.[23]

Nonetheless, Deutch argues that government corporations offer an important organizational option.[24] He draws three lessons from the Synthetic Fuels Corporation (SFC) experience. First, indirect incentives (production payments, tax credits, loans or loan guarantees, or guaranteed purchases) for demonstrating the possibilities of new technology deployment to the private sector have important advantages over stand-alone, government-dominated demonstrations not well connected to potential users. Second, because large demonstration projects with large cash outlays attract congressional interference, a quasi-public corporation, such as SFC, provides insulation against congressional intervention. Third, it is important to build flexibility and resilience into the economic model, which the private sector is better able to do, so that the executors of the project can react to changing market conditions and not make the mistake, which plagued SFC, of designing the demonstration solely around the assumption that current economics will always continue.

Deutch further argues that managing a commercial demonstration requires management expertise of the kind found in the private sector. Since DOE lacks such expertise, a public corporation is a means to recruit people that do have it. A public corporation would also be able to operate outside the limits of government procurement systems in an environment comparable to that of a commercial firm. This private-sector expertise—in both major project financing and commercial-scale engineering—should be backed by the kinds of financial incentives described above and by access to a sufficient multiyear stream of assured funding to permit the efficient execution of a demonstration project. Cost sharing with industry can provide a further incentive to cost control and commercial discipline.

A public corporation could also address the problem of financing improved manufacturing processes for new technologies, and accelerating the expansion of manufacturing capacity for energy-conserving technologies, especially in the auto sector. This will be discussed in more detail in the next section.

(3) Filling the Gaps in Financing Support for Manufacturing Processes, Production Scale-Up, and Building Efficiency

Most new energy technologies must compete on price more or less from the beginning. There will therefore be a premium on cutting manufacturing costs. Small start-up firms and university researchers are not generally experienced or expert in supporting breakthroughs in manufacturing engineering.

Support for manufacturing process is not a new role for American government. The U.S. military has long played this role with American industry and continues to do so. Starting in the 1820s, the army, seeking less expensive muskets from manufacturing production at scale, sponsored long-term R&D in early machine tools and related manufacturing processes at its Harper's Ferry and Springfield Arsenals.[25] The resulting advance was interchangeable, machine-made parts for muskets, a manufacturing process that led over the next decades to profound advances in industrial production and shifted leadership of the industrial revolution from Britain to the United States. Since then, numerous U.S. manufacturing sectors, from shipbuilding to aircraft production, have benefited from federal R&D on manufacturing processes.

In a more recent example, Sematech, a nonprofit partnership of industry and government, performed research that gave rise to major improvements in semiconductor manufacturing technology, and in this way helped restore the United States to world leadership in semiconductor production after it had been surpassed by Japanese industry in the mid-1980s.

Conceived in 1986 through industry leadership from Intel's Robert Noyce,[26] it was formed in 1987 and began operating in 1988 as a partnership between the U.S. government and fourteen U.S.-based semiconductor manufacturers to solve common manufacturing problems, particularly those faced by equipment makers. Sematech was and is at heart an industry consortium that worked in partnership with a government agency, receiving federal backing for its first five years. It was funded over that period by $500 million in public applied R&D subsidies from DARPA.

An energy Sematech, if effectively administered, could play a significant role in boosting entry of new energy technologies by bringing improvements in manufacturing processes to areas like solar and batteries to cut production costs and multiply production levels. It could take advantage of the industry consortium model that was at the heart of Sematech's success, building consortia in sectors where industry collaboration appears beneficial and feasible.

DARPA played a support role for Sematech, and has periodically played this role vis-à-vis manufacturing in the defense industry. A federal role in Sematech and in defense manufacturing in general was supported by both political parties because semiconductors and related critical tech-nologies were recognized as a critical defense technology. DARPA's work on IT connectivity in manufacturing supply chains, for example, helped improve the efficiency and cut costs for defense-sector manufacturers. R&D in manufactur-ing process technology can be every bit as challenging as it is in the creation of new products, and so it has been recog-nized as appropriately "DARPA-hard"—a challenge worthy of DARPA.

A role for ARPA-E in supporting industry consortia would thus be consistent with its role of stimulating breakthrough R&D. Private-sector entities resembling Sematech could also coordinate the response effort across industry sectors. For example, if manufacturing process costs for solar PV are to be reduced, a coordinated industry effort, backed with R&D support from ARPA-E, could support the necessary research and test and implement its results, with appropriate cost sharing among firms and with government. If ARPA-E could play an R&D support role for an industry consortium somewhat comparable to Sematech for cost-cutting manufacturing technologies and processes, it could do so for manufacturing scale-up as well.

It is also essential to speed the expansion of manufacturing capacity in order to take advantage of economies of scale and lower unit costs. This expansion will often facilitate the adoption of improved manufacturing technologies. For example, if advances in batteries continue to make plug-in hybrids look like a winning technology, given the fifteen or more years it takes for the U.S. auto fleet to turn over and the time it takes to build in new production capacity, PHEVs will make only a marginal difference in CO_2 emissions from automobiles for decades.

Can this technology transformation, if it seems sound, be accelerated? There may well be a need for purchase incentives and low-cost financing to encourage prompt introduction of expanded production capacity.[27] The public corporation for energy technology demonstrations described in the previous section could be a mechanism to sponsor such a promotional program. As a precedent, the government has financed expansions of capacity for military equipment production when the private sector was reluctant to do so for fear of the absence of an assured and continuing market.[28] Such a financing effort could extend to financing infrastructure scale-up for innovative technologies. This is not a radical proposal. Both the Chairman and the Ranking (senior minority) Member of the Senate Energy Committee introduced bills in 2008 calling for a quasi-governmental entity for financing deployment of new energy technology.[29]

Finally, there is a significant need to speed the installation of conservation and energy efficiency technologies in existing residential and commercial building stock, given the glacial turnover in this sector and the quick payoff expected by both builders and homeowners. Establishing financing programs and perhaps a secondary market through the kinds of authority held by the Federal National Mortgage Association (FNMA or "Fannie Mae"), presents an additional option for the corporation's operations. While FNMA has come under attack during the 2008 subprime lending crisis, its model has allowed broadened mortgage underwriting and therefore expanded home ownership for decades. If properly managed and regulated, it remains a potential model for energy financing by the government. [30] Other financing models include the Export-Import Bank (which finances U.S. business exports) and the Overseas Private Investor Corporation (which promotes U.S. private investments overseas and corresponding economic development); these models are used in the pending Senate Energy Committee financing legislation noted above.

Such financing mechanisms could enhance the flow of credit to this targeted energy sector, speed the transition to energy conservation and improved end-use efficiency, and make capital market operation in these areas both more efficient and transparent. The proposed corporation would be self-financing, and its programs could serve the range of activities suggested above. In effect, it could be a bank to speed an energy technology transition, especially in a financial crunch, working in collaboration with the private sector.

Because the elements described in this section would be located in a corporation outside the government, away from existing oversight mechanisms, a continuous oversight and evaluation process will be needed to judge its ongoing performance and recommend improvements. The roadmapping process described below could assist and help inform this effort, but a separate evaluation mechanism should be put in place. This may need to be a governmental role, perhaps through the Chief Financial Officer at the Department of Energy.

In summary, there is a need for a major technology financing effort, which could occur through a wholly owned government corporation, or "bank." It could facilitate the evolution of new energy technologies in five areas:

• Financing for small- and large-scale commercial engineering demonstration projects
• Financing for manufacturing production scale-up for new energy technologies
• Financing for new cost-cutting manufacturing processes and technologies
• Financing infrastructure needed for scale-up of innovative energy technology
• Financing and secondary market financing for conservation technologies for smaller commercial and residential users

(4) Filling the Collaboration Gap: Improving Technology Collaboration through Roadmapping between Public and Private Sectors

Collaboration through industry consortia could play an important role in some parts of the energy economy, not only in manufacturing technology but also in the more general evolution of technology. Here DARPA is an instructive precedent. DARPA teamed up with industry through hybrid industry-university R&D teams, and launched many of its advances in information technology directly into the commercial sector. DOD was therefore able to use the resulting products without bearing their enormous development costs. In other words, DARPA used commercial industry as the "customer" for its dual-use information products, just as it used DOD as a customer for Stealth, an exclusively military product. In the same way, an ARPA-E may be able to work with industrial consortia to identify requirements for translational research and carry this research out. Such collaboration with industry could help generate the industrial support that an ARPA-E will need for its programs to succeed.

The difficulties here should not be underestimated, however. Overall, as previously discussed, industry inherently has a short-term horizon because of the need to realize returns on R&D investment on a reasonable timetable, and so lacks the incentive for the longer-term forms of energy innovation. If revolutionary technology developments are to make the transition to widespread deployment, industrial firms must be found that are interested in undertaking the kind of longer-term collaborations we have proposed. The established energy sector is largely mature from a technology standpoint, has been cutting R&D expenditures, and is generally resistant to change. However, firms involved in disruptive energy technologies that create new industry sectors—PV solar as opposed to coal— may prove likely partners and could tie in to angel and venture capital resources in the private sector. If at the same time, other parts of DOE and the federal government are promoting demonstration projects and providing incentives to industry for technology transition, these carrots could be used to help leverage industry interest in collaboration on the R&D innovation front end with ARPA-E.[31] The goal is collaboration, not stranded firms. The major problem will be to target the government role for optimum impact on an important technology that would otherwise be a market failure, and not address areas where the private sector is ready to run the risks of technology development.

Moving beyond collaboration on particular technologies, industry consortia will also be critical for the kind of detailed, multiyear technology roadmapping discussed in chapter 3. Once an ARPA-E or other source supports an initial technology breakthrough, an industry consortium will be needed to roadmap it to deployment, to ensure continuing incremental improvement and to assess the menu of available and needed front- and back-end support mechanisms.

Such a coordinated effort between the public and private sectors can optimize the government's role in identifying and addressing the most promising opportunities to overcome market failure. It would assess each technology, identifying areas of needed precompetitive research and likely launch obstacles, and then recommend appropriate packages of front- and back-end policies and incentives to facilitate their development and deployment. In addition, collaborative roadmapping can address the need for change in energy systems, taking an integrated view of the possible development paths of the various technological options and the policies needed to support them to avoid locking in technologies too early and ensuring ongoing advances.[32] It can also provide a means to offset the power of the congressional pork barrel machine discussed in chapter 7, by establishing tough-minded technology performance requirements and timelines that may be difficult for Congress to disrupt without substantial technical backing.

Such roadmapping has played an essential role, for example, in enabling the semiconductor sector to evolve continuously and systematically, and will be vital to encouraging multiple generations of advances in energy technology. Sematech, the consortium discussed above in the semiconductor industry originally funded by DARPA, serves as the model for what a well-organized, technically informed roadmapping exercise can accomplish.[33] It has performed remarkably well in helping to keep a major worldwide industry locked onto the intense technology challenge of Moore's law, by which semiconductor capability and speed double and price is cut in half every eighteen months or so. This challenge is a precedent with parallels to the kind of roadmapping exercise that will be needed in energy.

The roadmapping exercise proposed here differs from the Sematech model in that it would not propose a precise timeline for technological developments or the order in which technological challenges are to be addressed and solved. In addition to strictly technological issues, it would be addressed to foreseeable obstacles to the deployment of technology and proactive measures to overcome them.

While a collaborative industry consortium and private-sector leadership will be key to the success of this exercise, roadmapping should also draw on a combination of technological expertise and practical engineering and policy experience from inside and outside of government, buttressed by insights from scholarly research on energy science and technology, energy economics, and the management of innovation, so that it can investigate the fit between different innovation types and alternative methods for the promotion of innovation. This cross-sectoral effort could be housed in a think tank, like that of RAND or the Institute for Defense Analysis, that serves and is served by an industry consortium. Energy roadmapping would begin with a strategic planning exercise and, once launched, should be subject to periodic review and revision and open to change as new technology options or issues emerge.

DOE has had past experience in supporting industry consortia—for example, with the Gas Research Institute, the Advanced Battery Consortium, and the Partnership for a New Generation of Vehicles (PNGV)—and in providing encouragement to the Electric Power Research Institute (EPRI). It could be a supporting and budgeting entity for this roadmapping effort, buttressed by technology talent in an ARPA-E as well as in national laboratories and the DOE Office of Science. It is important, however, that the roadmapping effort be a joint effort by industry and government, located outside of government and protected from domination by contending DOE bureaucracies and interests.

On the government side, roadmapping could also serve as a mechanism for cross-agency coordination of the efforts of the many federal R&D programs in which potential energy-related technologies can arise, from DOE to DOD to the National Science Foundation (NSF), a chief sponsor of basic scientific research outside of the fields related to health. A formal coordinating effort among agencies by the National Science and Technology Council (NSTC) could accompany and back the roadmapping effort. In fact, government-wide coordination and synergy in this area is likely important enough to justify formal legislation creating an energy council under the DOE Secretary and the Director of the Office of Science and Technology (OSTP) in the White House, analogous to the National Security Council. Such a council is being considered by the Senate Energy Committee; participating programs could include energy R&D efforts at DOE, DOD, NSF, the Department of Agriculture, the National Institutes of Health (NIH), and the Environmental Protection Agency, climate research at National Oceanic and Atmospheric Administration and NASA, building standards efforts at the Department of Housing and Urban Development, and government procurement at the General Services Administration and DOD. On the industry side, roadmapping could be a focal point for the coordination of numerous technology components with overall energy systems and platforms, and for coordination between industry efforts and front- and back-end government interventions, both incentive and regulatory.

The government can also take advantage of the fact that it itself is a major energy technology customer. It could use its role as a participant in the roadmapping effort to help identify critical technology priorities worthy of support through government purchasing. Its purchases also could be coordinated and its purchasing power enlisted to promote advanced technologies developed by ARPA-E through a government-wide plan, which in turn could fit with the roadmap developed by the industrial consortium. With congressional approval, an administration could, for example, order a proportion of new federal construction to incorporate new solar PV nanotechnology membranes for electrical power generation, or could direct military transport to cut fuel consumption by using hybrids featuring new nano-derived batteries, once these technologies had reached an appropriate level of development. Government purchase incentives, which are a back-end incentive, could play a supporting role in promoting and achieving the goals of industry collaboration and roadmapping implementation timetables. In general, new energy technologies would not have a government customer base nearly as large, overall, as DOD's. On the other hand, in some niche areas, new emerging energy products could make good use of a government purchasing role. And these technologies potentially have a non-government customer base that is orders of magnitude larger than DOD.

In these ways, technology roadmapping through industry and government collaboration could be a key system-level tool in supporting the introduction of new technology and ongoing incremental improvements to it, with DOE and an ARPA-E playing a coordinating role in promoting this approach.

A detailed roadmap is not enough. Its proponents will have to convince the public if it is to be implemented, which requires that the roadmap be translated into a clear strategy with clearly stated steps and overall goals. The Bush administration, led by its Department of Energy, offered a 224-page *Strategic Plan* in 2006.[34] However, the chairman of the Senate Energy Committee, Senator Jeff Bingaman (D-NM), has characterized it as "basically only shopping lists of viable technologies. They lack concrete goals, roadmaps for making progress, and timelines for development. Such reports are not entirely without value, but what we have now is far from being a strategy."[35] Two leading Senate advocates on R&D policy and energy development, Senator Bingaman and Senator Lamar Alexander (R-TN), called in 2008 for detailed strategies built around these elements of specific goals, supporting coordinated technology roadmaps, and timetables for the development of technology.[36] The new president and Secretary of Energy, backed up by a detailed and ongoing technology roadmapping process, will need to articulate to the public a strategy that paints a clear overall view of the goals that will need to be reached and how we will get to them.

(5)   Filling Talent Gaps, Motivating That Talent through Prizes, and Deploying Talent

Because energy R&D has been underfunded on the public side for twenty-five years, and because federally funded, mentor-based research is the way we fund much of graduate science education, we have not been developing the depth of talent we likely will need in energy fields. Paul Romer has made the economic case for the importance of talent as a critical factor in nurturing R&D and corresponding innovation.[37] Just training the talent is not enough, however. We need, in his terms, "human capital engaged in research"—that is, to engage that talent in the R&D field where advance is sought. Romer's prospector theory is applicable here—science, he reasons, is a lot like prospecting. The nation or region that sends out the largest numbers of well-trained prospectors into a territory usually finds the most gold—that is, technical advances. We do not face a talent shortfall per se, but more of a problem of talent deployment. The doubling of the NIH budget between 1998 and 2003 demonstrated that there is enough flexibility and capacity in institutions that employ scientists and engineers that this workforce can and will shift to staff a major innovation initiative. We also have had stagnation in federal support to physical science since the end of the Cold War, and in recent years in the life sciences as well, so that there should be available troops. The issue is more one of getting the best-trained talent deployed on the problem, of inspiring new talent to enter the field, and of assuring sustained support for their work.

Because R&D, as noted, plays the dual role of supporting both research and our scientific talent base, sustained increases in the R&D budget should help encourage the best talent to work on energy and lure experts from the wide range of relevant fields. In addition, an increase in funding for graduate education, both in energy and in science and engineering fields directly related to energy, could also be important in fielding new talent. These efforts are particularly important in an era when more and more technological advance is coming from connected research carried out in collaboration between university researchers and industry.[38] The Sputnik challenge inspired a generation of science talent. The energy challenge could, as well, if the right investments in R&D are made and sustained. The key point is *sustained*. If energy R&D remains on an on-again, off-again rollercoaster, even an energized talent pool cannot commit to a sustained research endeavor.

Prizes could be another source of inspiration. They are another tool with which to promote advances in technology. There is a distinguished history of prizes that successfully induced new discoveries and inventions by combining the allures of fame, fortune, and perhaps most importantly, the plain challenge ("because it's there"). The development of the chronometer for navigation is perhaps the most noted historical example.[39] Prizes constitute an instrument of technology supply strategy and rely on taking advantage of the greater knowledge of researchers of the state-of-the-art of a technology—rather than the inevitably more limited knowledge of those offering and selecting R&D grants in a grant-making agency or firm—and directing the attention of these researchers to a clearly articulated national goal. Congressional Energy Committees have recognized this option. The 2005 Energy Act proposed "Prizes for Achievement in Grand Challenges of Science and Technology,"[40] and the 2007 Energy Act called for prizes for lighting and for hydrogen advances.[41] A number of private firms and foundations have announced prizes in energy as well.[42]

Coming up with the right list of energy challenges that could lead to significant advances and then judging the results of the competition are not simple tasks, and require an informed and technically sophisticated process.[43] An ARPA-E may be in a good position to convene a process to do this, and to advise the Secretary of Energy on how to offer prizes that meet the most important challenges in energy technology. A variant on the prize concept is to tie a significant monetary reward to achieving a technology standard in a commercialized product—for example, highly efficient appliances or low-emission residences—to induce technological advance. The standard is set in advance, and if a commercial technology implements it, the monetary reward, which can be a purchase order, (sometimes called a "golden carrot") and corresponding public recognition are awarded.

All this having been said, prizes are not a magic substitute for a strong R&D program. That foundation, which builds a pool of potential prize competitors and the knowledge base they can work from, is still mandatory. Prizes can build an additional motivation on top of a system of support to R&D.

Still another issue concerning R&D talent is the question of how to deploy this talent effectively. Innovation is increasingly understood to be organized by region and locality. What is more, innovation is a social and cultural phenomenon; it comes from diverse ecosystems of institutions, firms, researchers, and entrepreneurs, who must be linked together.

Because of their growing role in technological innovation since the Second World War, universities have become innovation hubs for the regional economies around them.[44] Yet universities often feel abiding ambivalence about this "third stream" economic role, which they have accepted as an addition to their age-old roles in education and research. To be sure, the connections and the tensions among these three roles are inevitable in a modern knowledge-based economy. While universities celebrate this economic role when they advocate increases in R&D funding before Congress, it still violates older canons whose origins lie in their early monastic traditions calling for the separation of the life of the mind from worldly forms.

A central rationale advanced by Vannevar Bush in 1945 for the creation of the modern, federally funded research university was that basic research conducted there with federal support would lead to economic well-being for society. Yet as we have suggested in chapter 2, the organizational model for moving from university discoveries to technology commercialization has been imperfect at best. Gradually, through mechanisms such as the Bayh Dole Act that endows them with the intellectual property rights for discoveries from federally funded research, universities are learning the intricacies of technology transition.

Given the low level of industrial energy R&D discussed in chapter 5 and the general decline in basic R&D by industry, universities must play a critical role in solving the profound challenges in energy technology if a new paradigm for energy innovation is to emerge. This means that universities will need to place more focus on their organizational models for technology transition. If further resources are to be placed on university-based energy research, as indeed they must be, universities will need to sharpen their abilities to move their technological concepts toward commercial markets. This does not mean commercialized universities, but does mean better connections and collaborations with commercial forces.

As universities have learned from their own experience, particularly in the biotech area, these connections are not simple. But as former NSF Director Erich Bloch once suggested, technology breakthroughs that remain on the shelf might as well not exist. In an area as critical as energy, for promising technology to remain on the shelf is simply not an acceptable option. Universities should take on this transition task themselves and not wait for government intervention. They should explore their own most successful models and make their best organizational approaches and practices widely known so that others can experiment with and implement them.

After all, universities themselves are the institutions best suited to finding approaches that respond to a profound societal challenge that their students and faculty increasingly care deeply about while at the same time safeguarding their culture of learning and experimentation. But they cannot ignore this transition task. On the contrary, they will need to confront it.

(6) Filling the "Back-End" Gap: The Package of Incentives and Mandates for Technology Deployment

An earlier section summarized the range of back-end incentives and regulatory mandates, carrots and sticks that could be available to promote the introduction of new energy technologies, pending the enactment of a carbon charge or other macropricing system for energy. We argued that back-end incentives at the later stages of innovation should seek to create a level playing field for competing advances in technology. Except for those involving taxes, these incentives could be consolidated and institutionalized for general supervision at the Department of Energy, perhaps as one of the programs of the Chief Financial Officer. This office is now implementing DOE's new loan guarantee financing authority and may be able to build capability in this related area. The roadmapping effort described above could provide advice to this office on the applicability and advisability of particular incentives to particular technologies.

The more potentially relevant back-end measures are spelled out in more detail below. A rigorous analysis is needed to evaluate the current incentives in place and alternative incentives, reviewing their relative efficiency and cost in delivering technology implementation results. On the incentive/carrot side, the overall menu includes the following:

Tax incentives and credits for the adoption of specific technologies. These are currently the largest tool the government exercises to intervene in energy markets, far exceeding federal energy R&D investments.[45] They could be made available to consumers, for example, as they are now for other technologies, for purchasing low-emission plug-in hybrid vehicles, or to industries installing new low-emission technologies.[46]

Public-private partnerships (PPPs). The government offers revenue for capital investment or R&D. In a typical pattern, a business venture is formed with one or more private firms, and the effort is bound together with a contract for joint performance between firm and government actors, with cost sharing from both parties. Alternatively, the private sector invests capital based on a contract with the public sector participants for the performance of services, such as R&D, prototyping, or pilot project construction or operation. This approach could be tied to the consortium model described above.

Loan guarantees and low-cost loans. These could be used, for example, to encourage an auto manufacturer to rapidly speed up production of breakthrough low-emission vehicles such as plug-in hybrids. Reduced-rate loans could be available to offset the major costs of retooling assembly lines. A new federal or public-private financing entity may be required for the financing of this scale-up, as suggested above.

Government promotion programs, such as government procurement programs for promotion of the new technologies (discussed above), as well as government purchase promotion and buy-down programs.

On the regulatory mandate ("stick") side of the back end, which as we have seen is politically much more difficult to impose than incentives, the most relevant are:

Government standards, including appliance standards and energy technology standards in the building and construction sectors. These can be tied to incentives, such as a requirement that the government procurement programs purchase technologies that meet the standards.

Regulatory mandates, such as renewable portfolio standards requiring utilities to use a portion of renewable sources in their electricity production, and fuel standards, such as the current system for a 10 percent blend of ethanol in gasoline and improved CAFE fuel economy standards.

Other possibilities in this regulatory/stick part of the back-end menu include emissions fees and emissions taxes, although a carbon charge or other demand-side pricing scheme for energy would be a preferable and more effective way to drive the market in price-sensitive sectors. On the carrot side, a problem with incentives is that they are inefficient in differentiating among technology advances unless they are carefully packaged so as to be made available across comparable technologies. This problem is exacerbated by the fact that there is a massive existing subsidy structure benefiting incumbent energy sectors,[47] to the detriment of newer entrants. Rationalization of this maze of existing subsidies, while politically difficult, should accompany any new wave of incentives if they are to be effective and if something resembling a level playing field among low-emission technology options is to evolve to promote competition among competing technologies.

Such a rationalization of subsidies, along the lines of both technology neutrality and energy efficiency, could create major tax savings, likely more than enough to fund a sound replacement incentive structure while avoiding additional losses to the federal treasury. In other words, a new incentive program, if accompanied by a cleanup of the existing subsidy morass, could pay for itself. Recent House energy legislation attempted to adopt that approach but, as noted above, faced administration opposition.[48] However, the simple existence of that morass signals that a demand-side pricing system may prove a cleaner approach than the political complexities of attempting to redesign the system of subsidies.

There is another potential back-end pathway, aside from federal policy. A number of states and regions are already designing and implementing their own, often significant systems of subsidies and mandates. These typically take the form of tax subsidies for renewables, renewable portfolio standards, and vehicle standards, but sometimes also include appliance standards, building codes, climate policies, distributed generation policies, smart growth, and other tax incentives and utility policies.[49] If federal efforts at a demand pricing system for some reason fail, and if incentives for back-end energy technology alternatives remain distorted at the federal level, a group of Western states, led by California, and a group of Northeastern states, could take the lead. These states form an economic bloc that exceeds the size of all but the largest of the world's national economies. Assuming that their congressional delegations protect them from federal preemption under the Commerce Clause of the U.S. Constitution, these states constitute a sizable enough bloc, if they can succeed in coordinating their policies, to drive a significant shift toward standing up alternative energy technologies.[50]

Summary of New Institutional Arrangements to Meet Energy Innovation Gaps

This book does not propose an explosion of the government's role in energy. This sector is already laced with a network of contradictory government incentives and regulations, which should be rationalized along lines proposed here if they are to serve a new set of national environmental and security policy imperatives pending introduction of a demand pricing system. We have proposed in this section three new institutional elements related to identified gaps in the current energy innovation system: an ARPA-E translational R&D entity; a wholly owned government corporation for financing commercial demonstrations, manufacturing scale-up, and implementation of technology for energy efficiency; and a think tank for roadmapping energy technology. The latter two would be located outside government in public-private partnerships; the former would also seek private sector connections. We reemphasize that because solutions to our energy problems will have to be based in the private sector, each of these elements must be closely tied to and collaborate with the private sector. The function of each of these elements is summarized in table 6.2.

Will New Energy Technology Provide Economic Gains? Will It Create New Functionality?

Energy is a major economic sector, approaching 10 percent of U.S. GDP, with multitrillions in infrastructure, investment,

Table 6.2
Proposed new institutional elements for the promotion of innovation in energy technology

Proposed new innovation institutional element	Functions
ARPA-E	• Translational energy R&D • Manufacturing process and efficiency R&D for energy technologies, current and new • Support for industry-government consortia
Energy corporation	• Small- and large-scale commercial engineering demonstration projects • Financing for scale-up of manufacturing • Financing and incentives for industry consortia to address cost-cutting manufacturing technologies and processes • Financing infrastructure for scale-up of innovative technology • Financing and secondary financing market through GSE authority for conservation technologies for small commercial and residential building users
Roadmapping thinktank	• Developing and updating, on an ongoing basis, an energy innovation roadmap tied to industry consortia, combining industrial, government, and academic expertise to assess technologies and to identify areas of pre-competitive research and likely obstacles to launch and recommend appropriate policies

and revenues. Major new investments will be flowing world-wide into the kinds of new energy technology enumerated in chapter 4. If the United States sits this out and lets others lead, it will miss the economic opportunities for the production and sale of goods and services embodying these new technologies. One survey suggests that clean energy markets may grow from $55 billion in 2006 to $226 billion by 2016.[51]

On the other hand, the question remains, will new energy technology create new functionality in the rest of the economy? As Robert Solow established three decades ago, economic growth in advanced countries comes predominantly from technological and related innovation.[52] Others have argued that the "enabling" technologies that can come from this innovation extend into many applications across many sectors in the economy and can in turn improve productivity and therefore translate into real gains in societal wealth.[53] Can we play this out in energy as we did in the innovation wave in information technology (IT)?[54]

Energy technology presents a more complicated story regarding this kind of new economic functionality than does IT. IT was launched into a niche without initial competitive pressures, with front- and back-end support funded initially by the government, largely through the Defense Department. IT transformed productivity and therefore raised societal wealth. Energy will be different. Energy will not change functionality in the same way as did IT, which presented predominantly radical innovation as opposed to the predominantly secondary innovation that new energy technology will bring. Autos will still be autos even if they plug in, and electricity will still flow from wall plugs to appliances. Aspects of an energy technology transformation will likely lead to new enabling technologies, but this likely will proceed in a series of more gradual steps than IT.

Thus, new energy technology will not necessarily lead to the major productivity gains that IT has made possible, and may not be as profitable as IT, when viewed purely from the standpoint of its prospective contribution to economic growth. Of course, it took some time for this IT-induced increase in productivity to become apparent. DARPA contracted for the ARPAnet in 1969, widespread Internet use did not occur until the 1990s, and it took some years after that before the IT revolution showed up in productivity statistics. The timing of the impact of an energy transformation may not be all that different.

The main difference will be that the impact of IT was much bigger and it was and is easier to put your finger on it. IT was built around a mix of radical innovations, which multiply profitability through the operation of "increasing returns."[55] The gains from improved energy technology will at first be largely in efficiency, which, although significant, cannot offer the same multiplier. Unlike IT, then, an energy revolution through its initial phases will not necessarily pay for itself by creating a virtuous cycle of sectoral deflation and new productivity in the way that IT did.

To be sure, there will be significant economic and productivity gains from energy innovation. Energy inefficiency is economic waste, and there will be productivity gains from efficiency gains, as well as from the advent of disruptive new energy technologies. The first phase of an energy shift will lead to energy conservation and efficiency throughout many sectors, established products, and energy systems. This will generate savings and productivity gains; we will be getting more for less input. These will generate jobs throughout the economy. But these gains—and these jobs—will not necessarily be obvious to anyone but close observers to an energy transformation. Construction workers installing insulation will still be construction workers, not working at identifiable "green jobs." Companies of all kinds likely will have to implement "sustainability" models to improve energy efficiency throughout their operations and supply chains to stay competitive,[56] but this will not be their predominant focus. Because energy is a huge economic sector all over the world, there are major profits to be made throughout the economy from conservation and efficiency savings and from introducing advances in energy technology. Even so, we must be careful not to oversell at these early stages what new energy will do for employment and economic growth. In particular, politicians must be careful about what they promise; the economic and employment gains will be there, but it may be hard to cite them.

The next phase will likely emerge from adding secondary or component technologies to existing products, systems, or platforms. Energy transformation for a long period will likely be predominantly embodied in a shift in the components of existing systems and platforms. These will consist of secondary rather than of radical innovations; while there will likely be some disruptive technologies introduced (such as off-grid solar), component technologies will lead. An autoworker installing a lithium ion battery in a hybrid will still be an autoworker, and will not be working at a "green job." However, the employee of the company that makes the new component will have such a job. This stage of component introduction will thus start to show more identifiable gains in both incomes and productivity.

A third phase may introduce something different; it is possible that disruptive or radical innovations will evolve. We might reach decentralized renewable power systems for homes or business. Experimental technologies now evolving could have disruptive effects, introducing enabling technologies that create new functionalities with corresponding economic gains more like those of the IT revolution. But overall, the incumbent energy system is so huge that it will be harder to introduce new functionality; even if we are persistent, the process will be gradual and initially not very visible. As previously noted, because an energy transformation will land largely in occupied territory—unlike IT, which landed in a comparatively unoccupied field—its innovation benefits will likely evolve over time and be harder to distinguish.

What is more, the phases we have outlined will not be clearly differentiated. They will overlap each other, and aspects of one phase may leapfrog over the others because the pace of technology advance, as noted above, is not truly linear and predictable. However, energy technology advance will likely contain these three broad elements. Export markets for both incremental and radical technologies will accelerate this process; this underscores the need for the United States to take prompt advantage of the economic opportunities for technological leadership in energy.

In sum, there will be real economic gains from energy innovation, but these will be evolutionary. The justification for the major program we are proposing, then, lies not so much in the prospects for purely economic gain—although these remain real and significant—but in the imperative to protect our critical interests in the environment and our geopolitical interests. New energy is a sector we have to be in because of these overriding environmental and security demands.

7

All Pumping Together? Prospects for International Collaboration

Global warming, energy security, and economic competitiveness are inextricably linked, a fact that greatly complicates any national effort to stimulate innovation in energy technology. Both global warming and energy security are inherently international problems, to which purely national solutions can at best offer only partial answers. At the same time, there are inescapable conflicts between this common interest and the issues of international competitiveness and commercial competition, not to mention the geopolitical conflicts resulting from the interest of some nations in perpetuating the current energy paradigm. From the point of view of the firm, after all, the whole point of an innovation is to take advantage of so-called economic rents, the profits resulting from the temporary monopoly it provides. Resolving the tension between the international stake in safeguarding the Earth's climate and the national and commercial interest in economic competitiveness is critical to the revolution in energy technology that we seek to structure. The situation is further complicated by the growth of the developing countries, especially China and India. These countries did not create the problem of global warming but are now major contributors to it.

The Growing Role of China and India

Two thirds of cumulative fossil-fuel CO_2 emissions stem from the industrialization of Europe and the United States, which after all has been ongoing since the late eighteenth century.[1] In per capita CO_2 emissions, the United States remains the overwhelming leader, with 19.4 tons per American, compared to 11.8 tons per Russian, 8.6 tons per EU European, 5.1 per Chinese, and 1.8 per Indian.[2]

On the other hand, economic growth in the developing world now threatens to swamp the greenhouse gas controls evolving in the developed world. China has now passed the United States as the world's leading CO_2 emitter. China's GHG emissions doubled from 47 percent of U.S. levels to nearly 100 percent in the five years ending in 2005.[3] In 2006 alone, China installed an estimated 105 gigawatts (billion watts, or GW) of electric power capacity, an amount equal to what the entire world installed in 2004.[4] Its emissions grew by 8 percent in 2007 alone, exceeding U.S. emissions for that year by 14 percent and alone accounting for two-thirds of the world's annual growth in GHGs.[5] It is installing an average of two 500 MW coal-fired power plants a week,[6] adding new capacity each year that exceeds the energy output of Great Britain. Its CO_2 growth is accelerating. By 2030, the U.S. Energy Information Agency estimates that China alone will produce a quarter of the world's CO_2 emissions, while the United States will have fallen to less than 20 percent.[7] On the other hand, the less-developed nations will not catch up with the accumulated CO_2 emissions of the OECD countries for many decades.

When developed countries insist that developing countries reduce their carbon dioxide emissions before they reach American or European levels of development—an argument that has played an important role in American discussions of international measures to limit CO_2 emissions—their discourse lends itself to caricatures of American drivers of SUVs lecturing Indian oxcart drivers on the virtues of energy conservation. Even so, the need for the implementation of new energy technology clearly exists worldwide. Virtually all nations have an interest in limiting the impact of climate change and their dependence on oil imported from countries that are often unstable and unfriendly. From this point of view, there is every reason for scientists, technologists, investors, and governments all over the world to collaborate in addressing these global environmental and geopolitical problems.

Here a story told by a British diplomat about a liner in a storm at sea may shed light on the ethics of the situation. Some passengers, without necessarily intending to have done so, have stowed baggage that causes punctures in the hull. The ship begins to fill with water. The passengers who did not cause the hull damage refuse to help pump the oncoming water from the hold because it is not their fault. But without their help the ship will sink, drowning all the passengers. Will the passengers not initially at fault eventually come around and pump?

To this, the developing countries (the "innocent" passengers, in our story) have argued, in effect, we are willing do our share, but you have to give us extra time, and you have to help us, both technically and financially. In China and India, the two most important CO_2 emitters among the developing countries, the problem is complicated by two facts: first, that both countries are investing heavily in research and development in an effort to launch competitive, innovation-based industries of their own, and second, that the decisions that are accelerating CO_2 emissions in these countries are generally decentralized to regional and local governments and to corporate actors not controlled by the central government.[8]

Mechanisms for International Coordination

A number of mechanisms are now in place to help developing countries "work the pumps," using existing technologies to conserve energy or develop renewable sources of energy. The directive establishing the EU Emissions Trading System allows CO_2 emitters in EU countries to count reductions in GHG emissions generated outside the EU (except for nuclear power and CO_2 sinks such as forests) toward their compliance obligations inside the system, as long as at least half of the expected reductions occur within the country in which the emitter is located.[9]

This system of "linkages" or "joint implementation" between countries, which is consistent with the Kyoto Protocol, has its defects but is still useful.[10] Because GHGs are a global problem (technically, because they mix into all parts of the atmosphere no matter where they originate), reductions anywhere achieve the same gains. Linkage devices reward lower-cost mitigation approaches wherever they are located, so that countries facing relatively high costs for mitigation can limit their costs by achieving low-cost mitigation elsewhere. In principle, this should make it possible for a given level of GHG emission to be achieved at lower cost. An added advantage comes from the fact that this use of offsets from outside the EU through linkage is limited to countries that have agreed to participate in Kyoto. Because the resulting investments in developing countries can be quite significant, linkage is also a device to leverage participation in Kyoto (or its successor) and support broader progress on emissions reductions.

The leading cap-and-trade legislation pending in 2008 in the U.S. Congress, the 2008 Lieberman-Warner bill, takes a somewhat similar approach to linkages. That legislation allows owners and operators of facilities required to reduce emissions under the bill to satisfy a modest percentage of a given year's compliance obligation with "international allowances" purchased from a foreign GHG emission trading market certified by the U.S. Environmental Protection Agency as having a system comparable to that established by the bill.[11] Other provisions in the bill establish an international partnership fund to deploy clean energy technology, and an international climate fund to assist affected developing nations in adapting to disruptive consequences of climate change. Meanwhile, the World Bank's "Clean Development Fund" makes loans and grants to developing countries to finance renewable and alternative energy installations.[12]

Where these and other mechanisms seek to encourage developing countries to invest in renewable sources of energy to help mitigate the global problem of climate change, energy-intensive industries like steel in advanced countries are preparing the ground for measures to protect themselves against competition from imports from nations that are avoiding the costs of controlling emissions. The pending cap-and-trade bill in the Senate creates an "international reserve allowance" as an attempt at a trade adjustment mechanism to undertake this.[13] Without such an adjustment, a carbon charge could alter the competitive position of these industries, with the perverse effect of allowing goods made from high-carbon production processes to drive out goods made with lower-carbon production techniques. On the other hand, establishing carbon-controlled versus non-carbon-controlled manufacturing costs will not be a simple process, and the exercise risks becoming a tariff barrier, with implications for the World Trade Organization (WTO) agreement.

Where Will Energy Innovation Leadership Come From?

Installing new equipment based on existing technology is one problem, but innovating is another. Where will the innovations come from that will enable a worldwide energy technology transition to take place? Once these innovations have taken place, how are the poorer countries of the world to be induced to import technology and equipment they need to deal with a climate change problem they did not create? And are even advanced and innovative developing countries like China and India, which have made major investments in their R&D capacity, to be relegated to mere acceptors of advanced energy technology developed in the OECD countries?

If there is a reasonable possibility of new technology implementation in both the developed world and the expanding parts of the developing world, one might argue that the world does not need the United States to provide innovation leadership if it does not choose to do so. Perhaps, the argument might continue, innovation has become so international that there is no basis for concern about national innovation support in the United States or elsewhere. In other words, how viable are national systems of innovation in an increasingly globalized world? Is a national innovation systems analysis even a viable approach given the fact of globalization?

We would argue that, on the contrary, national innovation systems are growing in importance and are not declining as globalization increases.[14] The World Economic Forum, supported by numerous economic and innovation scholars worldwide, conducts a highly publicized biannual survey that analyzes the innovation capacity of over a hundred world economies, based on a system of metrics for measuring national innovation.[15] While it is true that late-stage development and production are carried out by corporations that are becoming more and more international, the survey in effect confirms that two fundamental factors are still dominated by the nation-state: research investment and support for scientific talent via investment in higher education. In other words, although the later stages of innovation are internationalizing, the critical early stages—on which the later stages depend—still rely on support from the nation-state.

Innovation in energy technology, although a global imperative, thus depends on R&D at the national level. The U.S. innovation system, which was ranked number one in the above global survey in 2008, remains stronger than any other and is entirely capable of meeting this challenge.[16] But if it does not rise to the occasion, are there alternatives to its leadership in energy innovation: the EU? China? Japan? We will briefly review these in succession. We shall conclude that U.S. leadership is still essential if innovation is to occur with the urgency we need.

First, let's look at the EU. While some European nations, led by Germany, are using subsidies to enable a shift to the implementation of new energy technologies, the EU is relying on cap-and-trade demand pricing for new energy technology and is not investing strongly in energy technology innovation.[17] Under the EU cap-and-trade system, nation-states control the revenue from permitting and auctions, and it appears that many EU countries will allocate that revenue to their social welfare systems, which face a severe demographic challenge. While EU countries like Germany are building a strong base of manufacturing jobs from clean energy, there is apparently less focus in the EU overall on the earlier innovation stage, as this revenue situation suggests.

China is racing to launch an advanced innovation system, investing heavily in the two key factors of innovation-led growth—R&D and talent. China is already attempting to become the leading world manufacturing center for solar and wind equipment,[18] and is working on development and deployment of new nuclear power technologies. These are entirely reasonable aspirations for a country that is already the world's leading platform for export manufactures.

Even so, Chinese capacity in this area is a work in progress. The world should not assume this system will be fully stood up in depth to develop and launch the transformative[19] energy technologies that must evolve in the coming decade and a half if they are to have an effect by midcentury. The discussion of China's national lighting initiative in chapter 4 suggests what China's strategy may be like in the coming years: a strong emphasis on building up production capacity in new technologies.

India is also installing wind-power equipment at a growing rate. It has the fifth highest level of electricity production from wind in the world,[20] and is home to the world's fifth largest wind-turbine manufacturer.[21] The resulting trade relations may help bring China and India into the international system of emission controls.

As for Japan, while Japan's innovation system is emerging from its painful economic decline in the 1990s, it has focused on the need to strengthen its ability to undertake innovation rooted in basic research.[22] Japan's decision makers generally understand better than their U.S. counterparts the connection between growth and innovation. Japan is working vigorously in such energy technology fields as autos, where it is already the world's innovation leader, and solar, and could provide technology leadership in other new energy technology sectors as well. It has long been outinvesting other nations in energy R&D—in part because of its own historic lack of energy resources—spending close to 1 percent of GDP on energy R&D between 1992 and 2005, more than twice the percentage of competitor nations, including the United States, Germany, France, and the United Kingdom.[23] Japan could play a significant role.

On balance, while other nations are making efforts to strengthen their innovation capabilities, the U.S. innovation system has led the world for many decades and is likely to continue to do so for some time, although major challenges are looming.[24] Given the long implementation period for new advances in technology, typically ten to twenty years, and the problem of energy scale, innovations need to start accelerating now if stabilization is to become attainable in upcoming decades.

Our brief survey of possible substitutes thus leads us to conclude that there is no easy substitute for U.S. technology leadership in this arena if a new energy paradigm is to be implemented with the speed and urgency that we and the rest of the world require. Besides, the United States would be missing an important economic bet if it failed to invest in leadership in an area that is likely to set the pattern of global technological development for decades to come. As Thomas Friedman puts it,

We are not going to regulate our way out of the problems of the Energy-Climate Era. We can only innovate our way out, and the only way to do that is to mobilize the most effective and prolific system for transformational innovation and commercialization of new products ever created on the face of the earth—the U.S. marketplace.[25]

Collaboration on Innovation

Innovative technology is the chief source of competitiveness of advanced countries, especially the United States. At the firm level, the lure of profits is the indispensable incentive for private investments in innovation. This argues for a purely capitalist system of encouraging the development of exclusive proprietary innovations and exporting them to the rest of the world. Developing countries will be major potential markets for such exports. It is important to keep incentives for innovation strong and healthy.

But it is also in the common global interest that all countries, and especially China and India given their growing emissions, make maximum efforts to reduce their CO_2 emissions.

To complicate matters further, some of these technologies, especially carbon capture and sequestration, will when adopted add considerably to the costs of exploiting the coal reserves that are China and India's chief domestic energy resources. On the other hand, China and India share the global interest in limiting the effects of global warming, if only to limit the sea level rise that may threaten over time their coastal cities with flooding and to slow the melting of the glaciers that constitute the sources of their major rivers.

This leads to an interesting balancing act. Internationally collaborative precompetitive research on problems of common interest—i.e., research on underlying questions that are not directly related to the development of proprietary products—is the most straightforward approach to this dilemma. For example, while the specific design and manufacture of carbon capture technology for coal-fired power plants may prove an area of great commercial promise, understanding the geological formations best suited to CO_2 storage may not be, and it may be useful for governments to collaborate on this kind of research and disseminate that information internationally in order to promote CCS implementation. It would be critically important to share information of this kind derived from major demonstration projects. The policy issues surrounding carbon dioxide storage and geothermal energy may be another area for research collaboration. Similarly, there is every reason to collaborate on research in the natural and social sciences related to the environmental, economic, and social impacts of biofuels, a subject that has attained recent prominence because of the spike in food prices.

The 2006 *Stern Review* made useful general recommendations for areas where international cooperation at the research and related stages could be promising.[26] It recommended sharing information on research results, including between developed and developing nations, coordinating government-supported R&D priorities across national programs, and pooling risk and reward for major R&D investments, particularly at the demonstration stage. It suggested that the portfolio of individual national R&D priorities and deployment support may not be sufficiently diverse or in depth for adequate progress, and that shared national gains could occur to the mutual benefit of participants on technologies with global potential, such as biomass and bioenergy.

Innovation in equipment and services embodying new technology (especially for CCS equipment and associated consulting services, which are the critical technologies for coal-dependent countries like China and India) presents a more difficult problem. Such innovation is, after all, at the heart of the competitiveness of the technologically advanced countries. Firms that have invested in R&D will be loath to share their hard-won proprietary technology in the name of the global interest in reducing CO_2 emissions. If they move production facilities offshore, even for products to be exported to developing countries, they will be accused of exporting "green jobs" at a time when unemployment is an increasingly serious problem.

At the same time, developing countries are likely to protest that they are being asked to pay for expensive, imported technology in order to solve a problem that they did not create. They are likely to argue that they, too, should be helped to innovate in energy technology and not simply be expected to import equipment or designs developed elsewhere. China and India in particular are making serious efforts to build up their own innovative capacity through major investments in science and technology. They are likely to see carbon-free energy sources as an area in which they, too, can gain competitive advantage through investment in the development of innovative technology, and will be more interested in collaboration with multinational firms than in government-to-government assistance, or in striking out on their own with their own capital goods and technical services.

For countries at an earlier stage of scientific and technological development, the most practical approach may be to help them develop the capacity to innovate—or at least to participate in the value-added connected with innovation—through investments in education and other aspects of scientific and technological capacity. In the short run, the objective would be to ensure that their trained people will be employed and their firms will be welcomed by foreign firms as vendors and perhaps as partners in the implementation of innovative energy products and processes. In the longer run, the hope and expectation would be that they will eventually develop the capacity to innovate on their own in areas where they find comparative advantage. Another area for the development of local capacity in these developing countries is in fields of science and technology in which local knowledge is the most critical, as for example environmental impact assessment, energy conservation services, agricultural research on biofuels, natural resources and biological surveys, and the technoeconomic and legal aspects of policy research.

In summary, new energy technology must be implemented worldwide, and cap-and-trade linkage programs offer one leverage mechanism to encourage such a global effort. Because of the historic strength of its innovation system, the United States likely will be needed to play a significant role in energy innovation if progress is to be made in coming decades. However, there should be an international dimension to collaboration on innovation. As discussed, the key is to maintain a sound balance between commercialization and collaboration, with commercial competition in innovation prevailing unless there is market failure or delay, in which case government support or collaboration can play a role. Basic and precompetitive R&D present particular collaboration opportunities, and collaborations in general may offer participating nations expanded innovation resources and opportunities for market entry they would not have on their own. There is an even stronger case for international collaboration at the technology implementation stage, particularly for developing nations. In a competitive but expanding global economy, there should be market enough for all to share.

8

Political Prospects and Conclusions

The Politics of Energy Innovation

Returning to efforts in the United States, how viable politically are the proposals for changes at the federal level advanced in this book? The proposals for federal government policy can be broken down into three broad categories: front-end investment in research, development, and demonstration; back-end incentives and regulatory mandates for technology implementation; and related institutional reforms in the innovation system. We believe there are signs as of late 2008, including recent elections, that each of these is coming into the range of the politically possible.

In the first category, that of R&D spending, Congress and the president took the initiative in putting DOE in 2007 on the road to doubling its energy science investment in a decade.[1] Although appropriations ran into difficulty in FY 2008, Congress has been supportive of meeting those R&D spending targets. Energy technology legislation emerging from the energy committees followed later in 2007, as noted above, to increase R&D and implementation incentives. Appropriations legislation is pending for FY 2009 to raise these R&D benchmarks. These are still a long way from the level that is needed, but indicate that there is a political consensus at least for a significant increase in energy R&D spending. To be sure, this consensus on the energy committees has not carried over to cap-and-trade legislation, which is under the control of different Congressional committees, and which, as we have seen, neglected the need for R&D support.

In the second, more difficult category of innovation institutional reform, ARPA-E legislation has now passed both houses of Congress[2] and been signed by the president, although it has not yet been implemented. As we have noted earlier, the Chairman and Ranking Member on the Senate Energy Committee each introduced 2008 bills for financing the deployment of new energy technologies.[3] This suggests that modest institutional reforms along the lines of those proposed in this book are possible and that Congress, despite parochial pressures from established energy institutions, could create the new entities that are required to fill the gaps in the current energy innovation system. To be sure, passing laws does not create the innovation culture that will be needed for these entities to work; only strong leadership in the executive branch and its political backing, and sound oversight and funding from Congress, can direct that process.

In the third category of back-end incentives, Congress has considered energy legislation[4] that suggests that both tax and policy-driving incentives are within the range of the politically possible. Congress is much better at carrots than at sticks, but nonetheless there were some significant regulatory mandates in that legislation. It also contained an initial attempt, blocked by the executive branch, to level the playing field of energy incentives that favor incumbent technologies and resources by reducing tax subsidies to the oil industry.

What about a carbon charge, such as from a cap-and-trade system? We saw earlier that the high-water mark in the 2008 consideration of a cap-and-trade bill was fifty-four votes in the Senate. In addition to a president willing to sign it, this legislation will need sixty votes to withstand the inevitable filibuster and pass. That goal still appears some distance away. Meanwhile, Congress is already moving down the parallel technology supply-side track, passing major energy technology bills in 2005 and in 2007.[5]

The menu of policies suggested above is possible. Congressional consensus is starting to build around each of the three major policy directions proposed here. Yet despite some progress, Congress, as discussed, has failed to approach energy technology as a systems problem, placing each technology on a separate pathway, with separate schemes of R&D and incentives depending on the political clout each technology can muster. This unbalanced approach precludes technology neutrality and will not result in optimal technological choices. What is missing is a unifying vision that would unite the three broad categories identified here, bring far greater coherence to the details, and make things happen. The executive branch could provide that leadership.

In the innovation arena, passing laws often means little. Much of the effect of new legislation with new ideas lies in their execution, which is squarely in the hands of the executive branch. Determined leadership, prepared to build working alliances with industry, can ensure effective implementation. This will need to be put over time into a strategy and then into a detailed roadmap that the executive branch must tackle in cooperation with industry and universities.

Given the growing clamor over energy security, the new President, who campaigned on these issues, may see the political need for new directions in energy policy. The signals we have des-cribed suggest that energy has truly become a political driver that can move the political system. Therefore, the idea of a new *technological/economic/political paradigm* for energy might, just might, become a political and then an economic reality.

The Problem of Pork

Where there is government money there is politics, and where there is politics there is the pork barrel. Can the proposed supply-side program for energy innovation be protected from gross political distortion? The short answer is yes, but only with difficulty.

Cohen and Nolte made a sober assessment of the United States' last experience with major programs to stimulate the development of innovative commercial technology, an effort that peaked in the 1970s. Their case studies illustrate the many political hazards to which such programs are subject.[6] Once a program has exceeded the threshold of congressional attention, they found, politics become at least as important as technical validity and the chances of a useful technical result dwindle. Relatively small-scale R&D grants historically faced only limited intrusion from pork-barrel politics, and entire R&D agencies, such as NSF, NIH, and DARPA, have been exempted from them, although earmarking from some universities is a growing problem in the defense and energy fields. But when the economic and job consequences of commercial demonstrations and back-end subsidies become apparent, the political system goes into overdrive and tends to interfere and preempt sound technical choices. In several of the cases they studied, projects that needed a sustained level of support were instead subjected to boom-and-bust financing as the political saliency of their objective waxed and waned. Support for politically charged fields like nuclear and solar energy has depended more on shifting political winds than on their technical or commercial prospects.

A RAND report assessed the results of a number of civilian technology demonstration projects of the same general period.[7] The RAND study concluded that demonstration programs of under a certain size—at the time about $50 million—stayed under the congressional radar screen and could be run as technical programs. Many of these—from a solid-waste-to-fuel conversion plant to a nuclear power reactor—were judged to have "stimulated diffusion significantly." In these cases, strong commitment and cost sharing by the private sector were found to have been essential.

On the other hand, both the RAND report and the Cohen and Nolte study found frequent pressure to carry out expensive but job-creating demonstrations on unproven technological ideas that should have remained in the laboratory at bench or pilot scale, to set unrealistic goals for politically desirable projects, to insist on time limits more demanding than was consistent with proper technology management, and to continue with failed programs long after their justification had disappeared.

A program of the magnitude we are proposing cannot remain purely technical. A certain amount of geographic distribution of the funds will be essential to attract the necessary public and political support. This is accepted as a fact of life in the case of the military and aerospace budgets. The danger is that a civilian energy technology program could become such a magnet for special interests that its technical and policy objectives will be lost.

Curiously, a major source of pressure for geographically oriented pork, both on the front and back ends, comes not so much from private firms or the lobbyists that represent them, but from within the innovation system itself, namely, the national laboratories run by the Department of Energy. These are major employers in the states that house them, whose representatives tend to place themselves on congressional committees with jurisdiction over one or another aspect of the energy budget. This has meant that proposals to emphasize technology produced by the national laboratories are able to marshal disproportionate political power. The national laboratories are also likely to be the source of pressure to weaken the proposed ARPA-E, should it be funded, by turning it into a vehicle for additional funding for their own activities. A goal of a transformational energy research program should be to get the very best researchers from everywhere at work on the problems; while many will come from the labs, they are not the only source from which staff should be recruited.

National R&D laboratories all over the world are both a major resource and a major problem. Their assured funding and long-term staff tenure make them ideally suited to carrying out long-range research on important problems that are unlikely to attract commercial interest. On the other hand, countries as different as India, China, and the United States have found it a substantial (although not insurmountable) challenge to create sustained interest in tackling practical problems of immediate interest to the productive sector, or even in the investments of money and personnel needed to transfer technology already developed into private hands.

The major instrument for this purpose in the United States is the Cooperative Research and Development Agreement (CRADA), by which a firm and a national laboratory agree to collaborate on research on a technical problem of generic interest that can be commercialized.[8] An interesting approach to this problem attempted in a few nations is to establish a matching fund for the promotion of innovation to which firms may apply but that does not specify the source of the technology. This means that government-financed research laboratories must compete for contracts with private sources of technology, such as private research laboratories.

The most important lesson of past pork is that determined executive-branch leadership will be needed to limit this risk. Pork is most likely a problem at the demonstration-project level and can also be limited through such features as required cost sharing with industry wherever possible; funding technologies only when truly ready for initial deployment; insisting on projects proposed and led by industry and not government; including the range of affected parties, such as potential purchasers, customers, regulators, and manufacturers, in the program design; and setting realistic timeframes.[9] The political influence of the regional federal laboratories can be mitigated by sound requirements for competition.

The political design of proposed new mechanisms for innovation is also critical. Effective programs require both effective political and substantive design; the trick is getting the political design to support the substantive design, not subvert it to pork. Building distance between the program and the politics can help. The government corporation proposed here for demonstration and financing—the main locus of major financing—would be outside the government, with advance funding and self-financing authority to make it less vulnerable to political disruption, although strong oversight is mandatory to avoid the 2008 housing finance authority problems. The roadmapping entity would likewise be outside government. Even so, both of these institutions will require links to government so as to ensure its participation, support, and oversight.

Conclusion: Achieving a Revolution in Energy Technology

The energy crisis presents a unique challenge to the American innovation system: the promotion of a technological transformation through long-term collaboration between public and private sectors on a massive scale. The American political system, together with the traditional adversarial relationship of government and business during peacetime, dictates that this collaboration will be neither neat nor orderly. The scale of the resources that need to be involved ensures that it will not be free of pork-barrel politics. Even so, the transformation is essential, and so is the role of government in that transformation.[10]

This technological transformation and this collaboration will require a substantial change in economic policies and hence in public attitudes—what we have called a *technological/economic/political paradigm*. Voters will need to support politicians who will authorize major increases in carbon energy prices in tandem with large subsidies for the development of new energy sources and for innovative ways to increase energy efficiency, and at the same time will need to maintain sufficient interest in the progress of the work that their political representatives will exercise vigilance and keep pork-barrel politics within reasonable limits.

Such a program will require support for technological innovation going well beyond the support to research that is the traditional mainstay of American science policy. It will require support for the entire innovation process across a broad range of sectors, including both basic and applied research, demonstration, and the bridging of the "valley of death" separating invention from innovation, as well as at the stage of technology launch emphasized in this work. It will require reexamination of long-standing policies that have blocked desirable innovation, especially in energy conservation.

The innovation trajectories for different technologies, and the policies needed to encourage their widespread adoption, differ from technology to technology. Some, like wind and solar, may require only a modest push; others, like carbon sequestration and fuel cells, will require major programs of research or large-scale demonstration, sometimes complemented by substantial subsidy and back-end mandates. A wide variety of policy instruments are available for this purpose. These in turn will require institutional innovations. DARPA, a relatively freewheeling agency in the Defense Department, provides a useful model for some of the mechanisms that will be required. Others may be best suited to a public corporation or a think-tank mechanism. Still others will need to be developed in the Department of Energy and, on the tax incentive side, even the Treasury.

A program of this magnitude likely requires presidential leadership and a major effort at the same time to sell the public and the business community on the need for such a program, involving them in its planning and using this approach to create sufficient political support for its sustained technological integrity. This transformation will require attention to the wild variations in the price of energy that have hitherto discouraged private investment in the sector. However desirable such policies may be, the political consensus for them may still be some time in coming. We must therefore seek ways to promote innovation on the technology supply side while we await their enactment. In the end, however, technology supply-and-demand oriented policies must proceed in parallel.

An instructive precedent from a quite different context is the Marshall Plan, the product of a comparable crisis in a very different political situation some sixty years ago.[11] In those days, America feared, not a terrorist attack, but an invasion of Western Europe by Russian communists under Stalin. President Truman, then intensely unpopular, named the proposed plan after the deeply respected World War II leader George Marshall. At his instruction, a nationwide public relations campaign, involving Marshall himself, Dean Acheson, and elements of the State Department, was carefully planned and executed, explaining why the Marshall Plan was essential to the survival of a democratic Western Europe.[12] Conservative Republican Senator Arthur Vandenberg of Ohio, who before the war had been an isolationist, shepherded the bill through the Republican 80th Congress.[13] When the plan became law, a Republican business executive, Paul Hoffman, was named as its director. Not only was the Marshall Plan kept pork-free, but its recipients were forbidden to purchase anything in the United States if it was priced too high in relation to other international suppliers.[14]

Granted, we are not still in the late 1940s. But the crisis we face is not so different in its magnitude and importance. With the president in the lead, when Americans really wanted to move a major program and keep it politically clean, they found a way to do it. The "full-court press" needed to enact the Marshall Plan arguably is a useful precedent. It may well take a major effort to enact the program we are proposing in a form that will avoid the pitfalls described. Will such an effort exhaust the political system and delay the push for higher carbon energy and carbon emission prices through demand-side policies? There are three answers. First, forewarned is forearmed. Second, the technology train is already departing the station; the congressional energy committees are already well down the track of new technology legislation, which is in need of a larger framework and greater coherence. Finally, what we propose is important in any case for an effective demand-side program and we might as well get cracking.

Is a presidential top-down effort the only way to do this? Taking a chapter from the history of American social and political reform movements, a bottom-up model is harder and slower but conceivable. The American people increasingly have come to understand that energy security is a key national security vulnerability. There is growing concern about climate change, which could accelerate as the early effects of global warming become more apparent to the public in areas like the Rocky Mountain West, the Gulf Coast, and the Arctic. A grassroots movement, expanded beyond the current environmental movement, is conceivable, which could translate into further state legislation and then into Congressional legislation.

Some of the institutional reforms suggested here could come about through a bottom-up, "just do it" approach. A major roadmapping and technology strategy exercise could be assembled by cooperating universities, independent think tanks, and interested industry, with participation and monitoring from government agencies, and a respected convener capable of creating an expandable initial network, much as the Intergovernmental Panel on Climate Change (IPCC) self-assembled, building on initiatives from the scientific community.

Congress is already moving major technology legislation, so that financing mechanisms and R&D increases could arise from federal legislative rather than executive branch leadership. Some private companies could reverse past trends and greatly increase their support to energy-related R&D, in addition to the commercialization of existing technology, and even undertake translational research and finance the bridging of the "valley of death." Foundations could play a greater supporting role in R&D as well as policy.

To be sure, presidential leadership and mobilization would make all of the above steps easier. A demand-side pricing strategy, necessary to complement a technology supply-side strategy, may require broad public political support, regardless of presidential leadership and interest, but this, too, is possible over time.

A prerequisite for such a top-down, bottom-up or combined approach is a workable policy framework for structuring the energy technology revolution we need. To summarize the ideas we have presented in this book, we have distinguished six sets of innovative energy technologies, based on an analysis of the paths they are likely to take when they are launched into energy markets and the measures needed to help them bridge the "valley of death" and, more importantly in the case of the energy sector, overcome the launch obstacles between invention and innovation. Our analysis suggests development of packages of policy measures that can be tied to particular technology launch categories, to speed the development and deployment of a large set of evolving future technology choices without favoring any single technology.

This analysis has also enabled us to identify important gaps in the present U.S. institutional system of support for energy innovation. Specifically, we find that there is a need for new attention to public support for the translation of research into innovation, for the careful monitoring of demonstrations of engineering-intensive technology, for the improvement of manufacturing technology and the speeding of its scale-up, for the facilitation of the installation of technology for conservation and energy efficiency, and for roadmapping of the requirements for the development and launch of promising technologies for energy conservation and efficiency.

The problem is huge; R&D and getting prices to reflect environmental and security externalities are only part of the answer. The adoption of technology needs to be accelerated over and above the natural response to market forces, even if prices are right. We need to speed both the deployment of energy technology that is already competitive or nearly so, and the development of a broad range of new technology for every aspect of the energy economy. We have provided a definition of the problem and a multistep conceptual framework that should be of broad application, even if there is disagreement on the details of particular recommendations.

While it may be argued that the approach we suggest may divert political attention away from the "real" problem of getting carbon and energy prices to reflect externalities, the converse is also true—namely, that if policymakers and the public view getting prices right by imposing a carbon charge or otherwise ensuring sustained high carbon energy prices as the whole answer even if the political effort takes a long time, such an effort will have ignored the need for a complementary supply-side effort, and we will still face a serious gap in technology implementation. What is more, a successful supply-side effort may diminish opposition to demand-side measures by showing what is actually possible by advancing technology solutions.

In practice, Congress is already paying attention to interventions on both the supply and demand side, although with a mind set far from the long-term approach and technology neutrality we have advocated in this book. Legislative advocates of cap-and-trade measures do view a supply-side technology program as the other side of the coin to their demand-side program. Pending cap-and-trade legislation recognizes the need for intervention on the supply side and allocates billions of dollars in anticipated revenues to the implementation of new energy technology, although not to the required R&D.[15]

A key problem lies in the fact that the massive energy technology legislation passed by Congress in 2005 and 2007 legislates technology by technology, with separate and often contradictory support pathways for each. There is no technology neutrality to these bills, and little support for longer-range research. The different policies they provide for different technologies jeopardize the prospects for optimal patterns of technological advance. It is important to bring a much more coherent approach to the technology supply side, such as the four-step framework proposed here, so that new technologies evolve to feed into a demand-side approach when the latter is eventually enacted.

To be sure, innovation in the energy sector would without question be greatly facilitated by the adoption of demand-side measures that increase the price of energy or impose a carbon charge and so limit the emission of carbon dioxide. However, the political consensus, despite the 2008 elections, for the major readjustments that would be required by such measures is still likely to take time to develop, due to the economic drop of late 2008. Even if sound and desirable demand-side measures come to pass more quickly than expected, they will need to be complemented by a strong "technology push" to support research and prototyping, and to speed the development and large-scale deployment of many generations of a broad range of technological innovations.

It will not be simple to keep energy technology innovation efforts apart from disruptive political tampering. Presidential leadership, combined with grassroots support, will likely be required for this to work. As Machiavelli observed in 1513, "There is nothing more difficult to carry out, nor more doubtful of success, nor more dangerous to handle, than to initiate a new order of things."[16] There is every reason to get a head start on the supply side of energy innovation even if the important demand-side measures are delayed; there is little time to lose.

Glossary

Terms in boldface are defined in the glossary. Italicized technical terms, for example synonyms of defined terms, are not defined in the glossary.

Back-end the phase of the innovation cycle in which a demonstrated technology idea becomes a commercialized product or process and generally uses private funding mechanisms (angel and venture capital, initial public offering, equity, lending) instead of public "**front-end**" funding. However, in some sectors, notably defense, public-sector back-end support may be available through government procurement, incentives, favorable tax treatment, or regulation.

Baseload power power to meet the basic load of an electric utility, typically from capital-intensive sources with relatively low-cost fuel sources. See **peaking power**.

"Black boxing" assessing the impacts of a given technology without understanding its inner technical or scientific workings.

Cap-and-trade an emission trading system in which a maximum amount of emission of a given pollutant is set (the *cap*) and in which potential polluters are allocated or sold (often by auction) allowances to emit that pollutant (also called *emission credits*) that they may trade among themselves.

Carbon charge any system for increasing the cost to the emitter of emitting carbon dioxide (or by extension, of other greenhouse gases) into the atmosphere. The most prominent examples are **carbon taxes** and **cap-and-trade** regimes.

Carbon-free energy   an energy source that does not result in the net emission of carbon dioxide (or by extension, other greenhouse gases) as a result of the overall process of energy generation.

Carbon tax   a direct tax imposed in proportion to the carbon dioxide emitted.

Carrots and sticks   "carrots" are incentives like tax credits, price guarantees, or government purchasing programs; "sticks" are regulatory mandates like renewable portfolio standards, emission taxes, and fuel economy standards.

Component technology   a technology that is part of a larger **platform** or system containing other related technologies or systems. For example, coal sequestration technology is a component of a larger system for carbon capture, transport, and sequestration.

Contested launch   a technology launch that faces political or non-market economic opposition from competitors or from the industrial sectors that must absorb them.

Demand for energy   total market demand for energy use throughout the economy.

Demand for energy technology   total market demand for innovative energy technology, as embodied in products and services, including research, development, and engineering services.

Demand-oriented policy   a policy intended to influence the demand for energy or energy technology, which can be through a *demand-pricing* or **macropricing** system such as a **cap-and-trade** regime or **carbon tax**. This is also termed a *demand-side* policy.

Demand pull   a model of the process of **technological innovation** that portrays innovation as being driven by the pull of the market, rather than by advances in science and technology. See **market pull**.

Demonstration   A full-scale operating model of a new technology, intended to show its practical utility to potential users and to gather data on its technical and economic characteristics under realistic conditions.

Deployment (or *implementation*)   installation and use of a technology or equipment on a substantial scale. See **technological innovation**.

Development   The process of turning an **invention** or discovery into a marketable product.

Disruptive technology a **technological innovation** that begins in lower-profit market segments ignored by larger firms (which typically concentrate on adding extra functions to high-profit products) and improves, expands, and displaces well-established **incumbent technologies**. Examples include the personal computer displacing mainframes, or low-cost airlines displacing legacy carriers.

Dominant design The design of an innovative product that comes to dominate the market and to set customers' expectations regarding appearance, performance and other user characteristics.

Enabling innovation a major innovation that stimulates innovation throughout the economy. Such an innovation typically creates a new function (termed *functionality*) in the economy and corresponding productivity gains. Examples include interchangeable machine parts, aircraft, computing, the Internet, and spaceflight.

Equipment hardware embodying a technology.

Externality a cost or benefit that is not counted in the accounting framework of a project or policy, such as an impact on environment, safety, or public health.

Feed-in tariff tariffs paid by utility companies in Germany and other EU countries for electric power from decentralized sources of renewable energy that the utility companies do not themselves own but from which they are required to buy. These tariffs are typically set at rates well above market rates in order to encourage investments in renewable energy.

Front end the phases of the innovation process that precede commercialization: research, **technology development**, and (in some cases) initial prototyping and **demonstration**.

Generic or precompetitive research research on generic problems affecting an entire industry that do not lend themselves to the development of proprietary products.

Incremental innovation relatively small improvements to the functionality of a technology—such as lowering costs or improving features. See also **technological innovation, radical innovation,** and **secondary innovation.**

Incumbent ("legacy") technology an established technology.

Induced innovation an innovation provoked by a change in prices, and thus costs. For example, rising energy prices may stimulate more rapid innovation in energy efficiency than would otherwise occur. More generally, an innovation provoked by a change in market conditions or policies, such as those for environment or safety. See **demand pull** and **policy pull**.

Invention   the first reduction to practice of a new technological idea. This typically includes *proof of concept* and the production of a *prototype*.

Level playing field   an environment in which any technology has the same chances and is given the same support as other technologies, in particular as compared to **incumbent technologies** that are already established.

Linear model of innovation   a model of the process of **technological innovation** that portrays innovation as beginning with basic scientific research, then progressing through early- and late-stage **development**, including *proof of concept* or *prototyping*, leading to **invention**, design and **demonstration**, manufacturing, and commercialization. Also called the *pipeline* or *technology-push* model.

Macropricing scheme   a policy regime intended to influence the price of energy or greenhouse gas emission throughout the economy.

Mandates   government-imposed requirements like standards and taxes, such as renewable portfolio standards, fuel economy standards, or emission taxes.

Market pull   a model of the process of **technological innovation** that portrays innovation as being driven by market forces, rather than by advances in science and technology. See **demand pull**.

Moore's law   the prediction, made by Intel cofounder Gordon Moore in 1965, that the number of transistors able to fit on an integrated circuit increases exponentially, doubling approximately every two years. The time frame has since been reduced to eighteen months, and a sublaw added, that the price per transistor will drop in half in the same period.

National innovation system   The network of public and private institutions within a country that contribute to the development and diffusion of technology and provide a framework for the implementation of the government's technology policy. The network includes university and laboratory research, government research funding agencies, mechanisms of capital support to innovation, companies, and organizations that assess the strength of the research and commercialization effort.

New-product buy-down a government program intended to lower the price of a new product entering the marketplace by providing subsidized funding or financing to the seller to make up the difference between the sale offered price and the cost of production, so as to encourage public purchase and spread of a socially beneficial good.

Niche market a specialized segment of a larger market.

Options value the value to an investor of having an additional possible course of action and hence the amount he or she should be willing to invest in order to have this additional choice. Certain kinds of analysis assume that the function of research is to provide options rather than new functionality.

Organizational mechanisms for innovation systems and organizations used by institutions, such as universities, government and firms, to support innovation, and the connections between them; also termed *innovation organization.*

Pasteur's quadrant basic research inspired not by pure curiosity but by the hope of practical application.

Peaking power power to meet the extra demands placed on a utility at particular times of the day or year, typically met by sources with relatively high fuel costs but relatively low up-front capital costs. See **baseload power.**

Perverse incentives incentives, such as tax breaks or direct subsidies, to environmentally harmful or other socially undesirable activities or products.

Platform a unit holding a variety of energy-related technologies and systems (by extension of the military term for a multicomponent weapon system such as a ship or tank). For example, a plug-in hybrid car is a platform that contains a complex mix of energy-related technologies and systems, including an engine, advanced battery, electric power drive system, aerodynamic exterior design, and devices that connect to the electric grid and fuel infrastructure systems. These constitute **components** of the overall system.

Point of market launch the point and time a technology is launched into the market. In part because of the scale required, this is the most difficult step in the development and deployment of new energy and other comparable complex technologies. This point contrasts with the "**valley of death,**" deemed the most difficult point in the launch of less complex technologies in the innovation literature, especially those innovations governed by the **technology push** model.

Policy pull   a model of the process of **technological innovation** that portrays some kinds of innovation as being driven by changes in policy, such as for environment, safety or energy conservation, rather than by advances in science and technology.

Pork barrel   a government project whose primary purpose is to spend funds or create jobs in the state or district of the political representatives who supported it.

Prototype   a preliminary working model of a new technological product, meant as a basis for later revisions to the product's design or function.

Radical innovation   an innovation that creates new products with new functional capabilities in an economy, typically giving rise to significant productivity gain. See also **secondary** and **incremental innovation.**

Renewable portfolio standard   a law requiring a certain percentage of the power-plant or generation capacity of an electric utility to come from renewable sources (i.e., solar, wind, hydro, geothermal) by a given date.

Research-and-development intensity   the ratio of the cost of research and development to a firm's overall revenues.

Roadmapping   an analysis that considers each technology element and its possible and preferred evolution pathways, including appropriate milestones, and then ties each to the appropriate elements of **front-** and **back-end** support.

Secondary innovation   a **technological innovation** that makes major improvements in the functionality of an existing technology. See also **incremental innovation** and **radical innovation.**

Silver bullet   a single solution purported to solve a number of complicated problems at the same time.

Structuring a technological revolution   providing a policy and institutional framework that can remove obstacles and promote major change in a **technological/economic/political paradigm.**

Supply-oriented policy   a policy to promote the entry or supply of new technology, also known as a *technology supply-side* or *technology-push* policy, usually through **front-end** but sometimes also through **back-end** support.

Technoeconomic feasibility   the ability of a technology to be successfully implemented, as judged by two criteria: its capacity to reliably fulfill its function, and a satisfactory financial or economic rate of return.

Technological/economic/political paradigm the combination of policies, regulations, incentives, institutions, public understanding, and political support that provides a stable environment for introduction and evolution of a particular technology or set of related technologies.

Technological innovation commercialization or widespread use of a technology. See also **deployment** (or *implementation*).

Technology a means of using technical knowledge to solve a practical problem. Contrary to frequent usage, this is not the same thing as the **equipment** that embodies that technology, and is not limited to information and computing.

Technology lock-in the influence of a **dominant design** in limiting the possibility of alternative pathways for the evolution of a technology.

Tilted playing field A nonlevel playing field on which some technologies are disadvantaged compared to others, typically incumbent technologies that are already established. See also **level playing field**.

Translational research breakthrough research tied to needed technologies, followed in an integrated manner by translation of these research results into technologies and launch of these technologies through the **prototype** stage, keeping in mind the requirements of deployment and commercialization.

Uncontested launch technology launch that will not be resisted by competitors or recipient industry if the new technology passes tests of **technoeconomic feasibility**. See **contested launch**.

Valley of death the stage of technological innovation between the early-stage development and proof of concept of an invention and its successful commercialization, a stage often shunned by private capital markets and traditionally deemed the most critical moment in technology launch in the innovation literature.

Note: A number of the above terms and definitions derive from the existing innovation literature. Sources for these terms are set out in the text and their accompanying notes.

Abbreviations

ARPA-E Advanced Research Projects Agency [for] Energy

ATP Advanced Technology Program [a NIST program, renamed TIP]

CSP Concentrating solar power

CCS Carbon capture and sequestration

DARPA Defense Advanced Research Projects Agency

DOD [U.S.] Department of Defense

DOE [U.S.] Department of Energy

EERE Office of Energy Efficiency and Renewable Energy [of DOE]

EGS Enhanced geothermal systems

EJ Exajoules (10^{18} joules, or a quintillion joules)

EPRI Electric Power Research Institute

EU European Union

GHGs Greenhouse gases

GNEP Global Nuclear Energy Partnership [a DOE program]

GW Gigawatts (10^9 watts, or a billion watts)

HEVs Hybrid electric vehicles

IC Internal combustion

IGCC Integrated gasification combined cycle

IPCC Intergovernmental Panel on Climate Change

kWh Kilowatt hours

LEDs Light-emitting diodes

MW   Megawatts (10^6 watts, or a million watts)

NASA   National Aeronautics and Space Administration

NCEP   National Commission on Energy Policy

NGNP   Next Generation Nuclear Plant

NIH   National Institutes of Health

NIST   National Institute of Standards and Technology

NREL   National Renewable Energy Laboratory

NSF   National Science Foundation

NSTC   National Science and Technology Council [a panel under OSTP]

OLEDs   Organic light-emitting diodes

OSTP   Office of Science and Technology Policy [in U.S. White House]

P&D   Prototyping and demonstration

PEM   Proton exchange membrane

PHEVs   Plug-in hybrid electric vehicles

PNGV   Partnership for a New Generation of Vehicles

PURPA   Public Utility Regulatory Policies Act

PV   Photovoltaic

R&D   Research and development

RD&D   Research, development and demonstration

SBIR   Small Business Innovation and Research [program]

SFC   Synthetic Fuels Corporation

TIP   Technology Innovation Program [a NIST program, formerly ATP]

VHTR   Very-high-temperature [nuclear] reactor

WTO   World Trade Organization

Notes

Chapter 1

1. Nicholas Stern, *Stern Review on the Economics of Climate Change* (London: H. M. Treasury, 2006), chap. 16, http://www.hm-treasury.gov.uk/media/4/3/Executive_Summary.pdf. (carbon pricing alone will not be sufficient to reduce emissions at the scale and pace required; government R&D and early-stage commercialization support will be needed); IEA, *Energy Technology Perspectives 2008: Scenarios and Strategies to 2050*, June 6, 2008, http://www.iea.org/Textbase/npsum/ETP2008SUM.pdf (major public and private investments will be required to implement new energy tehnologies); John Alic, David Mowery, and Edward Rubin, *U.S. Technology and Innovation Policies: Lessons for Climate Change*, ii. Washington, DC: Pew Center on Global Climate Change, November 2003) (R&D support will not be enough; the federal government will need to back a balanced portfolio of technology support policies).

2. Robert H. Socolow and Stephen W. Pacala, "A Plan to Keep Carbon in Check," *Scientific American* 295, no. 3 (September 2006): 50–57 (energy technologies can meet the goal of stabilizing carbon by midcentury); Stephen W. Pacala and Robert H. Socolow, "Stabilization Wedges: Solving the Climate Problem for the Next 50 Years with Current Technologies," *Science* 305 (August 13, 2004): 968, http://carbonsequestration.us/Papers-presentations/htm/Pacala-Socolow-ScienceMag-Aug2004.pdf.

3. Stern. *Stern Review on the Economics of Climate Change*, chap. 16 (carbon pricing will need to be supplemented by government

All links are accurate as of September 19, 2008.

R&D and early-stage commercialization support); compare Alic, Mowery, and Rubin, *U.S. Technology and Innovation Policies*, ii (suggestions for federal government support beyond R&D for energy technology implementation). A notable exception is Thomas L. Friedman, *Hot, Flat and Crowded: Why We Need a Green Revolution and How it Can Renew America* (New York: Farrar, Straus and Giroux, 2008), which advocates a strong focus on R&D and innovation spending.

4. IPCC, *Fourth Assessment, Climate Change 2007, Synthesis Report—Summary for Policymakers* (Geneva, Switzerland: IPCC, November 17, 2007): 22 (Citing Section 5.5 of longer report). http://www.ipcc.ch/pdf/assessment-report/ar4/syr/ar4_syr_spm.pdf.

5. Socolow and Pacala, "A Plan to Keep Carbon in Check"; Pacala and Socolow, "Stabilization Wedges"; IPCC, *Climate Change 2007—Fourth Assessment Report, Synthesis Report*, table SPM 7, 23. http://www.ipcc.ch/pdf/assessment-report/ar4/syr/ar4_syr_spm.pdf (available and planned technologies could halt emission growth at a cost of around 3 percent of global economic output by 2030).

6. Compare *Stern Review on the Economics of Climate Change* (estimates costs of global warming using an intergenerational discount rate equal to about 5 percent of annual global GDP, up to potentially 20 percent of global GDP or more, supporting a 60 to 80 percent reduction below 1990 levels), with, William Nordhaus, *A Question of Balance: Weighing the Options for Global Warming Policies* (New Haven, CT: Yale University Press 2008)(a nearly zero-time discount rate which values the welfare of future generations at the same level as today's as used in the 2006 *Stern Review* arguably lacks economic justification, so climate change costs are less severe, which justifies stretching out climate emissions reductions to 25 percent by 2050 and 45 percent by 2100).

7. Michael Abramowitz, "U.S. Joins G-8 Plan to Halve Emissions," *Washington Post*, July 9, 2008, http://www.washingtonpost.com/wp-dyn/content/article/2008/07/08/AR2008070800285.html; Sheryl Gay Stolberg, "Richest Nations Pledge to Halve Greenhouse Gas—G8 Call for GHG Reductions beyond Stabilization," *New York Times*, July 9, 2008, Science/Environment section, http://www.nytimes.com/2008/07/09/science/earth/09climate.html.

8. Alic, Mowery, and Rubin, *U.S. Technology and Innovation Policies*, ii.

9. The Intergovernmental Panel on Climate Change (IPCC), in agreement with previous reports (Socolow and Pacala, "A Plan to Keep Carbon in Check"; Stern, *Stern Review on the Economics of Climate Change*), has determined that atmospheric CO_2 levels can be stabilized by "a portfolio of technologies that are either currently available or expected to be commercialized, assuming appropriate incentives are in place for their development, acquisition, deployment and diffusion and addressing related barriers" (as previously noted). The table that follows this quotation sets forth a list of policy measures, each of which would be demanding politically, if "key mitigation technologies and practices" are to "create the incentives for mitigation action" (IPCC, *Fourth Assessment, Climate Change 2007—Synthesis Report*, 22, http://www.ipcc.ch/pdf/assessment-report/ar4 /syr/ar4_syr_spm.pdf). This point is discussed further later in this chapter.

10. John P. Holdren, "The Energy Innovation Imperative," *Innovations* 1, no. 2 (spring 2006): 3–23; President's Council of Advisors on Science and Technology (PCAST), *The Energy Imperative: Technology and the Role of Emerging Companies* (Washington, DC: Executive Office of the President of the United States, November 2006), http://www.ostp.gov/pcast/PCAST-EnergyImperative_FINAL .pdf.

11. The European Union is implementing a demand-side cap-and-trade pricing system applicable to two energy sectors, large-scale power and industrial emitters. Because this approach is relatively narrow, it contrasts with the broader-front, multisector approach under consideration in the United States to meet higher U.S. emission levels, which will necessitate more new technologies and therefore greater technology supply-side intensity across numerous sectors. See, generally, European Union, *EU Action against Climate Change*, 2005, http://ec.europa.eu/environment/climat/pdf/emission_trading3_en .pdf; A. Denny Ellerman and Barbara K. Buchner, "The European Union Emissions Trading Scheme: Origins, Allocation, and Early Results," *Review of Environmental Economic Policy* 1, no. 1 (2007): 66–87. EU nations rely on already high national fuel taxes, not their multinational cap-and-trade program, to improve efficiency in the transport sector. Expected auction revenues from the European Union's cap-and-trade system will go to each nation and be allocated by different rules in each nation, as discussed in chapter 7, on international collaboration.

12. See Richard R. Nelson, *National Systems of Innovation*, 3–21, 505–523 (New York: Oxford University Press, 1993) (national innovation system institutional and policy elements); Bengt-Ake Lundvall, *Innovation, Growth and Social Cohesion*, 53, 58–59 (Cheltenham, UK: Edward Elgar, 2002) (the importance of national innovation systems, with organizational and talent features in a geographic base, grows as global competition increases, and forces nations to exploit specialized innovation advantages to do well). See more detailed discussion of this topic in chapter 7.

13. Carlota Perez, *Technological Revolutions and Financial Capital*, 3–46 (Cheltenham, UK: Edward Elgar, 2002); Robert D. Atkinson, *The Past and Future of America's Economy: Long Waves of Innovation That Power Cycles of Growth*, 3–40 (Cheltenham, UK: Edward Elgar, 2004).

14. World Economic Forum, *Global Competitiveness Report*, October 31, 2007, 3–50, http://www.gcr.weforum.org/ (U.S. economy rated first in the world due to its innovation capacity).

15. WTRG Economics, *Oil Price History and Economics*, 2007, wtrg.com/prices.html.

16. Council on Competitiveness, *Energy Security, Innovation and Sustainability Initiative* (project summary) (Washington, D.C.: IEA, World Energy Outlook, November 12, 2008, 2).

17. John Carey, The Real Question: Should Oil be Cheap? *Business Week*, Aug. 4, 2008, 54 (business case for price floor for sustained high energy prices).

18. Richard S. Eckaus and Ian Sue Wing, "Implications of the Historical Decline in U.S. Energy Intensity for Long Run CO_2 Emission Projections," *Energy Policy* 35, no. 11 (Nov. 2007): 5267–5286 (U.S. emissions may grow at a faster rate in the next fifty years than in the past fifty from further technology advance; demand-side pricing will be a key strategy); Philip E. Auerswald, "The Myth of Energy Insecurity," *Issues in Science and Technology*, summer 2006, http://www.issues.org/22.4/auerswald.html (high energy prices are required for diversification from oil dependence).

19. A carbon tax is explored in, Robert Shapiro, Nan Phan, and Arun Malik, *Addressing Climate Change without Impairing the U.S. Economy: The Economics and Environmental Science of Combining a Carbon-Based Tax and Tax Relief* (Washington, DC: U.S. Climate

Task Force, June 2008), http://www.climatetaskforce.org/pdf/CTF
_CarbonTax_Earth_Spgs.pdf.

20. MIT, *The Future of Coal*, 89–93 (Cambridge, MA: MIT, March
14, 2007) (polling data indicates public attitudes shifting toward
climate change measures); S. J. Paltsev, J. Reilly, H. Jacoby, A. Gurgel,
G. Metcalf, A. Sokolov, and J. Holak, *Assessment of U.S. Cap-
and-Trade Proposals*, Report No. 146 (Cambridge, MA: MIT
Joint Program on the Science and Policy of Global Change, April
2007), http://web.mit.edu/globalchange/www/MITJPSPGC_Rpt146.
pdf.

21. Joseph I. Lieberman, "Global Warming Goes to Market," *The
American Interest* 1, no. 1 (autumn 2005) (critique of the economic
effects of cap-and-trade legislative proposals with exemptions for
limited compliance).

22. *Stern Review on the Economics of Climate Change*, chap. 16,
http://www.hm-treasury.gov.uk/media/4/3/Executive_Summary.pdf.

23. Jeffrey Sachs, "Technological Keys to Climate Protection,"
Scientific American 297, March 2008 http://www.sciam.com/article
.cfm?id=keys-to-climate-protection. See also Jeffrey Sachs, The
Road to Clean Energy Starts Here, *Scientific American* 2007, http://
www.sciam.com/article.cfm?id=the-road-to-clean-energy&SID=mail
&sc=emailfriend.

24. Daniel Kammen and Gregory Nemet, "Real Numbers: Reversing
the Incredible Shrinking Energy R&D Budget," *Issues in Science
and Technology* (fall 2005). This issue is discussed in detail in
chapter 5.

Chapter 2

1. IEA, *Energy Technology Perspectives 2008: Scenarios and Strategies to 2050,* June 6, 2008, http://www.iea.org/Textbase/techno/etp/
ETP_2008.pdf.

2. Jonathan Zittrain, *The Future of the Internet—And How to Stop
It* (New Haven, CT: Yale University Press, 2008).

3. A radical innovation creates new functional properties. A secondary innovation makes major improvements in existing functionality.
Incremental innovations, taken one at a time, make more minor
improvements. Over time, they can accumulate and become major

effects. See Frederick Betz, *Strategic Technology Management* (New York: McGraw-Hill, 1993); Melissa Schilling, *Strategic Management of Technological Innovation*, 38–39 (New York: McGraw-Hill, 2005).

4. See Michael Heller *The Gridlock Economy: How Too Much Ownership Wrecks Markets, Stops Innovation, and Costs Lives* (New York: Basic Books 2008)(suggests a problem where an economic sector is afflicted with networks of over-abundant rights and interests that preclude the ability to reform policy in that sector, preventing market entry of preferable solutions—in effect, an "anticommons").

5. See, generally, James M. Utterback, *Mastering the Dynamics of Innovation* 18, 23–55 (Boston: Harvard. Business School Books, 1996).

6. Vernon W. Ruttan, *Technology Growth and Development: An Induced Innovation Perspective* (New York: Oxford University Press 2001).

7. Vannevar Bush, *Science: The Endless Frontier* (Washington, DC: Government Printing Office, July 1945), http://www.nsf.gov/od/lpa/nsf50/vbush1945.htm.

8. See, for example, Dale Jorgenson, "U.S. Economic Growth in the Information Age," *Issues in Science and Technology*, fall 2001, http://www.issues.org/18.1/jorgenson.html (the role of IT and semiconductors in 1990s growth).

9. Lewis M. Branscomb and Philip E. Auerswald, *Taking Technical Risks: How Innovators, Executives, and Investors Manage High-Tech Risks* (Cambridge, MA: MIT Press, 2001). See, also, Lewis Branscomb and Philip Auerswald, *Between Invention and Innovation: An Analysis of Funding for Early-State Technology Development, Part I—Early Stage Development*, NIST GCR 02–841, Washington, DC: National Institute for Standards and Technology/ATP, November 2002, http://www.atp.nist.gov/eao/gcr02–841/contents.htm.

10. Donald E. Stokes, *Pasteur's Quadrant: Basic Science and Technological Innovation* (Washington, DC: Brookings Institution Press, 1997).

11. Branscomb and Auerswald, *Between Invention and Innovation*. An exception lies in biotechnology where new technologies have received venture capital support ten years or more from expected

commercialization, based in part on the importance of intellectual property rights and FDA product certification in this field.

12. Vernon W. Ruttan, *Is War Necessary for Economic Growth? Military Procurement and Technology Development* (New York: Oxford University Press, 2006).

13. Ruttan, *Technology Growth and Development*; Vernon W. Ruttan and Yujiro Hayami, *Agricultural Development: An International Perspective* (Baltimore, MD: Johns Hopkins University Press, 1985 ed.); Vernon W. Ruttan and Yujiro Hayami, "Induced Innovation Model of Agricultural Development," in Carl K. Eicher and John M. Staatz, eds., *International Agricultural Development* (Baltimore, MD: Johns Hopkins University Press 1998, 3rd ed.) 163–178.

14. Richard G. Lipsey, *Economic Transformations: General Purpose Technologies and Long-Term Economic Growth* (New York: Oxford University Press, 2005).

15. See, for example, Fred Block and Matthew R. Keller, *Where Do Innovations Come From, Transformations in the U.S. National Innovation System 1970–2006*, Washington, DC: Information Technology and Innovation Foundation (ITIF) Report, July 2008, http://www.itif.org/files/Where_do_innovations_come_from.pdf (since the 1970s, a significant majority of innovations have derived from partnerships involving government funded research, through universities, laboratories and firms).

16. IEA, *Energy Technology Perspectives 2008*.

17. Richard R. Nelson and Sidney G. Winter, *An Evolutionary Theory of Economic Change* (Cambridge, MA: Harvard University Press 1982).

18. Richard R. Nelson, *National Systems of Innovation*, 3–21, 505–523 (New York: Oxford University Press 1993).

19. National Research Council, Science, Technology, and Economic Policy Board, *SBIR: Challenges and Opportunities*, 15–27 (introduction), 41–51 (comments of Roland Tibbetts, NSF), 52–61 (comments of Josh Lerner) (Washington, DC: National Academy Press, 1999); National Research Council, Board on Science, Technology, and Economic Policy *The Advanced Technology Program: Challenges and Opportunities*, 11–25 (Washington, DC: National Academies Press, 1999); Christopher T. Hill, "The Advanced Technology Program: Opportunities for Enhancement," in Lewis M. Branscomb and James

H. Keller, eds., *Investing in Innovation: Creating a Research and Innovation Policy That Works*, 144–173 (Cambridge, MA: MIT Press, 1998); Josh Lerner, "The Design of Effective Public Venture Capital Programs", paper in NIST, *Managing Technical Risk*, NIST GCR 00-787 (April 2000), 80–93; Glenn R. Fong, "Repositioning the Advanced Technology Program," *Issues in Science and Technology*, fall 2001, 65–70, http://www.issues.org/18.1/fong.html.

20. William B. Bonvillian, "Power Play—The DARPA Model and U.S. Energy Policy," *The American Interest*, November–December 2006, 39–48 (argues that innovation organization is a critical innovation factor, citing DARPA as a case study); Glenn R. Fong, "ARPA Does Windows: The Defense Underpinning of the PC Revolution," *Business and Politics* 3, no. 3 (2001): 213–237; National Research Council (NRC), Science and Telecommunications Board, *Funding a Revolution: Government Support for Computing Research*, 85–157 (Washington, DC: National Academy Press, 1999); Richard Van Atta, Sidney G. Reed, and Seymour J. Deitchman, *DARPA Technological Accomplishments: An Historical Review of Selected DARPA Projects* (Alexandria, VA: IDA, 1991); James C. Goodwyn DARPA Technology Transition (Washington, DC: DOD, 1997) http://www.darpa.mil/body/pdf/transition.pdf.

21. Vaclaw Smil, *Energy in Nature and Society: General Energetics of Complex Systems* (Cambridge, MA: MIT Press 2008).

22. Ruttan, the leading exponent of induced innovation, wrote a separate book—*Is War Necessary for Economic Growth?*—to capture a subject not covered in his previous work on induced theory, the role of the Defense Department in supporting technological advance. The book effectively draws on what we label pipeline theory (pp. 4–5).

Chapter 3

1. The electric power and the transport sectors are connected in the longer run: first, because battery storage technologies may overlap both, and second, because any move to plug-in hybrid electric cars has implications for electric power and hence for coal and climate change.

2. Brian Arthur, *Increasing Returns and Path Dependence in the Economy*, 34–44 (Ann Arbor: University of Michigan Press, 1994); M. Mitchell Waldrop, *Complexity*, chap. 1 (New York: Simon &

Schuster, 1992) (discussion of economist Brian Arthur's work on technology lock-in).

3. "Venture Capital Investment in Renewable Energy Soars to $3.4 Billion in 2007," Reuters, *Business Wire*, January 16, 2007 (citing Greentech Media data), http://www.reuters.com/article/pressRelease/idUS153866+16-Jan-2008+BW20080116 (investment in solar power led renewable investment in 2007 with over $1.05 billion invested in more than 70 VC financing rounds; VC investment in battery technology was $433.9 million; investment in the energy efficiency/smart grid sector was $419.1 million, and investment in biofuels, such as cellulosic ethanol and biodiesel, was some $750 million).

4. This boomlet could become a bubble if more is not is done to avoid the "blend wall" that effectively caps the ethanol mix in gasoline at 10 percent of gasoline in the absence of major investments in new pipeline and pump infrastructure for ethanol. See the discussion below. Also see Clifford Krauss, "Ethanol's Boom Stalling as Glut Depresses Prices," *New York Times*, September 30, 2007, business section.

5. See, generally, Jan Kalicki and David Goldwyn, eds., *Energy Security in the 21ˢᵗ Century* (Baltimore: Woodrow Wilson Center/Johns Hopkins University Press 2005), especially the contribution therein by Melanie A. Kenderdine and Ernest J. Moniz, "Technology Development and Energy Security," 425–459 (technology strategy for energy security).

6. The 2005–2007 movement of venture capital into new energy technology has been oriented toward "magic bullets" like corn ethanol that benefit from subsidies, state and federal, aimed at specific technologies with strong lobbies in Washington. That new investment level still amounts to less than two-tenths of 1 percent of the more than $1.5 trillion U.S. energy and transportation markets (Senate Committee on Energy and Natural Resources, Hearing to Investigate Market Constraints on Large Investments in Advanced Energy Technologies, Senate Hearing 110–63, 100th Cong., 1st sess., March 7, 2007, 53 (testimony of John Dennison of Perkins Caulfield)) (2006 venture capital investment in new energy technology was $2.5 billion, of which $1 billion was for ethanol plants; U.S. energy and transport markets at that time were approximately $1.5 trillion). See, for 2007 VC data, "Venture Capital Investment in Renewable Energy Soars to $3.4 Billion in 2007," Reuters, *Business Wire*. The 2008 economic decline will curtail VC energy support.

7. Energy Information Administration, *International Energy Outlook 2008*, Report No. DOE/EIA 0484, Highlights–Figure 1 (Washington, DC: EIA, 2008), http://www.eia.doe.gov/oiaf/ieo/ (world market energy consumption is projected to increase by 57 percent from 2004 levels by 2030; total energy demand in the non-OECD countries to increase by 95 percent, compared with an increase of 24 percent in OECD countries). Compare Energy Information Administration, *International Energy Outlook 2007*, Report No. DOE/EIA 0484, chap.1, table 8 (Washington, DC: EIA, 2007), http://www.eia.doe.gov/oiaf/ieo/index.html.

8. See, for example, Kenneth J. Arrow, "Economic Welfare and the Allocation of Resources for Invention," in Richard Nelson, ed., *The Rate and Direction of Inventive Activity: Economic and Social Factors*, 609–625 (Princeton, NJ: Princeton University Press, for NBER, 1962) (concept of nonappropriability); Kenneth J. Arrow, "Global Climate Change: A Challenge to Policy," *The Economists' Voice* 4, no. 3, article 2 (2007), http://www.bepress.com/ev/vol4/iss3/art2; Kenneth J. Arrow, *Intergenerational Equity and the Rate of Discount in Long Term Social Investment*, Stanford University Working Papers in Economics 97-005, December 1995 (government intervention role appropriate given economic costs shown by intergenerational discounting required by climate change).

9. This list is drawn from Michael D. Yokell, "The Role of the Government in Subsidizing Solar Energy," *American Economic Review* 69, no. 2, containing Papers and Proceedings of the Ninety-First Annual Meeting of the American Economic Association (May 1979), 357–361. See also Gregory F. Nemet, *Policy and Innovation in Low Carbon Energy Technologies*, unpublished doctoral dissertation, UC Berkeley, 2007, 3–7.

10. Yokell, "The Role of the Government in Subsidizing Solar Energy"; Roger H. Bezdek and Robert M. Wendling, "Real Numbers: The U.S. Energy Subsidy Scorecard," *Issues in Science and Technology*, spring 2006, http://www.issues.org/22.3/realnumbers.html. See also Energy Information Administration, *Report on Federal Financial Interventions and Subsidies in Energy Markets 1999: Primary Energy*, table ES-1 (Washington, DC: EIA, 1999), http://www.eia.doe.gov/oiaf/servicerpt/subsidy/table_es1.html (federal FY 1999 subsidies as federal support for all primary energy sources); Joint Committee on Taxation, *Estimated Budget Effects of the Conference Agreement for*

Title XIII of H.R. 6, the Energy Tax Incentives Act of 2005, JCX 59–05, July 27, 2005, http://www.house.gov/jct/x-59-05.pdf (table on the extent of subsidies passed in the 2005 energy legislation). Renewables advocates have argued this case; see, for example, Scott Sklar, "The Solar Subsidy Crutch or an Uneven Playing Field?" *Renewable Energy Access*, April 25, 2006, http://www.renewableenergyaccess.com/rea/news/story?id=44723.

11. See, for example, the discussion in Tim McGee, "Cut Solar Subsidies? Update with Vinod Khosla," *Los Angeles Times*, October 24, 2006, http://www.treehugger.com/files/2006/10/cut_solar_subsi_1.php.

12. Clayton Christensen, Scott Anthony, and Erik Roth, *Seeing What's Next*, xv–xvii (Boston: Harvard Business School Press, 2004). Disruptive technologies typically begin with a minor market segment that is neglected or missed by established firms. This market grows and the technology improves in quality and performance until it dominates and expands the niche, displacing the occupants in related markets. A disruptive technology may begin in a down-market, low-profit market segment ignored by larger firms that are concentrating on adding extra functions to existing high-profit products (such as low-cost airlines). Alternatively, it can serve a new market segment with a different value chain (such as the asynchronous communication offered by the Internet).

13. *See* Robert W. Fri, "From Energy Wish Lists to Technological Realities," *Issues in Science and Technology*, fall 2006, http://www.issues.org/23.1/fri.html (proposes a priority order of types of energy research for government support).

14. See, for example, John Reilly and Sergey Palsev, *Biomass Energy and Competition for Land*, Report No. 145 (Cambridge, MA: MIT Joint Program on the Science and Policy of Global Change, April 2007) http://web.mit.edu/globalchange/www/MITJPSPGC_Rpt145.pdf.

Chapter 4

1. Nancy Stauffer, *Research Spotlight: Algae System Transforms Greenhouse Emissions into Fuel*, research of Isaac Berzin, MIT ERC, 2006, http://web.mit.edu/erc/spotlights/alg.html.

2. Nancy Stauffer, *Research Spotlight: Engineering Viruses: Using Biology to Assemble Materials, Devices*, research of Angela Belcher, MIT ERC, 2006, http://web.mit.edu/erc/spotlights/vir.html.

3. Department of Energy, Office of Basic Energy Sciences, Workshop Reports, Abstracts of BES Workshop and Technical Reports, http://www.sc.doe.gov/bes/reports/abstracts.html, and The Basic Research Needs Workshop Series, http://www.sc.doe.gov/bes/reports/files/BRN_workshops.pdf.

4. IEA, *Energy Technology Perspectives 2008: Scenarios and Strategies to 2050*, June 6, 2008, http://www.iea.org/Textbase/techno/etp/ETP_2008.pdf.

5. The data in this section is from Joan Ogden, "High Hopes for Hydrogen," *Scientific American* 295, no. 3 (September 2006): 94–101; Yang Shao-Horn, "An Alternative Technology for Transportation: Fuel Cell Hybrid Vehicles," presentation at CSIS Energy Technology Forum, Washington, DC, September 28, 2006; Ahmed F. Ghoneim, "Meeting the Global Energy Challenge—Hydrogen," MIT Congressional Seminar, April 19, 2006.

6. Fuel cells can use a variety of feedstocks or reactants—a hydrogen fuel cell uses hydrogen as the fuel feedstock and oxygen as oxidant. Other reactants include hydrocarbons (diesel, methanol, and chemical hydrides) and alcohols; other oxidants include air, chlorine, and chlorine dioxide. For example, first-generation fuel cells made by a leading manufacturer (UTC) for NASA were phosphoric acid based; the firm's current commercial fuel cell uses as a feedstock anaerobic digester gas (ADG), a byproduct of wastewater treatment that contains methane.

7. For instance, low-temperature phosphoric acid fuel cells manufactured by United Technologies (UTC) produce 250 kW, alkaline fuel cells for the space shuttle produce 12 kW, and a Proton Exchange Membrane fuel cell made by Ballard produces 50 kW. High-temperature solid oxide fuel cells manufactured by Siemens-Westinghouse produce 100 kW and molten carbonate fuel cells made by Fuel Cell Energy produce 250 kW (Millie Dresselhaus, "Basic Research Need for a Hydrogen Economy," Presentation at DOE BES Workshop, May 13–15, 2003, Washington, DC June 24, 2004, https://public.ornl.gov/conf/nanosummit2004/talks/3_Dresselhaus.pdf.

8. Richard Anthony, "Powering Up—Roll-up Fuel Cells", *Spectrum* (MIT winter 2007) 7 (research of Paula Hammond).

9. Ghoneim, "Meeting the Global Energy Challenge—Hydrogen"; Ulf Bossell, Baldour Eliasson, and Gordon Taylor, *The Future of the Hydrogen Economy, Bright or Bleak?*, European Fuel Cell Forum Report, 2003 (updated 2005), http://www.efcf.com/reports/E08.pdf; Reuel Shinnar, "The Hydrogen Economy," *Technology and Society* 25, no. 4 (2003): 455–476; Frank Kreith and Ron West, "The Fallacies of a Hydrogen Economy," *Journal of Energy Resources Technology* 126, no. 4 (December 2004): 249–257; Joseph J. Romm, *Hell and High Water: Global Warming—the Solution and the Politics—and What We Should Do* (New York: William Morrow, 2007).

10. Department of Energy, Office of Basic Energy Sciences, *Basic Research Needs for the Hydrogen Economy*, http://www.sc.doe.gov/bes/hydrogen.pdf.

11. The data cited in this subsection is drawn from Vladimir Bulovic, "Identifying a New Primary Energy Source," presentation at CSIS Energy Technology Forum, Washington, DC, September 28, 2006; Daniel M. Kammen, "The Rise of Renewable Energy," *Scientific American* 295, no. 3 (September 2006): 86–89.

12. There are a series of solar heating approaches not focused on here for incorporation into buildings to provide hot water and space heating, such as passive solar collection (through sunspaces and trombe walls). Solar chimneys can be used as well for heating, cooling, and ventilation. There are also solar thermal collectors, which are classified by the U.S. Energy Information Administration into three categories, low, medium, or high temperature; low-temperature collectors are typically collectors with pumps used to warm swimming-pool water; medium-temperature collectors are typically flat-plate solar panels and can be passive or active with pumps, for heating hot water for domestic use; and high-temperature collectors are solar concentrators described in the text.

13. "Solar PV Set to Grow," *Oxford Analytica*, May 9, 2008, 1.

14. Table 3.1 suggests that potentially disruptive innovations that are not secondary or component technologies do not necessarily require government "back-end" support in the form of incentives or regulatory mandates. The table suggests that this step be taken on a case-by-case basis depending on the needs of the particular technology. That is particularly true in the United States, where there is a capital infrastructure (venture, angel, and IPO capital) available from past radical technology revolutions, particularly IT and biotech, to

support disruptive innovation; it is less true in Europe and Asia, where such infrastructure is still emerging. EU and Japanese policies have subsidized existing technology partly to facilitate economies of scale and potential technology manufacturing economic leadership, and partly in the hope that the subsidy will be used for innovation, although without clear assurance that the latter will be the case.

15. European Union, Directorates for Energy and Transport and for General Research, *Concentrating Solar Power: From Research to Implementation*, 2007, http://ec.europa.eu/energy/res/publications/doc/2007_concentrating_solar_power_en.pdf.

16. Department of Energy, Climate Change Technology Program, *Strategic Plan*, DOE/PI-0005 (Washington, DC: Department of Energy, September 2006), http://www.climatetechnology.gov/stratplan/final/tbc.pdf.

17. Department of Energy, Climate Change Technology Program, *Strategic Plan*, 99.

18. "Solar PV Set to Grow," *Oxford Analytica*, 2 (source of this market and production data).

19. Department of Energy, Climate Change Technology Program, *Strategic Plan*, 99.

20. Nancy Stauffer, *Research Spotlight: Making Solar Cells from Ribbons*, research of Emanuel Sachs, MIT ERC, 2006, http://web.mit.edu/erc/spotlights/solar_cells.html.

21. Jefferson W. Tester, Elisabeth M. Drake, Michael J. Driscoll, Michael W. Golay, and William A. Peters, *Sustainable Energy: Choosing among Options* (Cambridge, MA: MIT Press, 2005), 576–582.

22. Department of Energy, Climate Change Technology Program, *Strategic Plan*, 102.

23. Bulovic, Identifying a New Primary Energy Source (the research projects listed are the work, respectively, of Bulovic, Moungi Bawendi, and Mark Baldo; Mark Baldo; Yoel Fink; and Daniel Nocera); David Talbot, "Emerging Technologies 2007—Nanocharging Solar," *Technology Review*, March/April 2007, 49–50 (research of Arthur Nozik), http://www.technologyreview.com/energy/18285; and interview with Bulovic, June 13, 2008.

24. Jason Pontin, "Vinod Khosla, Veteran VC's New Energy: Q and A," *Technology Review*, March/April 2007, 32, www.technologyreview.com/energy/18299.

25. Department of Energy, Climate Change Technology Program, *Strategic* Plan, 102.

26. Department of Energy, "California Utility to Buy 500 Megawatts of Solar Thermal Power," *EERE Network News*, August 16, 2006, http://apps1.eere.energy.gov/news/archive.cfm/pubDate =%7Bd%20'2006–08–16'%7D#10199.

27. "UD-Led Team Sets Solar Cell Record," University of Delaware Daily, July 23, 2007, http://www.udel.edu/PR/UDaily/2008/jul/ solar072307.html; "UD Team Sets Solar Record," *Science Daily*, July 30, 2007, http://www.sciencedaily.com/releases/2007/07/070726210931 .htm.

28. See summary in Ashlea Ebeling, "Do Solar While the Credit Shines," *Forbes Magazine*, December 12, 2005, http://www.forbes .com/investmentguide/free_forbes/2005/1212/192.html.

29. Ashlea Ebeling, "Do Solar While the Credit Shines," *Forbes Magazine*.

30. Ryan H. Wiser and Galen Barbose, *Renewable Portfolio Standards in the U.S.: A Status Report with Data through 2007* (Berkeley: Lawrence Berkeley National Laboratory, April 10, 2008), http://eetd .lbl.gov/ea/ems/re-pubs.html><http://eetd.lbl.gov/ea/ems/emp-ppt .html.

31. Ryan H. Wiser and Galen Barbose, *Renewable Portfolio Standards in the U.S.: A Status Report with Data through 2007*.

32. "Solar PV Set to Grow," 2–3 (source for cost estimates in this paragraph).

33. Matthew W. Kanan and Daniel G. Nocera, "In Situ Formation of an Oxygen-Evolving Catalyst in Neutral Water Containing Phosphate and Co^{2+}," *Science Online DOI*: 10.1126/science .1162018, July 31, 2008, http://www.sciencemag.org/cgi/content/ abstract/1162018; "Glowing After Dark," *The Economist* (Aug. 7, 2008); Anne Trafton, Major Discovery from MIT Primed to Unleash Solar Revolution, MIT News Office (July 31, 2008) http://web.mit .edu/newsoffice/2008/oxygen-0731.html.

34. Michael J. Currie, Jonathan K. Mapel, Timothy D. Heidel, Shalom Goffri, and Marc Baldo, High-Efficiency Organic Solar Concentrators for Photovoltaics, *Science* 321, no. 5886, July 11, 2008, 226–228. http://www.sciencemag.org/cgi/content/abstract/321/5886/ 226; Elizabeth A. Thompson, "MIT Opens New 'Window' on Solar

Energy," MIT News Office (July 10, 2008), http://web.mit.edu/newsoffice/2008/solarcells-0710.html.

35. National Academy of Sciences, Board on Energy and Environmental Systems, *Energy: What You Need to Know* (Washington, DC: National Academy of Sciences, 2008), 22. Electricity consumed by residential, commercial, and industry users accounts for some 42 percent of U.S. CO_2 emissions. See also Energy Information Administration, *Commercial Buildings Energy Consumption Survey*, Report DOE.EIA-871 (Washington, DC: EIA, 1995), as well as Energy Information Administration, *Commercial Buildings Characteristics*, Report DOE/EIS-E-0109 (Washington, DC: EIA, 1997), cited in Susan W. Sanderson, Kenneth L. Simons, Judith L. Walls, and Yin-Yi Lai, "Lighting," in National Research Council, Board on Science, Technology and Economic Policy, *Innovation in Global Industries*, 170–172 (Washington, DC: National Research Council, 2008) (this paper is relied on throughout this subsection).

36. E. Hong, L. A. Conroy, and M. J. Scholand, *U.S. Lighting Market Characterization: Energy Efficient Lighting Technology Options*, vol. 2, Technical Report (Washington, DC: Department of Energy, EERE, 2005); Sanderson et al., "Lighting."

37. EIA, *Commercial Buildings Characteristics* (1995).

38. Hong, Conroy, and Scholand, *U.S. Lighting Market Characterization: Energy Efficient Lighting Technology Options*, vol. 2.

39. Sanderson et al., "Lighting."

40. Sanderson et al., "Lighting," citing 2004 data from the U.S. International Trade Commission.

41. National Academy of Sciences, Board on Energy and Environmental Systems, *Energy: What You Need to Know*, 23.

42. Holonyak holds the National Medal of Technology and some thirty patents, including one on the red-light semiconductor laser used in CD and DVD players and cell phones. He was double-Nobelist John Bardeen's first PhD student when he went to the University of Illinois at Champaign-Urbana after his work on the transistor at Bell Labs; Holonyak has spent most of his career as an electrical and computer engineer at that university but was consulting to GE when he devised what is generally considered the first practical LED. He predicted in 1963 that the LED would replace Edison's incandescent lightbulb. In 2006 the American Institute of Physics

selected the top five papers published over the years in its publication *Applied Physics Letters*; two of them were coauthored by Holonyak.

43. National Academy of Sciences, Board on Energy and Environmental Systems, *Energy: What You Need to Know*, 22.

44. National Academy of Sciences, Board on Energy and Environmental Systems, *Energy: What You Need to Know*, 8, 22.

45. Sanderson et al., "Lighting," 174–175.

46. Sanderson et al., "Lighting," 180–182, 184–186.

47. Sanderson et al., "Lighting," 174–175.

48. National Academy of Sciences, Board on Science Technology and Economic Policy, *Partnerships for Solid State Lighting* (Washington, DC: National Academy of Sciences, 2002), 66–78, 175.

49. Sanderson et al., "Lighting," 191–199.

50. See, generally, Interacademy Council, "Lighting the Way," October 22, 2007, 42–44, http://www.interacademycouncil.net/ ?id=12161, for menu of government support options.

51. HR 6, Public Law 110–140, *The Energy Independence and Security Act of 2007* (December 19, 2007), Subtitle B, Sections 321–324.

52. Tester et al., *Sustainable Energy: Choosing among Options*, 614–616 (source of historical material in this subsection).

53. "Wind Power Expands in Renewables Search," *Oxford Analytica*, November 15, 2007, 2 (source for data on European developments).

54. National Academy of Sciences, Board on Energy and Environmental Systems, *Energy: What You Need to Know*, 26–27.

55. "Wind Power," 1.

56. Alan Yung Chen Cheng, *Economic Modeling of Intermittency in Wind Power Generation*, master's thesis in Technology and Policy and Civil and Environmental Engineering, MIT, 2005, http://web .mit.edu/globalchange/www/docs/Cheng_MS_05.pdf.

57. Tester et al., *Sustainable Energy: Choosing among Options*, 617–619.

58. Tester et al., *Sustainable Energy: Choosing among Options*, 635–637 (source for summary of environmental effects and externalities).

59. Federal Non-Nuclear Energy Research and Development Act of 1974, Public Law 93–577, 68 Stat. 1894, 42 U.S.C. 5913 (1974).

60. Tester et al., *Sustainable Energy: Choosing among Options*, 635.

61. "Wind Power Expands in Renewables Search," 2.

62. "Wind Power Expands in Renewables Search," 2.

63. Tester et al., *Sustainable Energy: Choosing among Options*, 638.

64. Tester et al., *Sustainable Energy: Choosing among Options*, 628–629.

65. Department of Energy, Climate Change Technology Program, *Strategic Plan*, 101.

66. Nancy Stauffer, *Research Spotlight: Giant Wind Turbines Floating Out of Sight* (Cambridge, MA: MIT ERC, 2008) (Research of Paul D. Sclavounos), http://web.mit.edu/erc/spotlights/wind.html.

67. "Wind Power Expands in Renewables Search," 1–2.

68. "Wind Power Expands in Renewables Search," 2.

69. HR 6, Public Law 110–140, *The Energy Independence and Security Act of 2007* (December 19, 2007), Subtitle B, Sections 321–324.

70. Cheng, *Economic Modeling of Intermittency in Wind Power Generation*, 49–53. In a carbon-stabilized scenario, despite its intermittency, study argues wind power could achieve 22 percent world market penetration by 2055.

71. The discussion in this section is drawn from Gerbrand Ceder, presentation at the CSIS Energy Forum, Washington, DC, September 28, 2006; *Testimony of Yet-Ming Chiang on Breakthrough Battery Technology at the Center of the Plug-in Hybrid Revolution, Senate Committee on Environment and Public Works, Subcommittee on Global Warming, Hearing on Emerging Technologies and Practices for Reducing Greenhouse Gas Emissions*, 110th Cong., 1st sess., May 8, 2007. We thank Professor Chiang for his thoughtful review of and suggestions for this section, although any errors remain our own.

72. Kevin Bullis, "An Electrifying Startup," *Technology Review* 111, no. 3 (May–June 2008): 68–71, http://www.technologyreview.com/Energy/20570/.

73. The question is often asked whether PHEVs, by relying for recharging on the grid, are simply running cars on coal, not oil. Coal-fired power plants provide roughly half of U.S. electricity overall; nuclear and hydro, which are CO_2-free, provide much of the rest, so PHEVs looked at nationwide will have a significant CO_2 advantage over oil. Since PHEVs will generally recharge off peak at night, when nuclear and hydro provide a higher portion of baseload power, the CO_2 reduction likely will be higher. Nonetheless, PHEV technology is optimal only when coupled with the introduction of technologies to reduce coal dependence or to reduce coal CO_2 emissions. PHEVs thus offer an example of the connectedness of energy technology across sectors.

74. MIT, Energy Research Council, *Report of the Energy Research Council*, Cambridge, MA: MIT, May 3, 2006, 22–23.

75. Jonathan Rauch, "Electro-Shock Therapy," *Atlantic*, July/August 2008, http://www.theatlantic.com/doc/200807/general-motors.

76. Discussion with Ric Fulop, vice president and co-founder, A123 Systems, June 24, 2008.

77. HR 6, Public Law 110–140, *The Energy Independence and Security Act of 2007* (December 19, 2007), Title I.

78. The discussion and data in this section are based on MIT, *The Future of Geothermal Energy—Impact of Enhanced Geothermal Systems (EGS) on the U.S. in the 21st Century*, Cambridge, MA: MIT, February 2007 (Jefferson W. Tester, chair; study supported by NREL). We thank Professor Tester and MIT researchers Hildigunnur Thornsteinsson and Chad Augustine for their careful review of this section and comments on and suggestions for it, although any errors remain our own.

79. Bruce Green and Gerald Nix, *Geothermal—the Energy under Our Feet*, NREL/TP 840–40665, Golden, CO: National Renewable Energy Laboratory (NREL), November 2006), 5–7.

80. MIT, *The Future of Geothermal Energy—Impact of Enhanced Geothermal Systems (EGS) on the U.S. in the 21st Century*.

81. An *exajoule*, which is equal to a quintillion (10^{18}) joules, is a standard unit of national energy consumption, equivalent to 0.948 quads, or quadrillion (10^{15}) British thermal units (BTU).

82. Ronald Dipippo, "Ideal Thermal Efficiency for Geothermal Binary Plants," *Geothermics* 36, no. 3 (June 2007): 276–285.

83. MIT, *The Future of Geothermal Energy—Impact of Enhanced Geothermal Systems (EGS) on the U.S. in the 21st Century*, sections 1.4–1.5.

84. H. Thorsteinsson, C. Augustine, B. Anderson, M. Moore, P. von Rohr, T. Rothenfluh, and J. Tester, "Sustainable Energy Opportunities with the Geothermal Continuum," paper, *NSTI Nanotech* 2008, June 1–5, 2008; see also Hildigunnur Thorsteinsson, Chad Augustine, Brian Anderson, Michal Moore, and Jefferson Tester, "The Impacts of Drilling and Reservoir Technology Advances on EGS Exploitation," *Proceedings of the Thirty-Third Workshop on Geothermal Reservoir Engineering*, January 28–30, 2008.

85. HR 6, Public Law 110–140, *The Energy Independence and Security Act of 2007* (December 19, 2007), Title VI, Subtitle B, Sections 613–625.

86. The data for this section is drawn from *Testimony of Kristala Jones Prather, Senate Committee on Energy and Natural Resources Conference on Accelerated Biofuels Diversity*, 110th Cong., 1st sess., February 1, 2007, and accompanying *Comments Submitted to the Committee on Question 5 on Required R&D*, January 26, 2007. We thank Prof. Jones Prather for her thoughtful review of and suggestions and comments on this section, although any errors remain our own.

87. David Rotman, "The Price of Biofuels," *Technology Review* 111, no. 1 (January–February 2008): 42, http://www.technologyreview.com/Energy/19842/.

88. HR 6, Public Law 110–140, *The Energy Independence and Security Act of 2007* (December 19, 2007), Title II.

89. Nancy Stauffer, "Ethanol Study Shows Biofuel Benefits," *MIT Tech Talk* 51, no. 15 (January 24, 2007), 1, http://mit.edu/newsoffice/2007/techtalk51-15.pdf; Tiffany A. Groode, Review of corn Based Ethanol Use and GHG Emissions (Cambridge, MA: MIT LFEE Working Paper, June 2006) http://lfee.mit.edu/metadot/index.pl?id=2334.

90. C. Ford Runge and Benjamin Senauer, "How Biofuels Could Starve the Poor," *Foreign Affairs* 86, no. 3 (May–June 2007): 41–53. To avoid problematic food price increases worldwide, ethanol's production inputs, these authors argue, must be diversified away from corn. See also Robbin S. Johnson and C. Ford Runge, "Ethanol: The Train Wreck Ahead," *Issues in Science and Technology* (Fall 2007), 25–30, http://www.issues.org/24.1/p_johnson.html. Compare Robert Zubrin, "In Defense of Biofuels," *New Atlantis: A Journal of Tech-*

nology and Society (spring 2008), http://www.thenewatlantis.com/
publications/in-defense-of-biofuels.

91. Donald Mitchell, World Bank Policy Research Working Paper
4682, "A Note on Rising Food Prices" (The World Bank Development Prospects Group, July 2008): 16–17; see also other studies cited
therein at pp. 4–5 http://www.wds.worldbank.org/external/default/
WDSContentServer/IW3P/IB/2008/07/28/000020439_20080728103002/
Rendered/PDF/WP4682.pdf.

92. MIT Joint Program on the Science and Policy of Global Change,
*The Environmental and Policy Issues Posed by New Concept Energy
Technologies Operating at the Scale Required to Impact the Climate
Problem*, unpublished study proposal, February 21, 2007. See also
Angelo Gurgel, John M. Reilly, and Sergey Paltsev, "Potential Land
Use Implications of a Global Biofuels Industry," *Journal of Agricultural and Food Industrial Organization 5*, no. 2 (December 10, 2007)
http://works.bepress.com/angelo_gurgel/1/. (forced intensification of
production from a global biofuels industry could affect pasture and
grazing land and lead to significant deforestation unless the nonmarket value of land is reflected in land conversion decisions).

93. HR 6, Public Law 110–140, *The Energy Independence and
Security Act of 2007* (as noted, in the text above, Title II raises the
renewable fuels standard to nine billion gallons in 2008 with increases
in progressive steps to thirty-six billion gallons by 2022; of that total,
cellulosic-based advanced biofuels are required to make up twenty-
one billion gallons by 2022).

94. See, generally, Wilfred Vermerris, ed., *Genetic Improvement of
Bioenergy Crops* (New York: Springer, 2008).

95. "Grow Your Own—the Biofuels of the Future Will Be Tailor-
Made" in "The Future of Energy," *The Economist*, June 2–27, 2008
(special report): 16–20.

96. IEA, *Energy Technology Perspectives 2008: Scenarios and Strategies to 2050*, 307ff.

97. Department of Energy, Office of Basic Energy Sciences, *Basic
Research Needs: Catalysis for Energy*, Report of Workshop, August
6–9, 2007, http://www.er.doe.gov/bes/reports/files/CAT_rpt.pdf.

98. Gurgel, Reilly, and Paltsev, "Potential Land Use Implications of
a Global Biofuels Industry."

99. Drawn from Testimony of Kristala Jones Prather, *Senate Committee on Energy and Natural Resources Conference on Accelerated*

Biofuels Diversity, February 1, 2007, and accompanying *Comments Submitted to the Committee on Question 5 on Required R&D*, January 26, 2007. See also Gregory Stephanopoulos, "Challenges in Engineering Microbes for Biofuels Production," *Science* 315 (February 9, 2007): 801–804.

100. Jay D. Keasling and Howard Chou, "Metabolic Engineering Delivers Next-Generation Biofuels," *Nature Biotechnology* 263 (March 26, 2008): 298–299.

101. Ana Campoy, "Betting on a Biofuel—Butanol Has Several Advantages over Ethanol and One Big Disadvantage," Report on Energy (special supplement), *Wall Street Journal*, June 30, 2008, R14.

102. Donald Kennedy, "The Biofuels Conundrum," *Science* 316 (April 27, 2007): 515.

103. Energy Information Administration, *Emissions of Greenhouse Gases in the United States*, Report No. DOE/EIA-0573(2001) (Washington, DC: EIA, December 2002). By comparison, 42 percent of total U.S. CO_2 emissions come from petroleum combustion and 21 percent from natural gas.

104. Energy Information Administration, *International Energy Outlook 2007*, Report No. DOE/EIA-0484 (Washington, DC: May 2007), chap. 5, www.eia.doe.gov/oiaf/leo/index.html. Some 67 percent of world coal resources are held by four nations: the United States, 27 percent; Russia, 17 percent; China, 13 percent; and India, 10 percent.

105. The discussion in this section is drawn from MIT, *The Future of Coal*, March 14, 2007, http://web.mit.edu/coal/The_Future_of _Coal.pdf. See also D. Hawkins, D. Lashof, and R. Williams, "What to Do about Coal," *Scientific American* 295, no. 3 (September 2006): 69–75; John Deutch and Ernest J. Moniz, *Testimony before the Senate Committee on Energy and Natural Resources, Hearing on the Future of Coal*, 110th Cong., 1st sess., March 22, 2007; Howard J. Herzog, *Testimony before the House Committee on Natural Resources, Hearing to Explore Carbon Sequestration Technologies*, 110th Cong., 1st sess., May 1, 2007; James Katzer, *Testimony on Coal-Based Power Generation with CO_2 Capture and Sequestration, Senate Committee on Commerce, Science, and Transportation, Science, Energy, and Innovation Subcommittee*, 110th Cong., 1st sess., March 20, 2007. We thank Principal Research Engineer Howard J. Herzog, of the Laboratory for Energy and the Environment at MIT, for his thoughtful review of and suggestions and comments on this section, although any errors remain our own.

106. MIT, *The Future of Coal*, 111–112, http://web.mit.edu/coal/The_Future_of_Coal.pdf.

107. Edward S. Steinfeld, *Testimony to the House Committee on Energy and Commerce, Hearing on Climate Change—International Issues, Engaging Developing Countries*, 110th Cong., 1st sess., March 27 2007: "China over the next twenty-five years is expected to account for more than half of global growth in coal supply and demand. The country today is world's largest producer of coal (2.23 billion tons in 2005), and coal accounts for over two-thirds of China's primary energy supply. Electricity generation accounts for just over half of all coal utilization in China, and about 80 percent of Chinese electricity generation is fueled by coal. . . . Growth of the power sector is arguably the single most important factor driving China's impact on carbon emissions and global climate change. In 2005, approximately 70 GW of new generating capacity was brought into service in China (an addition nearly the size of the UK's entire power grid). In 2006, 102 GW of capacity was added, again primarily in the form of coal-burning power plants."

108. Eric Williams, Nora Greenglass, and Rebecca Ryals, *Carbon Capture, Pipeline, and Storage: A Viable Option for N.C. Utilities?* Report No. CC PP WP 07–01 (Durham, NC: Nicholas Institute for Environmental Policy, Duke University, March 8, 2007). The one area of the U.S. very dependent on coal-fired electricity plants but lacking geological storage formations suited to CO_2 is the Southeast. However, this study estimates that even in a state like North Carolina, if cap-and-trade prices are set at a sound level, CO_2 transport and sequestration would not make the state's coal-generation costs uncompetitive.

109. Howard J. Herzog, "Coal and CCS," presentation at CSIS forum, Washington, DC (September 28, 2006). Eighty percent of the cost associated with CCS is related to CO_2 capture and compression, 20 percent with transport and injection.

110. MIT, *The Future of Coal*, 48–51, http://web.mit.edu/coal/The_Future_of_Coal.pdf.

111. MIT, *The Future of Coal*, chap. 4, http://web.mit.edu/coal/The_Future_of_Coal.pdf.

112. MIT, *The Future of Coal*, http://web.mit.edu/coal/The_Future_of_Coal.pdf. See, also, M. A. de Figueiredo, H. J. Herzog, P. L. Joskow, K. A. Oye, and R. M. Reiner, *Regulating Carbon Dioxide*

Capture and Storage, 07-003 (Cambridge, MA: MIT CEEPR, April 2007), http://web.mit.edu/ceepr/www/publications/workingpapers/2007-003.pdf; M. A. de Figueiredo, *The Liability of Carbon Dioxide Storage*, doctoral dissertation, MIT, 2007, http://sequestration.mit.edu/pdf/Mark_de_Figueiredo_PhD_Dissertation.pdf.

113. Department of Energy, Office of Basic Energy Sciences, *Basic Research Needs for the Geosciences: Facilitating 21st Century Energy Systems*, February 2007, http://www.sc.doe.gov/bes/reports/list.html.

114. Conversation with Howard J. Herzog, June 18, 2008.

115. "DOE Announces Restructured FutureGen Approach to Demonstrate Carbon Capture and Storage Technology at Multiple Clean Coal Plants," DOE Fossil Energy, *Techline,* January 30, 2008, http://www.fossil.energy.gov/news/techlines/2008/08003-DOE _Announces_Restructured_FutureG.html; see, also, the accompanying DOE Factsheet, http://www.fossil.energy.gov/programs/powersystems/futuregen/futuregen_revised_0108.pdf. The decision has been the subject of ongoing Congressional inquiries.

116. Howard J. Herzog, *Regulatory Framework for Carbon Capture and Storage (CCS): The Policy Problem*, MIT project proposal, December 8, 2006.

117. John M. Deutch and Ernest J. Moniz, "The Nuclear Option," *Scientific American* (September 2006): 76–83. See also MIT, *The Future of Nuclear Power*, 2003, http://web.mit.edu/nuclearpower.

118. Department of Energy, Office of Nuclear Energy, *Generation VI Nuclear Energy Systems: What is Generation IV?*, 2008, http://nuclear.energy.gov/genIV/neGenIV1.html.

119. Uranium Information Centre, *Nuclear Power in France*, Briefing Paper No. 28, April 2007, http://www.uic.com.au/nip28.htm.

120. Department of Energy, Office of Nuclear Energy, Office of Fuel Cycle Management, *Global Nuclear Energy Partnership Strategic Plan*, GNEP-167312, Rev. 0, January 2007, http://64.233.169.104/search?q=cache:aqcUqm5ezW8J:www.gnep.gov/pdfs/gnepStrategicPlanJanuary2007.pdf+Department+of+Energy,+Office +of+Nuclear+Energy,+Office+of+Fuel+Cycle+Management,+U.S. .+Global+Nuclear+Energy+Partnership+Strategic+Plan.+GNEP-167312, +Rev.+0.+January+2007&hl=en&ct=clnk&cd=1&gl=us&client =safari; Senate Committee on Energy and Natural Resources,

Hearing on the Global Nuclear Energy Partnership as It Relates to U.S. Policy on Nuclear Fuel Management, 110th Cong., 1st sess. (November 14, 2007), http://frwebgate.access.gpo.gov/cgi-bin/getdoc .cgi?dbname=110_senate_hearings&docid=f:41099.wais.

121. Department of Energy, Office of Nuclear Energy, *Generation IV Nuclear Energy Systems: Priorities and Strategic Goals*, 2008.

122. Senate Committee on Energy and Natural Resources, *Hearing on the Global Nuclear Energy Partnership as It Relates to U.S. Policy on Nuclear Fuel Management*, 110th Cong., 1st sess. (November 14, 2007), http://frwebgate.access.gpo.gov/cgi-bin/getdoc.cgi?dbname =110_senate_hearings&docid=f:41099.wais.

123. Department of Energy, Office of Basic Energy Sciences, *Basic Research Needs for Advanced Nuclear Systems*, August 2006, http://www.sc.doe.gov/bes/reports/files/ANES_rpt.pdf.

124. Department of Energy, Office of Basic Energy Sciences, *Basic Research Needs for the Geosciences: Facilitating 21st Century Energy Systems*, February 2007, http://www.sc.doe.gov/bes/reports/list.html.

125. Proposals for better waste and proliferation management systems are developed in MIT, *The Future of Nuclear Power*, 2003, 53–71, http://web.mit.edu/nuclearpower/.

126. Kelly Sims Gallagher, John P. Holdren, and Ambuj D. Sagar, "Energy Technology Innovation," *Annual Review of Environment and Resources* 31 (November 2006): 216 (broad range of innovations required for effect on energy issues).

127. The data in this section are from William H. Green, "Liquid Fuels for Transportation," presentation MIT, April 20, 2006.

128. Energy Information Administration, *Emissions of Greenhouse Gasses in the United States*, Report No. DOE/EIA-0573(2001), December 2002. By comparison, 37 percent of total U.S. CO_2 emissions come from coal and 21 percent from natural gas.

129. Communication from Daniel Cohn, Division Head and Senior Research Scientist, MIT Plasma Science and Fusion Center, May 31, 2008. We thank Dr. Cohn for his thoughtful review of and suggestions and comments on this section, although any errors remain our own.

130. Anup Banivadekar, Kristian Bodek, Lynette Cheah, Christopher Evans, Tiffany Groode, John Heywood, Emmanuel Kasseris, Mathew

Kromer, and Malcolm Weiss, *On the Road in 2035, Reducing Transportation's Petroleum Consumption and GHG Emissions.* Laboratory for Energy and the Environment, Report LFEE 2008–05RP (July 2008), http://web.mit.edu/sloan-auto-lab/research/beforeh2/otr2035/.

131. Kevin Bullis, "The Incredible Shrinking Engine," *Technology Review*, March/April 2007, 88–90, http://www.technologyreview.com/Energy/18304/. These technologies could not be combined before because of engine knock, which limits efforts to increase engine torque and power. But direct injection of ethanol provides a very large cooling effect when it vaporizes and thus prevents the rise in temperature that causes knock. By injecting ethanol from a small reservoir into the engine cylinders when needed to prevent knock, the required amount of ethanol can be limited to a small fraction of gasoline use. The refill interval for the ethanol reservoir can be every four to six months and the reservoir can thus be refilled at the time of regular servicing. The new system could offer hybridlike fuel efficiency at a much lower cost since hybrids require both IC and electric engine systems, including substantial battery capability. The system could also significantly improve the efficiency of the IC element of hybrid engines.

132. Energy Information Agency, *Emissions of Greenhouse Gases in the United States.* We thank Henry Kelly, president of the Federation of American Scientists, for his thoughtful review of and suggestions and comments on this section, although any errors remain ours alone.

133. Diana Urge-Vorsatz, L. D. Harvey, Sevastianos Mirasgedis, and Mark D. Levine, "Mitigating CO_2 Emissions from Energy Use in the World's Buildings," *Building and Research Information*, 2007 http://web.ceu.hu/envsci/publication/duv/BRImitiginbldgsppr2007.pdf. See also IPCC, Working Group III (Mark Levine, Diana Urge Vorsatz, Lead Authors, *IPCC Fourth Assessment Report*, Final Draft, chap. 6, "Residential and Commercial Buildings" Cambridge, UK and NY: Cambridge University Press, IPCC, 2007), http://www.mnp.nl/ipcc/pages_media/FAR4docs/chapters/CH6_Buildings.pdf.

134. Eberhard K. Jochem, "An Efficient Solution," *Scientific American* (September 2006): 64–67.

135. Urge-Vorsatz et al., "Mitigating CO_2 Emissions from Energy Use in the World's Buildings," 4–12.

136. Thomas L. Friedman, *Hot, Flat and Crowded: Why We Need a Green Revolution and How it Can Renew America* (New York: Farrar, Straus and Giroux, 2008), 246.

Chapter 5

1. Gregory Nemet and Daniel Kammen, "U.S. Energy R&D: Declining Investment, Increasing Need, and the Feasibility of Expansion," *Energy Policy 35* (2007): 747. See also President's Council of Advisors on Science and Technology (PCAST), *Report to the President on Federal Energy R&D for the Challenges of the 21st Century* (Washington, DC: PCAST, Nov. 1997), ES-11–14, http://www.ostp.gov/cs/report_to_the_president_on_federal_energy_research_and_development_for_the_challenges_of_the_twentyfirst_century_table_of_contents.

2. Nemet and Kammen, "U.S. Energy R&D," 747.

3. Nemet and Kammen, "U.S. Energy R&D," 747.

4. Nemet and Kammen, "U.S. Energy R&D," 748–749. The AAAS estimated actual energy R&D expenditures at the Department of Energy at $2.4 billion for FY 2008, out of basic and applied research budgets of $3.2 and $3.4 billion overall, at DOE's Office of Science and EERE. See American Association for the Advancement of Science (AAAS), *R&D Budget and Policy Program—FY 2009* (revised March 2008), http://www.aaas.org/spp/rd/fy09.htm.

5. Nemet and Kammen, "U.S. Energy R&D," 749–751. See also Antonia V. Herzog and Daniel Kammen, "Energy R&D: Investment Challenge," *Materials Today 5*, no. 5 (May 1, 2002): 28–33.

6. "Venture Capital Investment in Renewable Energy Soars to $3.4 Billion in 2007", Reuters, Business Wire, (Jan. 16, 2007).

7. IEA, *Energy Technology Perspectives 2008: Scenarios and Strategies to 2050*, June 6 2008, chap. 4, 186. VC funding to energy may drop in 2009 due to the 2008 economic decrease.

8. IEA, *Energy Technology Perspectives 2008*, 169.

9. IEA, *Energy Technology Perspectives 2008*, 178; Nemet and Kammen, "U.S. Energy R&D," 748–749.

10. IEA, *Energy Technology Perspectives 2008*, 178.

11. Nemet and Kammen, "U.S. Energy R&D," 752–753.

12. BIO, "Biotechnology Industry Facts," http://bio.org/speeches/pubs/er/statistics.asp.

13. Pharmaceutical Research and Manufacturers of America (PhRMA), "R&D Spending by Biopharmaceutical Reaches $58.8 Billion in 2007," March 24, 2008, http://www.phrma.org/news_room/

press_releases/us_biopharmaceutical_companies_r%26d_spending
_reaches_record_%2458.8_billion_in_2007/.

14. Pharmaceutical Research and Manufacturers of America (PhRMA), "R&D Spending by Biopharmaceutical Reaches $58.8 Billion in 2007."

15. Semiconductor Industry Association (SIA), "Industry Facts and Figures," 2007, http://www.sia-online.org/ind_facts.cfm.

16. Nemet and Kammen, "U.S. Energy R&D," 752.

17. Daniel Kammen and Gregory Nemet, Real Numbers: Reversing the Incredible Shrinking R&D Budget, *Issues in Science and Technology* (Fall 2005), 84.

18. Nemet and Kammen, U.S. Energy R&D, p. 747.

19. President's Council of Advisors on Science and Technology (PCAST), *Report to the President on Federal Energy R&D for the Challenges of the 21st Century*, ES-2–6.

20. Nicholas Stern, *Stern Review on the Economics of Climate Change* (London: H. M. Treasury, 2006), ix, http://www.hm-treasury .gov.uk/media/2/F/Chapter_24_Promoting_Effective_International _Technology_Co-operation.pdf.

21. National Commission on Energy Policy (NCEP), *Ending the Energy Stalemate: A Bipartisan Strategy to Meet America's Energy Challenges*, December 1, 2004, http://www.energycommission.org/ ht/a/GetDocumentAction/i/1088.

22. Graham A. Davis and Brandon Owens, "Optimizing the Level of Renewable Electric R&D Expenditures Using Real Options Analysis," *Energy Policy* 31 (2003): 1589–1608.

23. Robert N. Schock, William Fulkerson, Merwin Brown, Robert San Martin, David Greene, and Jae Edmonds, "How Much Is Energy R&D Worth as Insurance?", *Annual Review of Energy and the Environment* 24 (1999): 487–512.

24. IPCC, Working Group III (Nebojsa Nakicenovic and Rob Swart, eds.) *Special Report on Emissions Scenarios* (Cambridge UK: Cambridge University Press, IPCC, March 2000), http://www.grida .no/climate/ipcc/emission/.

25. Nemet and Kammen, "U.S. Energy R&D," 752–754.

26. IEA, *Energy Technology Perspectives 2008*, 38–39.

27. IEA, *Energy Technology Perspectives, 2008,* list from figure 4.2, 188–189.

28. IEA, *Energy Technology Perspectives, 2008,* 201.

29. IEA, *Energy Technology Perspectives, 2008,* 40.

30. IEA, *Energy Technology Perspectives, 2008,* 752.

31. Charles I. Jones and John C. Williams, "Measuring the Social Return to R&D," *Quarterly Journal of Economics* 13, no. 114 (1998): 1119–1135; M. Ishaq Nadiri, *Innovations and Technological Spillovers,* NBER Working Paper No. 4423 (Cambridge, MA: National Bureau of Economic Research, 1993); Zvi Griliches, "The Search for R&D Spillovers," *Scandinavian Journal of Economics* 94 (1992): 29–47; David Popp, "The Effect of New Technology on Energy Consumption," *Resource and Energy Economics* 23 (2001): 215–239.

32. Popp, "The Effect of New Technology on Energy Consumption," 753.

33. Communication from former Dept. of Energy senior official on August 27, 2007, and follow-up discussion on July 1, 2008.

34. David M. Walker, U.S. Comptroller General, "A Call for Stewardship," National Press Club speech, December 17, 2007, http://www.gao.gov/cghome/d08371cg.pdf (entitlement obligations not under fiscal control).

35. Wording and framing of this summary is from Robert Nordhaus and Kyle Danish, *Designing a Mandatory Greenhouse Gas Reduction Program for the U.S.,* Pew Center for Global Climate Change Report, Executive Summary (Washington, DC: Pew Center for Global Climate Change, May 2003), iii, http://www.pewclimate.org/docUploads/USGas.pdf.

36. Public Law 101–548 Clean Air Act Amendments of 1990 (November 15, 1991). See, generally, A. Denny Ellerman, Paul L. Joskow, Richard Schmalensee, Juan-Pablo Montero, and Elizabeth M. Bailey, *Markets for Clean Air: The U.S. Acid Rain Program* (Cambridge: Cambridge University Press, 2000).

37. See, for example, S. 1151, *The McCain-Lieberman Climate Stewardship and Innovation Act of 2005,* 109th Cong., 1st sess., http://thomas.loc.gov/cgi-bin/bdquery/z?d109:s.01151. The proposed legislation, a major early climate cap-and-trade bill, proposed to use

revenues generated from the sale of allowances to promote three different aspects of technology innovation and deployment: (1) first-of-a-kind engineering, (2) demonstration and deployment of the first generation of faci-lities that use substantially new technology, and (3) the marketing and procurement of low-/no-GHG-emitting power or low-GHG-producing products.

38. S. 2191, *The Climate Security Act,* introduced on October 18, 2007, 110th Cong., 1st sess., and debated on the Senate floor, as amended, as S. 3036, 110th Cong., 2nd sess., June 6, 2008. For a summary of S. 2191, see Andrea Hudson, Kyle Danish, and Alex Lazur, "Lieberman Warner Climate Change Cap and Trade Bill Seen as Framework for Senate Climate Debate", Report (Washington, DC: Van Ness Feldman, October 19, 2007), http://www.vnf.com/news-alerts-217.html. The legislation was named after its authors and initial sponsors, Senators Joseph I. Lieberman (I-CT) and John Warner (R-VA).

39. Robert Shapiro, Nan Phan, and Arun Malik, *Addressing Climate Change without Impairing the U.S. Economy: The Economics and Environmental Science of Combining a Carbon-Based Tax and Tax Relief* (Washington, DC: U.S. Climate Task Force, June 2008), http://www.climatetaskforce.org/pdf/CTF_CarbonTax_Earth_Spgs.pdf (proposes a carbon tax with a shift of 90 percent of the tax revenues for tax relief through rebates on Social Security payroll taxes to employees and employers; 10 percent of revenues used for R&D and technology development).

40. Public Law 109-058, *Energy Policy Act* of 2005 (July 29, 2005).

41. HR 6, *The Energy Independence and Security Act of 2007,* Public Law 110–140 (passed Congress and signed into law December 19, 2007). Title I of the original legislation passed by Congress repealed certain tax subsidies for the oil and gas industries, but these were deleted after Bush administration opposition.

42. HR 2272, *The America Competes Act,* Public Law 110–69 (signed into law August 9, 2007) (Title IV—DOE funding).

43. *The Energy Independence and Security Act of 2007.*

44. Stephen W. Pacala and Robert H. Socolow, "Stabilization Wedges: Solving the Climate Problem for the Next 50 Years with Current Technologies," *Science* 305 (August 13, 2004): 968. See also John Podesta, Todd Stern, and Kit Batten, *Capturing the Energy Opportunity: Creating a Low-Carbon Economy* (Washington, DC: Center for American Progress, November 27, 2007) (argues that the

technology needed for an energy low-carbon transformation exists and that the investment dollars are available, assuming adequate policies are implemented).

45. IEA, *Energy Technology Perspectives 2008*.

46. See, for example, H. Damon Matthews, and Ken Caldeira, "Stabilizing Climate Requires Near-Zero Emissions," *Geophysical Research Letters* 35 (February 27, 2008), http://www.agu.org/pubs/ crossref/2008/2007GL032388.shtml (study finds that because the CO_2 presence in the atmosphere appears far more enduring and long-lasting than previously thought, CO_2 emissions may have to be reduced to far lower levels than anticipated in order to reach climate stabilization). See, generally, House Select Committee on Energy Independence and Global Warming, *Briefing on the Climate Threat to the Planet*, Testimony of James Hansen, NASA, 110th Cong., 2nd sess., June 23, 2008.

Chapter 6

1. The Office of Science had a requested annual budget of $4.1 billion for FY 08; EERE had a budget request of $1.24 billion for FY 08 (American Association for the Advancement of Science, *Research & Development Report Fiscal Year 2008*, Report 32, 2007, chap. 8, tables I, II–11; Alexander Karsner, *Testimony of the Assistant Secretary for Energy Efficiency and Renewable Energy before the Subcommittee on Energy and Water Development, Committee on Appropriations, United States Senate*, April 11, 2007. Congress, however, in its omnibus appropriations bill for FY 08 reduced DOE science appropriations from the request to a 2.6 percent increase over FY 07.

2. Victor Reis, Senior Advisor, Department of Energy, "Nuclear Energy, Nuclear Weapons and Climate Change," unpublished presentation, June 2008.

3. See, generally, National Research Council, *Energy Research at DOE: Was It Worth It?* (Washington, DC: National Academy of Sciences, 2001) (limits to the role DOE R&D programs played in energy technology innovation; reforms required in DOE R&D management).

4. Reis, "Nuclear Energy, Nuclear Weapons and Climate Change."

5. Department of Defense/Jasons (advisory group)(Paul Dimotakis, Robert Grober, and Nate Lewis, study leaders), *Reducing DOD Fossil*

Fuel Dependence, JSR-06–135 (Mclean, VA: Mitre Corp., September 2006), http://stinet.dtic.mil/cgi-bin/GetTRDoc?AD=ADA459082 &Location=U2&doc=GetTRDoc.pdf (fossil-fuel dependence is not a major problem for DOD at this time; however, energy logistics reductions would be a prudent DOD policy).

6. President's Council of Advisors on Science and Technology (PCAST), *Report to the President on Federal Energy R&D for the Challenges of the 21st Century* (Washington, DC: PCAST, Executive Office of the President of the United States, 1997), 51, http://www .ostp.gov/cs/report_to_the_president_on_federal_energy_research _and_development_for_the_challenges_of_the_twentyfirst_century _table_of_contents (summary of spending on energy technology at federal agencies).

7. The detailed discussion below of the translational model is drawn from William B. Bonvillian, *Comments to the House Science and Technology Committee on HR 364 (ARPA-E Legislation)*, April 2, 2007; William B. Bonvillian, *Testimony to the House Committee on Science and Technology, Subcommittee on Energy and Environment, Hearing on Establishing ARPA-E*, HR 364, 110th Cong., 1st sess. (April 26, 2007), summarized in William B. Bonvillian, "Will the Search for New Energy Technologies Require a New R&D Mission Agency?", *Bridges*, July 14, 2007, http://www.ostina.org/content/ view/2297/721/.

8. William B. Bonvillian, "Power Play: The DARPA Model and US Energy Policy," *The American Interest*, November–December 2006, http://www.theamericaninterest.com/ai2/article.cfm?Id=183&MId=6 [portion of article].

9. The recent report by the National Academies of Sciences called for a DARPA-like "ARPA-E" at DOE. See National Academy of Sciences, *Rising above the Gathering Storm* (Washington, DC: National Academy of Sciences 2007). Congress picked up this argument. See HR 364, 109th Cong., 2nd sess.; S. 761, 110th Cong., 1st sess.; also see House Science Committee, *Hearings on ARPA-E Concept*, March 9, 2006, and April 26, 2007. ARPA-E legislation was passed in HR 2272, *The America COMPETES Act* (Conference Report H, Rep. 110–289, August 1, 2007), Sec. 5012, and was signed into law on August 9, 2007.

10. Aside from HSARPA, DARPA's success has encouraged other somewhat comparable models, including In-Q-Tel (see the discussion

of the relevance of this agency to ARPA-E in Bonvillian, *Comments to the House Science and Technology Committee on HR 364 (ARPA-E Legislation)*, April 2, 2007; see, generally, Rick E. Yanuzzi, "In-Q-Tel: A New Partnership between the CIA and the Private Sector," *Defense Intelligence Journal* 9, no. 1 (2000), https://www.cia.gov/library/publications/additional-publications/in-q-tel/index.html#author.

11. Bonvillian, "Power Play."

12. William A. Wulf and Thomas Leighton, *Testimony to the House Science Committee Hearing on the Future of Computer Science Research in the U.S.*, May 12, 2005 (Testimony by William A. Wulf, President, National Academy of Engineering; Thomas F. Leighton, Chief Scientist, Akamai Tech. Inc.; Joint Statement of the Computing Research Community; and Letters in Response to Committee Questions from W. Wulf and T. Leighton, July 2005); Edward D. Lazowska and David Paterson, "An Endless Frontier Postponed," *Science* 308 (May 6, 2005): 757; John Markoff, "Clouds over 'Blue Sky' Research Agency," *New York Times*, May 4, 2005, 12; President's Information Technology Advisory Committee, *Cybersecurity: A Crisis of Prioritization*, Report to the President, February 2005, http://www.nitrd.gov/pitac/reports/20050301_cybersecurity/cybersecurity.pdf; Defense Science Board, *High Performance Microchip Supply*, February 2005, 87–88, http://www.acq.osd.mil/dsb/reports/2005-02-HPMS_Report_Final.pdf. Compare DARPA's responses, House Science Committee Hearing, May 12, 2005 (DARPA Testimony with Appendices A–D).

13. See Donald E. Stokes, *Pasteur's Quadrant: Basic Science and Technological Innovation* (Washington, DC: Brookings Institution Press, 1997), 1–25, 45–89.

14. Richard Van Atta, Sidney G. Reed,and Seymour J. Deitchman, *DARPA Technological Accomplishments: An Historical Review of Selected DARPA Projects*, vols. 1–5 (Alexandria, VA: IDA, 1991).

15. William A. Wulf and Thomas Leighton, *Testimony to the House Science Committee Hearing on the Future of Computer Science Research in the U.S.*

16. Another option is to "let DARPA do it"—that is, to avoid having to create and launch institutional elements for new technology at DOE and instead relying on the residual talent and depth in the defense R&D and innovation system to tackle our energy problems. However, while it is a problem for DOD operations, energy is not a

central and deep enough problem for its core capability to drive the levels of component R&D investment and focus needed. DOD is also not focused at the level of the overall U.S. energy economy, but rather at the energy systems level for military platforms. See Department of Defense/Jasons (advisory group)(Paul Dimotakis, Robert Grober, and Nate Lewis, study leaders), *Reducing DOD Fossil Fuel Dependence*, http://stinet.dtic.mil/cgi-bin/GetTRDoc?AD =ADA459082&Location=U2&doc=GetTRDoc.pdf.

17. Some have suggested that ARPA-E be located outside of DOE in a government-owned corporation, and that such a corporation could house two efforts: breakthrough technology development and large-scale demonstrations (discussed below). There is a risk in combining the research and demonstration roles. As often seen in DOD agencies that combine R&D and acquisition roles, the cost demands of an ongoing new-technology-platform capital project tend to trump and devour the funding for high-risk, longer-term technology-breakthrough R&D projects. In addition, demonstrations call for very different kinds of personnel, with commercial management, financing, and late-stage engineering rather than breakthrough research expertise. If there is a divided agency mission, consisting of both R&D and dem-onstration, firewalls between these program elements would be required, and there is risk they will not be observed.

18. DARPA has been able to mitigate these problems with special hiring and contracting authorities; if it is located with DOE, an ARPA-E should have similar powers, which the new ARPA-E legisla-tion attempts to ensure.

19. HR 364, Establishing the Advanced Research Projects Agency-Energy (ARPA-E) Act, 109th Cong., 2nd sess.(2006), as reported from Committee; enacted in, HR 2272, *The America COMPETES Act*, Con-ference Report H. Rep. 110–289, 110th Cong., 1st sess. (passed Con-gress August 1, 2007; signed into law August 9, 2007), Sec. 5012.

20. Warren Bennis and Patricia Ward Biederman, *Organizing Genius: The Secrets of Creative Collaboration* (New York: Basic Books, 1997), 196–218.

21. EERE at DOE has demonstration authority in its portfolio, but its flexibility is limited by its presence inside a government bureau-cracy inevitably distanced from commercial operating procedures, and by its lack, as a civil service agency, of depth in the commercial management, financing, and project engineering required.

22. John Deutch, *What Should the Government Do to Encourage Technical Change in the Energy Sector?*, Report No. 120 (Cambridge, MA: MIT Joint Program on the Science and Policy of Global Change, May 2005), http://web.mit.edu/globalchange/www/MITJPSPGC_Rpt120.pdf.

23. The U.S. Synthetic Fuels Corporation (SFC), created by the Energy Act of 1980, was abandoned after energy prices collapsed from their 1980 highs to less than $20 a barrel (S. 932, Public Law 96–294 (June 23, 1980); Public Law 99–272, Termination of US SFC Act, April 7, 1986, Title VII, Subtitle E, 100 Stat. 143.

24. For a detailed discussion of government corporations, see A. Michael Froomkin, "Reinventing the Government Corporation," *Illinois Law Review* 543 (1995), http://osaka.law.miami.edu/~froomkin/articles/reinvent.htm.

25. Vernon W. Ruttan, *Is War Necessary for Economic Growth? Military Procurement and Technology Development* (New York: Oxford University Press, 2006), 21–31. See also Ruth Swartz Cowan, *A Social History of American Technology* (New York: Oxford University Press, 1996), 78–81.

26. Leslie Berlin, *The Man Behind the Microchip: Robert Noyce and the Invention of Silicon Valley* (New York: Oxford University Press, 2005), 257–304 (origins of Sematech); Larry Browning and Judy Shetler, *Sematech: Saving the U.S. Semiconductor Industry*, Kenneth E. Montague Series in Oil and Business History, No. 10 (College Station, TX: Texas A&M Press, 2000).

27. These incentives would have more or less the same purpose as the guarantees provided by the Japanese government during the 1970s and 1980s to make it possible for Japanese firms to expand their production capacity, even at the risk of overexpansion, so as to achieve the economies of scale needed to enable them to "price down the learning curve."

28. John Alic, *Trillions for Military Technology* (New York: Palgrave Macmillan, 2007).

29. S. 3233, 21st Century Energy Technology Deployment Act, 110th Congress, 2nd Session (introduced by Sen. Bingaman, July 11, 2008)(the primary function of the proposed government-controlled financing corporation would be to securitize private loans and sell bonds based on their revenues in order to allow a greater amount of less expensive lending in the private sector. The corporation also

would seek to accommodate riskier debt and thus provide a mechanism and an incentive for lenders to provide riskier loans.); S. 2730, Clean Energy Investment Bank Act, 110th Congress, 2nd Session (introduced by Sen. Domenici, March 6, 2008)(creates a clean energy bank, modeled on the Export-Import Bank and OPIC, to offer direct loans, loan guarantees and insurance products. It would have authority to take positions in commercially viable clean energy projects, and could manage the existing DOE Title 17 loan guarantee program for energy technologies). See, also, Senate Committee on Energy and Natural Resources, *Hearings on legislation to improve the availability of financing for deployment of clean energy and energy efficiency technologies and to enhance United States' competitiveness in this market,* S. 3233 and S. 2730, 110th Cong., 2nd sess. (July 15, 2008).

30. Federally chartered and sponsored Government Sponsored Enterprises (GSEs) date from 1916, and include the Federal National Mortgage Association, the Federal Home Loan Mortgage Corp. (Freddie Mac), and the Federal Agricultural Mortgage Corp. (Farmer Mac), which are investor owned, and the Federal Home Loan Bank System and the Farm Credit System, which are cooperatively owned by borrowers. The mortgage and banking GSEs are regulated under 12 U.S.C. 4501, et seq. GSEs can address risk premiums using a line of credit from the Treasury to issue bonds without a federal guarantee. Using this capital pool, they can offer a variety of instruments, from direct lending to loan guarantees to loan securitization for purchasing and trading existing loans. While, as noted, housing GSEs have been sharply criticized for sustaining losses during the subprime mortgage lending crisis of 2008, and for their dominant role in mortgage markets, they have been an effective model overall. Recent regulatory oversight failures and management errors do not necessarily mean the model itself, if properly implemented and supervised, is erroneous. Additional oversight protections could be provided through reauthorization and sunset requirements.

31. See also Paul M. Romer, "Implementing a National Technology Strategy with Self-Organizing Investment Boards," in Martin N. Baily and Peter C. Reiss, eds., *Macreconomics 1993*, Brookings Papers on Economic Activity (Washington, DC: Brookings Institution Press, 1993), 345.

32. See, generally, José Goldemberg, Thomas B. Johansson, Amulya K.N. Reddy, and Rob Williams, *Energy for a Sustainable World* (Washington, DC: World Resources Institute, 1987).

33. Browning and Shetler, *Sematech.*

34. U.S. Climate Change Technology Program, *Strategic Plan*, Report DOE/PI-0005 (September 2006).

35. Jeff Bingaman, "Strategies for Today's Energy Challenge," *Issues in Science and Technology*, summer 2008, 36, http://www.issues.org/24.4/bingaman.html.

36. Jeff Bingaman, "Strategies for Today's Energy Challenge," 33–38; Lamar Alexander, "A New Manhattan Project for Clean Energy Independence," 39–44. http://www.issues.org/24.4/alexander.html.

37. Paul H. Romer, "Endogenous Technological Change," *Journal of Political Economy* 98 no. 5 (1990): 72–102.

38. Fred Block and Matthew R. Keller, "Where Do Innovations Come From? Transformations in the U.S. National Innovation System 1970–2006," *ITIF Report*, July 2008, http://www.itif.org/files/Where_do_innovations_come_from.pdf (a survey of significant innovations selected by an R&D publication in the past forty years showed that while in the 1970s the great majority came from corporations acting on their own, in more recent years over two-thirds of the winners have come from partnerships involving business- and government-funded researchers, including at universities and labs. In 2006, 77 of 88 selectees in *R&D Magazine*'s top 100 innovations of the year received federal funding).

39. For a summary of the history of prizes across technology fields, see Richard G. Newell and Nathan E. Wilson, *Technology Prizes for Climate Change Mitigation: Resources for the Future*, RFF Discussion Paper 05-33, June 2005, 14–19, http://www.rff.org/RFF/Documents/RFF-DP-05-33.pdf.

40. Public Law 109–058, *Energy Policy Act of 2005*, 109th Cong. 1st sess. (2005), Title X, Section 1008. The Secretary of Energy was authorized to award $10 million in cash prizes for breakthroughs in research, development and demonstration.

41. HR 6, Public Law 110–140, *The Energy Independence and Security Act of 2007*, 110th Cong., 1st sess. (passed Congress and signed December 19, 2007). Section 654 calls for competitive cash prizes for RD&D and commercial application in hydrogen; Section 655 calls for three specific prizes for lighting advances.

42. A $10 million Automotive X-Prize for super-efficient vehicles has been announced, and Richard Branson has offered a $25 million "Virgin Earth Challenge" for GHG removal.

43. See the discussion of the process decisions for implementing prizes in Newell and Wilson, *Technology Prizes for Climate Change Mitigation*, 20–35.

44. See, generally, Richard K. Lester, *Universities, Innovation and the Competitiveness of Local Economies*, (Cambridge, MA: MIT Industrial Performance Center Working Paper 05-010 (Dec. 2005)).

45. Roger H. Bezdek and Robert M. Wendling, "Real Numbers: The U.S. Energy Subsidy Scorecard," *Issues in Science and Technology*, spring 2006, http://www.issues.org/22.3/realnumbers.html.

46. Robert W. Fri, "From Energy Wish Lists to Technological Realities," *Issues in Science and Technology*, fall 2006, http://www.issues.org/23.1/fri.html (technology standards are generally more economically efficient and so are preferable to production tax credits).

47. Bezdek and Wendling, "Real Numbers."

48. HR 3221, *New Direction for Energy Independence, National Security, and Consumer Protection Act*, 110th Cong., 1st sess. (passed the House August 4, 2007) (petroleum tax subsidies reduced to fund alternative energy programs). This provision was omitted in the final version of the act, as enacted (HR 6, Public Law 110–140, *The Energy Independence and Security Act of 2007*, 110th Cong., 1st sess. (passed Congress December 14, 2007)) because of presidential opposition.

49. William A. Pizer, *Discussion Paper: A U.S. Perspective on Future Climate Regimes*, RFF DP 07–04 (Washington, DC: Resources for the Future, February 2007), 3–4. Depending on the criteria used, some twenty-two to twenty-seven states now impose some form of renewable portfolio standards on state-regulated utilities.

50. See, generally, Meghan McGuinness and A. Denny Ellerman, *The Effects of Interactions between Federal and State Climate Policies*, Report 08-004 (Cambridge, MA: MIT Center for Energy and Environmental Policy Analysis, May 2008), http://web.mit.edu/ceepr/www/publications/workingpapers/2008-004.pdf.

51. "Clean Energy Trends 2007: Global Clean Energy Markets Projected to Exceed $220 Billion by 2016," *Clean Edge News*, March 6, 2007, http://www.cleanedge.com/reports/reports-trends2007.php.

52. Robert M. Solow, *Growth Theory: An Exposition*, 2nd ed. (New York: Oxford University Press, 2000), ix–xxvi (Nobel Prize Lecture, December 8, 1987).

53. Richard G. Lipsey, *Economic Transformations: General Purpose Technologies and Long-Term Economic Growth* (Oxford and New York: Oxford University Press, 2005). See, generally, Jonathan Zittrain, *The Future of the Internet—And How to Stop It* (New Haven, CT: Yale University Press, 2008).

54. Dale Jorgenson, "U.S. Economic Growth in the Information Age," *Issues in Science and Technology*, fall 2001, http://www.issues.org/18.1/jorgenson.html (central role of IT drivers in 1990s growth).

55. W. Brian Arthur, *Increasing Returns and Path Dependence in the Economy* (Ann Arbor: University of Michigan Press, 1994).

56. Council on Competitiveness, *Energy Security, Innovation and Sustainability*, project summary (Washington, DC: Council on Competitiveness, 2008), 2–3.

Chapter 7

1. Edward A. Cunningham, *Innovation Partnerships with China and India: Managing Global Climate Change and Clean Energy Systems*, Report. (Boston, MA: Mass Insight Corp, February 1, 2008), 3.

2. Elisabeth Rosenthal, "China Leads the World in Emissions of Carbon Dioxide," *New York Times*, June 14, 2008, A-5, http://www.nytimes.com/2008/06/14/world/asia/14china.html.

3. Cunningham, "Innovation Partnerships with China and India," 3.

4. Cunningham, "Innovation Partnerships with China and India," 4.

5. Rosenthal, "China Leads the World in Emissions of Carbon Dioxide."

6. MIT, *The Future of Coal*, March 14, 2007, 63, http://web.mit.edu/coal/The_Future_of_Coal.pdf.

7. Energy Information Agency, *International Energy Outlook 2007*, Report No. DOE/EIA 0484 (Washington, DC: May 2007), chap. 7, http://www.eia.doe.gov/oiaf/ieo/emissions.html.

8. MIT, *The Future of Coal*, 64–65, http://web.mit.edu/coal/The_Future_of_Coal.pdf.

9. A. Denny Ellerman and Paul L. Joskow, *The European Union's Emissions Trading System in Perspective*, Report of the Pew Center on Global Climate Change (Washington, DC: Pew Center on Global

Climate Change, May 2008), 43–44, http://www.pewclimate.org/docUploads/EU-ETS-In-Perspective-Report.pdf.

10. Judson Jaffe and Robert Stavins, *Linking Tradable Permit Systems for Greenhouse Gas Emissions: Opportunities, Implications and Challenges*, Report for the International Emissions Trading Association (Geneva Switzerland and Washington, DC: International Emissions Trading Association, November 2007), http://www.ieta.org/ieta/www/pages/getfile.php?docID=2733; Ellerman and Joskow, *The European Union's Emissions Trading System in Perspective*, 43–45. Linkage is not a perfect mechanism, however. It will create non-economic preferences and "winners and losers." A second problem is "additionality," according to which tons of emissions credited in one emission system may also be credited in another, or would have occurred anyway, referred to as "anyway tons." A third problem is that relatively easy-to-get outside linkage credits could create an oversupply of credits in the EU system, slowing the ability of the market trading system to drive change in energy practices within the EU. As a practical matter, linkages have had no real effect to date in the EU since the 2004 Directive, because the registry that would enable the credit system was not scheduled for completion until mid-2007.

11. S.2191, *The Climate Security Act*, as reported from the Senate Environment and Public Works Committee on December 5, 2007, 110th Cong., 1st sess. (*Lieberman-Warner bill*), Title II, Subtitle E; S. 3036, *Boxer-Lieberman-Warner Substitute Amendment to S. 2191*, 110th Cong., 2nd sess. (introduced May 21, 2008), Title III, Subtitle B, Sections 321–322.

12. World Bank, *Proposal for a Clean Technology Fund*, Report on Design Meeting on Climate Investment Funds (Washington, DC: World Bank April 3, 2008), http://siteresources.worldbank.org/INTCC/Resources/Proposal_For_A_Clean_Technology_Fund_April_3_2008.pdf; Subcommittee on Monetary Policy, Subcommittee of the House Financial Services Committee, *Testimony of Undersecretary of the Treasury for International Affairs David McCormick, Hearings on $2b Proposed U.S. Contributions to the $10b Clean Technology Fund* (June 6, 2008).

13. S. 3036, Title XIII, Subtitle A, Sections 1301–1307; Subtitle C, Section 1321; Subtitle D, 1331–1333.

14. Growth economist Christopher Freeman of the University of Sussex, in evaluating the Japanese economy in 1987, first used the

term *national innovation system.* Christopher Freeman, "Japan: A New National Innovation System," in G. Dosi, C. Freeman, R. R. Nelson, G. Silverberg, L. Soete, eds., *Technology and Economy Theory* (London: Pinter, 1988); Christopher Freeman, "The National System of Innovation in Historical Perspective," *Cambridge Journal of Economics* 19 (1995): 5–24. Economist Richard R. Nelson titled his 1993 book *National Systems of Innovation* and attempted to systematically characterize the national landscapes of varying innovation systems and the institutional actors that populate them. See Richard R. Nelson, *National Systems of Innovation* (New York: Oxford University Press, 1993), 3–21, 505–523 (national innovation system institutional and policy elements). Kenichi Ohmae has suggested, in contrast, that national systems are fading and a new system of techno-laissez-faire has evolved in which national technical competency does not necessarily generate national advantage. Kenichi Ohmae, *The End of the Nation State* (Simon & Schuster, 1995); Kenichi Ohmae, *The Next Global State—Challenges and Opportunities in Our Borderless World* (Philadelphia: Wharton, 2005). In contrast, other scholars continue to argue the importance of national innovation. Bengt-Ake Lundvall argues that as global competition increases, nations that have placed innovation features into their geographic base, are forced to exploit specialized innovation advantages in order to do well. In other words, he maintains that national innovation systems retain a central role. Bengt-Ake Lundvall, "National Innovation Systems— Analytical Concept and Development Tool," *Industry and Innovation*, February 2007 (different modes of innovation complement each other and find support in a national system); Bengt-Ake Lundvall, *Innovation, Growth and Social Cohesion* (Cheltenham, UK: Edward Elgar, 2002), 53, 58–59 (the importance of national innovation systems, with organizational and talent features in a geographic base, grows as global competition increases, and forces nations to exploit specialized innovation advantages to do well); Daniele Archibugi and Simona Iammarino, "The Globalization of Technology and National Models," in Daniele Archibugi and Bengt-Ake Lundvall, eds., *The Globalizing Learning Economy* (New York: Oxford University Press, 2002), 111–126 (Archibugi and Iammarino argue that nationally based innovation equips nations for technological progress and global competition; note Kenichi Ohmae's contrasting view of techno-laissez-faire, where national technical competency does not necessarily generate national advantage).

15. World Economic Forum, *2007–08 Global Competitiveness Report—National Competitiveness Rankings*, October 31, 2007, http://www.gcr.weforum.org/.

16. James Hosek and Titus Galama, US Competitiveness in Science and Technology, Report (Santa Monica, CA: RAND Corp., June 2008); Council on Competitiveness, Competitiveness Index: Where America Stands, Report (Washington, DC: Council on Competitiveness, January 2007), http://www.compete.org/images/uploads/File/PDF%20Files/Competitiveness_Index_Where_America_Stands_March_2007.pdf; World Economic Forum, 2007–08 *Global Competitiveness Report*, 3–50, http://www.gcr.weforum.org (U.S. economy rated first in world due to its innovation capacity). Compare Stephen Ezell and Robert Atkinson, *RAND's Rose-Colored Glasses* (Washington, DC: Information Technology and Innovation Foundation (ITIF), September 10, 2008) http://www.itif.org/index.php?=174 (U.S. faces major challenge to its innovation leadership, with emerging weaknesses in a series of technology fields).

17. The European Union is implementing a demand-side cap-and-trade pricing system applicable to two energy sectors, large-scale power and industrial emitters. Because this approach is relatively narrow, it contrasts with the broader-front, multisectoral approach under consideration in the United States to meet higher U.S. emission levels, which will require more technology supply-side intensity across numerous sectors. See, generally, European Union, *EU Action against Climate Change*, 2005, http://ec.europa.eu/environment/climat/pdf/emission_trading3_en.pdf; A. Denny Ellerman and Barbara K. Buchner, "The European Union Emissions Trading Scheme: Origins, Allocation, and Early Results," *Review of Environmental Economic Policy* 1, no. 1 (2007) 66–87. EU nations are relying on already high national fuel taxes, not their multinational cap-and-trade program, to improve efficiency in the transport sector. Because expected auction revenues from its cap-and-trade system will go to each nation and be allocated by different rules in each nation, the EU does not now plan for a multinational energy technology R&D program using these auction revenues, although individual nations may allocate some of these revenues to R&D.

18. "Solar PV Set to Grow," *Oxford Analytica*, May 9, 2008, 2 (China's PV production has grown rapidly and may pass U.S. and European solar production, as well as wind-power manufacturing, by 2010).

19. Carl J. Dahlman and Jean Eric Aubert, *China and the Knowledge Economy: Seizing the 21st Century*, Overview (Washington, DC: World Bank Institute, 2001), 1–27, http://info.worldbank.org/etools/docs/library/17281/Chinaoverview_0917.pdf.

20. "Wind Power Expands in Renewables Search," *Oxford Analytica*, November 15, 2007, 2.

21. Tom Wright, "Indian Wind Turbine Firm Hits Turbulence," *Wall Street Journal*, June 30, 2008, B1.

22. National Research Council (NRC), STEP Board, *21st Century Innovation Systems for Japan and the United States: Lessons from a Decade of Change*, 2008, http://dels.nas.edu/dels/rpt_briefs/climate_change_2008_final.pdf; Glenn R. Fong, "Follower at the Frontier: International Competition and Japanese Industrial Policy," *International Studies Quarterly* 42, no. 2 (1998) 339–366 (Japan's revised industrial policy approach to strengthen its ability to compete in basic research-driven breakthrough).

23. IEA, *Energy Technology Perspectives: Scenarios and Strategies to 2050*, June 6, 2008, figure 4.3, 172, http://www.iea.org/Textbase/techno/etp/ETP_2008.pdf.

24. Carlota Perez, *Technological Revolutions and Financial Capital* (Cheltenham, UK: Edward Elgar 2002), 3–46. See also Robert D. Atkinson, *The Past and Future of America's Economy: Long Waves of Innovation that Power Cycles of Growth* (Cheltenham, UK: Edward Elgar 2004).

25. Thomas L. Friedman, *Hot, Flat and Crowded: Why We Need a Green Revolution and How it can Renew America* (New York: Farrar Straus and Giroux, 2008), 243–244.

26. Nicholas Stern, *Stern Review on the Economics of Climate Change* (London: H. M. Treasury, 2006), part IV, 51, http://www.hm-treasury.gov.uk/media/2/F/Chapter_24_Promoting_Effective_International_Technology_Co-operation.pdf.

Chapter 8

1. HR 2272, *The America COMPETES Act*, Conference Report H. Rep. 110–289, 110th Cong., 1st sess. (passed Cong. August 1, 2007, signed into law August 9, 2007).

2. HR 2272, *The America COMPETES Act*, Sec. 5012.

3. S. 3233, 21st Century Energy Technology Deployment Act, 110th Congress, 2nd Sess. (introduced by Sen. Bingaman); S. 2730, Clean Energy Investment Bank Act, 110th Congress, 2nd Sess. (introduced by Sen. Domenici).

4. Compare HR 6 (110th Cong., 1st sess.) (passed the Senate June 2, 2007) with HR 3221 (110th Cong., 1st sess.) (passed the House August 4, 2007).

5. HR 6, Public Law 110–140, The Energy Independence and Security Act of 2007, 110th Cong., 1st sess. (passed Congress December 14, 2007).

6. Linda R. Cohen and Roger G. Noll, *The Technology Pork Barrel* (Washington, DC: Brookings Press, 1991), especially 259–320.

7. Walter S. Baer, Leland L. Johnson, and Edward W. Merrow, *Analysis of Federally Funded Demonstration Projects*, R-1925-DOC (Santa Monica, CA: RAND Corp., April 1976), http://www.rand.org/pubs/reports/2006/R1925.pdf.

8. CRADAs were created as a result of the *Stevenson-Wydler Technology Innovation Act of 1980*, Public Law 96–480, as amended by the *Federal Technology Transfer Act of 1986*, Public Law 99–502. They provide incentives to promote the commercialization of federally developed technology; protect proprietary information brought to the CRADA effort by the private-sector partner; allow all parties to the CRADA to keep research results emerging from the CRADA confidential and free from disclosure for up to five years; allow the government and the private-sector partner to share patents and patent licenses; and permit one partner to retain exclusive rights to patents or patent licenses.

9. Baer, Johnson, and Merrow, *Analysis of Federally Funded Demonstration Projects*, iv.

10. Thomas C. Schelling, "Climate Change: The Uncertainties, the Certainties and What They Imply about Action," *The Economists' Voice* 4, no. 3, article 3 (2007) http://www.bepress.com/ev/vol4/iss3/art3 (although the uncertainties regarding climate change are many, the certainties create some urgencies and inaction is an extreme position; technological advance and governmental sponsorship are required).

11. Forest C. Pogue, *George C. Marshall—Statesman 1945–1959* (New York: Viking Penguin, 1987), 200, 231, 251, 256; Theodore A. Wilson, *The Marshall Plan: An Atlantic Venture of 1947–51 and How It Shaped the World* (New York: Foreign Policy Association, June 1977), 36; Imanuel Wexler, *Marshall Plan Revisited* (Westport, CT: Greenwood Press, 1983), 32–33; Harry B. Price, *Marshall Plan and Its Meaning* (Ithaca, NY: Cornell University Press, 1955), 55–57.

12. John Bledsoe Bonds, *Bipartisan Strategy: Selling the Marshall Plan* (Westport, CT: Praeger, 2002).

13. Dean Acheson, *Present at the Creation* (New York: Norton, 1969), 221–225, 229–235, 241–242.

14. Charles Weiss, *The Marshall Plan: Lessons for U.S. Assistance to Central and Eastern Europe and the Former Soviet Union*, Atlantic Council Occasional Paper (Washington, DC: Atlantic Council, 1995).

15. See, for example, S. 2191, *The Climate Security Act*, 110th Cong., 1st sess. (introduced on October 18, 2007 by Senators Lieberman and Warner).

16. Niccolò Machiavelli, *The Prince and the Discourses* (New York: Modern Library, [1513] 1950), chap. 6, p. 21.

References

Abramowitz, Michael. U.S. Joins G-8 Plan to Halve Emissions. *Washington Post,* July 9, 2008. http://www.washingtonpost.com/wp-dyn/content/article/2008/07/08/AR2008070800285.html.

Acheson, Dean. *Present at the Creation.* New York: Norton, 1969.

Alexander, Lamar. A New Manhattan Project for Clean Energy Independence. *Issues in Science and Technology,* summer 2008, 39–44. http://www.issues.org/24.4/alexander.html.

Alic, John. *Trillions for Military Technology.* New York: Palgrave Macmillan, 2007.

Alic, John, David Mowery, and Edward Rubin. *U.S. Technology and Innovation Policies: Lessons for Climate Change.* Washington, DC: Pew Center on Global Climate Change, November 2003. http://www.pewclimate.org/global-warming-in-depth/all_reports/technology_policy.

American Association for the Advancement of Science. *Research & Development, Fiscal Year 2008.* Report 32. Washington, DC: American Association for the Advancement of Science, 2007.

American Association for the Advancement of Science. *R&D Budget and Policy Program—FY 2009* (revised March 2008). http://www.aaas.org/spp/rd/fy09.htm.

Anthony, Richard. Powering Up—Roll-up Fuel Cells (research of Paula Hammond). *Spectrum* (winter 2007), 7. Cambridge, MA.: MIT.

Archibugi, Daniele, and Simona Iammarino. The Globalization of Technology and National Models. In Daniele Archibugi and

Note: URLs for cited works were checked on September 19, 2008.

Bengt-Ake Lundvall, eds., *The Globalizing Learning Economy.* New York: Oxford University Press, 2002.

Arrow, Kenneth J. Economic Welfare and the Allocation of Resources for Invention. In Richard Nelson, ed., *The Rate and Direction of Inventive Activity: Economic and Social Factors.* Princeton, NJ: Princeton University Press, for NBER, 1962.

Arrow, Kenneth J. Global Climate Change: A Challenge to Policy. *The Economists' Voice* 4, no. 3, article 2 (2007). http://www.bepress .com/ev/vol4/iss3/art2.

Arrow, Kenneth J. *Intergenerational Equity and the Rate of Discount in Long Term Social Investment.* Stanford University Working Papers in Economics 97–005. December 1995. http://www-econ.stanford .edu/faculty/workp/swp97005.html.

Arthur, Brian. *Increasing Returns and Path Dependence in the Economy.* Ann Arbor: University of Michigan Press, 1994.

Atkinson, Robert D. *The Past and Future of America's Economy: Long Waves of Innovation That Power Cycles of Growth.* Cheltenham, UK: Edward Elgar, 2004.

Auerswald, Phillip E. The Myth of Energy Insecurity. *Issues in Science and Technology,* summer 2006. http://www.issues.org/22.4/auerswald .html.

Baer, Walter S., Leland L. Johnson, and Edward W. Merrow. *Analysis of Federally Funded Demonstration Projects.* R-1925–DOC. Santa Monica, CA: RAND Corp., April 1976. http://www.rand.org/ pubs/reports/2006/R1925.pdf.

Banivadekar, Anup, Kristian Bodek, Lynette Cheah, Christopher Evans, Tiffany Groode, John Heywood, Emmanuel Kasseris, Mathew Kromer, and Malcolm Weiss. *On the Road in 2035, Reducing Transportation's Petroleum Consumption and GHG Emissions.* Laboratory for Energy and the Environment, Report LFEE 2008–05RP (July 2008). http://web.mit.edu/sloan-auto-lab/research/beforeh2/otr2035/.

Bennis, Warren, and Patricia Ward Biederman. *Organizing Genius: The Secrets of Creative Collaboration.* New York: Basic Books, 1997.

Berger, Suzanne. *How We Compete.* New York: Doubleday Business, 2005.

Berlin, Leslie. *The Man behind the Microchip: Robert Noyce and the Invention of Silicon Valley.* New York: Oxford University Press, 2005.

Betz, Frederick. *Strategic Technology Management*. New York: McGraw-Hill, 1993.

Bezdek, Roger H., and Robert M. Wendling. Real Numbers: The U.S. Energy Subsidy Scorecard. *Issues in Science and Technology*, spring 2006. http://www.issues.org/22.3/realnumbers.html.

Bingaman, Jeff. Strategies for Today's Energy Challenge. *Issues in Science and Technology*, summer 2008, 33–38. http://issues.org/24.4/bingaman.html.

BIO. Biotechnology Industry Facts. http://bio.org/speeches/pubs/er/statistics.asp.

Block, Fred, and Matthew R. Keller. *Where Do Innovations Come From? Transformations in the U.S. National Innovation System 1970–2006*. Washington, DC: Information Technology and Innovation Foundation (ITIF) Report. July 2008. http://www.itif.org/files/Where_do_innovations_come_from.pdf.

Bonds, John Bledsoe. *Bipartisan Strategy: Selling the Marshall Plan*. Westport, CT: Praeger, 2002.

Bonvillian, William B. *Comments to the House Science and Technology Committee on HR 364 (ARPA-E Legislation)*, April 2, 2007.

Bonvillian, William B. Power Play: The DARPA Model and US Energy Policy. *The American Interest*, November-December 2006. http://www.theamericaninterest.com/ai2/article.cfm?Id=183&MId=6 [portion of article].

Bonvillian, William B. *Testimony to the House Committee on Science and Technology, Subcommittee on Energy and Environment Hearing on Establishing ARPA-E*, HR 364, 110th Cong., 1st sess. (April 26, 2007).

Bonvillian, William B. Will the Search for New Energy Technologies Require a New R&D Mission Agency? *Bridges*, July 14, 2007. http://www.ostina.org/content/view/2297/721/.

Bossell, Ulf, Baldour Eliasson, and Gordon Taylor. *The Future of the Hydrogen Economy, Bright or Bleak?* European Fuel Cell Forum Report. 2003, updated 2005. http://www.efcf.com/reports/E08.pdf.

Branscomb, Lewis, and Philip Auerswald. *Between Invention and Innovation: An Analysis of Funding for Early-State Technology Development*. NIST GCR 02–841. Washington, DC: National Institute of Standards and Technology/ATP, November 2002.

Branscomb, Lewis M., and Philip E. Auerswald. *Taking Technical Risks: How Innovators, Executives, and Investors Manage High-Tech Risks.* Cambridge, MA: MIT Press, 2001.

Browning, Larry, and Judy Shetler. *Sematech: Saving the U.S. Semiconductor Industry.* Kenneth E. Montague Series in Oil and Business History, No. 10. College Station, TX: Texas A&M Press, 2000.

Bullis, Kevin. An Electrifying Startup. *Technology Review,* May-June 2008: 68–71. http://www.technologyreview.com/Energy/20570/.

Bullis, Kevin. The Incredible Shrinking Engine. *Technology Review,* March–April 2007: 88–90. http://www.technologyreview.com/Energy/18304/.

Bulovic, Vladimir. Identifying a New Primary Energy Source. Presentation to CSIS Energy Technology Forum, Washington, DC, September 28, 2006.

Bush, Vannevar. *Science: The Endless Frontier.* Washington, DC: Government Printing Office, July 1945. http://www.nsf.gov/od/lpa/nsf50/vbush1945.htm.

Campoy, Ana. Betting on a Biofuel—Butanol Has Several Advantages over Ethanol and One Big Disadvantage. Report on Energy (special supplement). *Wall Street Journal,* June 30, 2008, R14.

Carey, John. The Real Question: Should Oil be Cheap? *Business Week,* August 4, 2008, 54.

Ceder, Gerbrand. Presentation to CSIS Energy Technology Forum, Washington, DC, September 28, 2006.

Cheng, Alan Yung Chen. *Economic Modeling of Intermittency in Wind Power Generation.* Master's thesis in Technology and Policy and Civil and Environmental Engineering, MIT, 2005. http://web.mit.edu/globalchange/www/docs/Cheng_MS_05.pdf.

Chiang, Yet-Ming. *Testimony on Breakthrough Battery Technology at the Center of the Plug-in Hybrid Revolution,* Senate Committee on Environment and Public Works, Subcommittee on Global Warming, Hearing on Emerging Technologies and Practices for Reducing Greenhouse Gas Emissions, 110th Cong., 1st sess., May 8, 2007.

Christensen, Clayton. *The Innovator's Dilemma: When New Technologies Cause Great Firms to Fail.* Boston: Harvard Business School Press, 1997.

Christensen, Clayton, Scott Anthony, and Erik Roth. *Seeing What's Next.* Boston: Harvard Business School Press, 2004.

Clean Energy Trends 2007: Global Clean Energy Markets Projected to Exceed $220 Billion by 2016. *Clean Edge News*, March 6, 2007. http://www.cleanedge.com/reports/reports-trends2007.php.

Cohen, Linda R., and Roger G. Noll. *The Technology Pork Barrel.* Washington, DC: Brookings Institution Press, 1991.

Council on Competitiveness. *Energy Security, Innovation and Sustainability Initiative.* Project summary. Washington, DC: Council on Competitiveness, 2008.

Council on Competitiveness. *Competitiveness Index: Where America Stands.* Report. Washington, DC: Council on Competitiveness, January 2007. http://www.compete.org/images/uploads/File/PDF%20Files/Competitiveness_Index_Where_America_Stands_March_2007.pdf.

Cowan, Ruth Swartz. *A Social History of American Technology.* New York: Oxford University Press, 1996.

Cunningham, Edward A. *Innovation Partnerships with China and India: Managing Global Climate Change and Clean Energy Systems.* Report. Boston, MA: Mass Insight Corp., February 1, 2008.

Currie, Michael J., Jonathan K. Mapel, Timothy D. Heidel, Shalom Goffri, and Marc Baldo. High-Efficiency Organic Solar Concentrators for Photovoltaics. *Science* 321, no. 5886 (July 11, 2008): 226–228. http://www.sciencemag.org/cgi/content/abstract/321/5886/226.

Dahlman, Carl J., and Jean Eric Aubert. *China and the Knowledge Economy: Seizing the 21st Century.* Overview. Washington, DC: World Bank Institute, 2001. http://info.worldbank.org/etools/docs/library/17281/Chinaoverview_0917.pdf.

Davis, Graham A., and Brandon Owens. Optimizing the Level of Renewable Electric R&D Expenditures Using Real Options Analysis. *Energy Policy* 31 (2003): 1589–1608. http://www.nrel.gov/docs/fy03osti/31221.pdf.

Defense Science Board. *High Performance Microchip Supply.* Report. Washington, DC: DSB, February 2005. http://www.acq.osd.mil/dsb/reports/2005-02-HPMS_Report_Final.pdf.

Dennison, John, of Perkins Caulfield. *Testimony to the Senate Committee on Energy and Natural Resources, Hearing to Investigate Market Constraints on Large Investments in Advanced Energy Technologies,* Senate Hearing 110–63, 100th Cong., 1st sess., March 7, 2007.

Department of Defense/Jasons (advisory group) (Paul Dimotakis, Robert Grober, and Nate Lewis, study leaders). *Reducing DOD Fossil Fuel Dependence.* JSR-06-135. McLean, VA: Mitre Corp., September 2006. http://stinet.dtic.mil/cgibin/GetTRDoc?AD=ADA459082&Location =U2&doc=GetTRDoc.pdf.

Department of Energy. California Utility to Buy 500 Megawatts of Solar Thermal Power. *EERE Network News,* August 16, 2006. http://apps1 .eere.energy.gov/news/archive.cfm/pubDate=%7Bd%20'2006–08 –16'%7D#10199.

Department of Energy, Climate Change Technology Program. *Strategic Plan.* DOE/PI-0005. Washington, DC: Department of Energy, September 2006. http://www.climatetechnology.gov/stratplan/final/toc.pdf.

Department of Energy. DOE Announces Restructured FutureGen Approach to Demonstrate Carbon Capture and Storage Technology at Multiple Clean Coal Plants. DOE Fossil Energy *Techline* January 30, 2008. http://www.fossil.energy.gov/news/techlines/2008/08003-DOE _Announces_Restructured_FutureG.html.

Department of Energy, Office of Basic Energy Sciences. Workshop Reports, Abstracts of BES Workshop and Technical Reports, 2003– 2007, http://www.sc.doe.gov/bes/reports/abstracts.html, and The Basic Research Needs Workshop Series, http://www.sc.doe.gov/bes/reports/files/BRN_workshops.pdf.

Department of Energy, Office of Basic Energy Sciences. *Basic Research Needs for the Hydrogen Economy: Report of the Workshop on Hydrogen Production, Storage and Use,* May 13–15, 2003. Washington, DC: Department of Energy, February 2004. http://www.sc.doe.gov/bes/hydrogen.pdf.

Department of Energy, Office of Basic Energy Sciences. *Basic Research Needs for Advanced Nuclear Systems.* August 2006. http://www .sc.doe.gov/bes/reports/files/ANES_rpt.pdf.

Department of Energy, Office of Basic Energy Sciences, *Basic Research Needs: Catalysis for Energy,* Report of Workshop, August 6–9, 2007. http://www.er.doe.gov/bes/reports/files/CAT_rpt.pdf.

Department of Energy, Office of Basic Energy Sciences. *Basic Research Needs for the Geosciences: Facilitating 21st Century Energy Systems.* February 2007. http://www.sc.doe.gov/bes/reports/list.html.

Department of Energy, Office of Nuclear Energy. *Generation IV Nuclear Energy Systems: Priorities and Strategic Goals.* 2008.

Department of Energy, Office of Nuclear Energy. *Generation VI NuclearEnergy Systems: What is Generation IV?.* 2008. http:// nuclear.energy.gov/genIV/neGenIV1.html.

Department of Energy, Office of Nuclear Energy, Office of Fuel Cycle Management. *Global Nuclear Energy Partnership Strategic Plan.* GNEP-167312, Rev. 0. January 2007. http://64.233.169.104/ search?q=cache:aqcUqm5ezW8J:www.gnep.gov/pdfs/ gnepStrategicPlanJanuary2007.pdf+Department+of+Energy,+Office +of+Nuclear+Energy,+Office+of+Fuel+Cycle+Management ,+U.S..+Global+Nuclear+Energy+Partnership+Strategic+Plan .+GNEP-167312,+Rev.+0.+January+2007&hl=en&ct=clnk&cd=1 &gl=us&client=safari.

Deutch, John M. *What Should the Government Do to Encourage Technical Change in the Energy Sector?* Report No. 120. Cambridge, MA: MIT Joint Program on the Science and Policy of Global Change, May 2005. http://web.mit.edu/globalchange/www/MITJPSPGC_Rpt120.pdf.

Deutch, John M., and Ernest J. Moniz. The Nuclear Option. *Scientific American*, September 2006. http://www.sciam.com/article .cfm?id=the-nuclear-option.

Deutch, John M., and Ernest J. Moniz. *Testimony before the Senate Committee on Energy and Natural Resources, Hearing on the Future of Coal*, 110th Cong., 1st sess., March 22, 2007. http://64.233.169.104/ search?q=cache:CepUKKbDyJAJ:energy.senate.gov/public/_files/ ProfessorsDuetchandMoniztestimony.doc+Deutch,+John+and+Ernest +J.+Moniz,+Testimony+before+the+Senate+Committee+on+Energy +and+Natural+Resources,+hearing+on+the+Future+of+Coal,+March +22,+2007.&hl=en&ct=clnk&cd=3&gl=us&client=safari.

Dipippo, Ronald. Ideal Thermal Efficiency for Geothermal Binary Plants. *Geothermics* 36, no. 3 (June 2007): 276–285.

Dresselhaus, Millie. Basic Research Need for a Hydrogen Economy. Presentation at DOE BES Workshop, May 13–15, 2003. Washington, DC, June 24, 2004. https://public.ornl.gov/conf/nanosummit2004/ talks/3_Dresselhaus.pdf.

Ebeling, Ashlea. Do Solar While the Credit Shines. *Forbes Magazine*, December 12, 2005. http://www.forbes.com/investmentguide/ free_forbes/2005/1212/192.html.

Eckaus, Richard S., and Ian Sue Wing. Implications of the Historical Decline in U.S. Energy Intensity for Long Run CO_2 Emission Projections. *Energy Policy* 35, no. 11 (November 2007): 5267–5286.

Ellerman, A. Denny, and Barbara K. Buchner. The European Union Emissions Trading Scheme: Origins, Allocation, and Early Results. *Review of Environmental Economic Policy* 1, no. 1 (2007): 66–87.

Ellerman, A. Denny, and Paul L. Joskow. *The European Union's Emissions Trading System in Perspective.* Report of the Pew Center on Global Climate Change. Washington, DC: Pew Center on Global Climate Change, May 2008. http://www.pewclimate.org/docUploads/EU-ETS-In-Perspective-Report.pdf.

Ellerman, A. Denny, Paul L. Joskow, Richard Schmalensee, Juan-Pablo Montero, and Elizabeth M. Bailey. *Markets for Clean Air: The U.S. Acid Rain Program.* Cambridge: Cambridge University Press, 2000.

Energy Information Administration. *Commercial Buildings Energy Consumption Survey.* Report No. DOE.EIA-871. Washington, DC: EIA, 1995.

Energy Information Administration. *Commercial Buildings Characteristics.* Report No. DOE/EIS-E-0109. Washington, DC: EIA 1997.

Energy Information Administration. *Emissions of Greenhouse Gasses in the United States.* Report No. DOE/EIA-0573(2001). Washington, DC: EIA, December 2002. http://www.eia.doe.gov/oiaf/1605/archive/gg02rpt/index.html.

Energy Information Administration. *International Energy Outlook 2007.* Report No. DOE/EIA-0484. Washington, DC: EIA, 2007. http://www.eia.doe.gov/oiaf/ieo/index.html.

Energy Information Administration. *International Energy Outlook 2008.* Report No. DOE/EIA-0484. Washington, DC: EIA, 2008. http://www.eia.doe.gov/oiaf/ieo/.

Energy Information Administration. *Report on Federal Financial Interventions and Subsidies in Energy Markets 1999: Primary Energy.* Table ES-1. Washington, DC: EIA, 1999. http://www.eia.doe.gov/oiaf/servicerpt/subsidy/table_es1.html.

European Union. *EU Action against Climate Change, 2005.* http://ec.europa.eu/environment/climat/pdf/emission_trading3_en.pdf.

European Union, Directorates for Energy and Transport and for General Research. *Concentrating Solar Power: From Research to Implementation.* 2007. http://ec.europa.eu/energy/res/publications/doc/2007_concentrating_solar_power_en.pdf.

Ezell, Stephen and Robert Atkinson. *RAND's Rose-Colored Glasses.* Report. Washington, DC: Information Technology and Innovation Foundation (ITIF) September 10, 2008. http://www.itif.org/index.php?=174.

Federal Non-Nuclear Energy Research and Development Act of 1974, Public Law 93–577, 68 Stat. 1894, 42 U.S.C. 5913 (1974).

Figueiredo, M. A. de. *The Liability of Carbon Dioxide Storage.* Doctoral dissertation, MIT, 2007. http://sequestration.mit.edu/pdf/Mark_de_Figueiredo_PhD_Dissertation.pdf.

Figueiredo, M. A. de, H. J. Herzog, P. L. Joskow, K. A. Oye, and R. M. Reiner. *Regulating Carbon Dioxide Capture and Storage.* 07–003. Cambridge, MA: CEEPR, MIT, April 2007. http://web.mit.edu/ceepr/www/publications/workingpapers/2007–003.pdf.

Fong, Glenn R. ARPA Does Windows: The Defense Underpinning of the PC Revolution. *Business and Politics* 3, no. 3 (2001): 213–237.

Fong, Glenn R. Follower at the Frontier: International Competition and Japanese Industrial Policy. *International Studies Quarterly* 42, no. 2 (1998): 339–366.

Fong, Glenn R. Repositioning the Advanced Technology Program. *Issues in Science and Technology* (fall 2001): 65–70. http://www.issues.org/18.1/fong.html.

Freeman, Christopher. The National System of Innovation in Historical Perspective. *Cambridge Journal of Economics* 19 (1995): 5–24. http://cje.oxfordjournals.org/cgi/reprint/19/1/5.

Freeman, Christopher. Japan: A New National Innovation System. In G. Dosi, C. Freeman, R. R. Nelson, G. Silverberg, L. Soete, eds., *Technology and Economy Theory.* London: Pinter, 1988.

Fri, Robert W. From Energy Wish Lists to Technological Realities. *Issues in Science and Technology,* fall 2006. http://www.issues.org/23.1/fri.html.

Friedman, Thomas L. *Hot, Flat and Crowded: Why We Need a Green Revolution and How it Can Renew America.* New York: Farrar, Straus and Giroux, 2008.

Froomkin, A. Michael. Reinventing the Government Corporation.1995 U. Ill. L. Rev. 543 (1995). http://osaka.law.miami.edu/~froomkin/articles/reinvent.htm.

Gallagher, Kelly Sims, John P. Holdren, and Ambuj D. Sagar. Energy Technology Innovation. *Annual Review of Environment and Resources* 31 (November 2006): 193–327.

Ghoneim, Ahmed F. Meeting the Global Energy Challenge—Hydrogen. MIT Congressional Seminar, April 19, 2006.

Glowing After Dark. *The Economist,* August 7, 2008.

Goldemberg, José, Thomas B. Johansson, Amulya K.N. Reddy, and Rob Williams. *Energy for a Sustainable World.* Washington, DC: World Resources Institute, 1987.

Goodwyn, James C. DARPA Technology Transition. Report. Washington, DC: DOD, 1997. http://www.darpa.mil/body/pdf/transition.pdf.

Green, Bruce, and Gerald Nix. Geothermal—the Energy under Our Feet. NREL/TP 840–40665. Golden, CO.: National Renewable Energy Laboratory (NREL), November 2006. http://www1.eere.energy.gov/geothermal/pdfs/40665.pdf.

Green, William H. Liquid Fuels for Transportation. Presentation, MIT, April 20, 2006.

Griliches, Zvi. The Search for R&D Spillovers. *Scandinavian Journal of Economics* 94 (1992): 29–47.

Groode, Tiffany A. Review of Corn Based Ethanol Use and GHG Emissions. MIT LFEE Working Paper. Cambridge, MA: MIT LFEE June 2006.

"Grow Your Own—the Biofuels of the Future Will Be Tailor-Made," in "The Future of Energy," *The Economist,* June 2–27, 2008 (special report): 16–20.

Gurgel, Angelo, John M. Reilly, and Sergey Paltsev. Potential Land Use Implications of a Global Biofuels Industry. *Journal of Agricultural and Food Industrial Organization* 5, no. 2 (December 10, 2007). http://works.bepress.com/angelo_gurgel/1/.

Hawkins, D., D. Lashof, and R. Williams. What to Do about Coal. *Scientific American* 295, no. 3 (September 2006): 69–75.

Heller, Michael. *The Gridlock Economy: How Too Much Ownership Wrecks Markets, Stops Innovation, and Costs Lives.* New York: Basic Books 2008.

Herzog, Antonia V., and Daniel Kammen. Energy R&D: Investment Challenge. *Materials Today* 5, no. 5 (May 1, 2002). http://www. sciencedirect.com/science?_ob=MImg&_imagekey=B6X1 J-45NFNNM -15-9&_cdi=7244&_user=10&_orig=search&_coverDate=05%2F01 %2F2002&_sk=999949994&view=c&wchp=dGLbVlz-zSkzV& _valck=1&md5=a1f71c7a47eca507334818fab2023985&ie=/sdarticle .pdf.

Herzog, Howard. Coal and CCS. Presentation to CSIS Energy Technology Forum, Washington, DC, September 28, 2006.

Herzog, Howard. *Testimony before the House Committee on Natural Resources, Hearing to Explore Carbon Sequestration Technologies,* 110th Cong., 1st sess., May 1, 2007.

Herzog, Howard J. *Regulatory Framework for Carbon Capture and Storage (CCS): The Policy Problem.* MIT project proposal, December 8, 2006.

Hill, Christopher T. The Advanced Technology Program: Opportunities for Enhancement. In Lewis M. Branscomb and James H. Keller, eds., *Investing in Innovation: Creating a Research and Innovation Policy That Works,* 144–173. Cambridge, MA: MIT Press, 1998.

Holdren, John P. The Energy Innovation Imperative. *Innovations* 1, no. 2 (spring 2006): 3–23. http://www.mitpressjournals.org/doi/pdf/ 10.1162/itgg.2006.1.2.3.

Hong, E., L. A. Conroy, and M. J. Scholand. *U.S. Lighting Market Characterization: Energy Efficient Lighting Technology Options.* Technical Report, vol. 2. Washington, DC: Department of Energy, EERE, 2005.

Hosek, James, and Titus Galama. US Competitiveness in Science and Technology. Report. Santa Monica, CA: Rand Corp., June 2008 House Science Committee. *Hearings on ARPA-E Concept,* 109th Cong., 2nd sess. And 110th Cong., 1st sess., March 9, 2006, and April 26, 2007.

House Select Committee on Energy Independence and Global Warming. *Testimony of James Hansen, NASA, at Briefing on the Climate Threat to the Planet,* 110th Cong., 2nd sess., June 23, 2008. http:// www.columbia.edu/~jeh1/2008/TwentyYearsLater_20080623.pdf.

HR 6, Public Law 110–140, *The Energy Independence and Security Act of 2007,* 110th Cong., 1st sess. (passed Congress and signed December 19, 2007); earlier Senate version, HR 6, 110th Cong., 1st sess. (passed the Senate June 2, 2007).

HR 364, *Establishing the Advanced Research Projects Agency-Energy (ARPA-E) Act,* 109th Cong., 2nd sess.

HR 2272, *The America COMPETES Act,* Conference Report H. Rep. 110–289, 110th Cong., 1st sess. (passed Congress August 1, 2007; signed into law August 9, 2007), particularly Sec. 5012.

HR 3221, *New Direction for Energy Independence, National Security, and Consumer Protection Act,* 110th Cong., 1st sess. (passed the House August 4, 2007).

Hudson, Andrea, Kyle Danish, and Alex Lazur. Lieberman Warner Climate Change Cap and Trade Bill Seen as Framework for Senate Climate Debate. Report. Washington, DC: Van Ness, Feldman, October 19, 2007. http://www.vnf.com/news-alerts-217.html.

IEA. *Energy Technology Perspectives 2008: Scenarios and Strategies to 2050.* June 6, 2008. http://www.iea.org/Textbase/techno/etp/ETP_2008.pdf.

IEA. *World Energy Outlook 2008.* November 12, 2008, http://www.iea.org/Textbase/npsum/WEO2008SUM.pdf (summary).

Interacademy Council. *Lighting the Way.* October 22, 2007, 42–44. http://www.interacademycouncil.net/?id=12161.

IPCC. *Fourth Assessment, Climate Change 2007 Synthesis Report— Summary for Policymakers.* Geneva, Switzerland: IPCC, November 17, 2007. (Citing Section 5.5 of longer report.) http://www.ipcc.ch/pdf/assessment-report/ar4/syr/ar4_syr_spm.pdf.

IPCC, Working Group III, Mark Levine and Diana Urge Vorsatz, lead authors. Chap. 6 (Residential and Commercial Buildings): 389–430. *IPCC Fourth Assessment Report.* Cambridge: Cambridge University Press, 2007. http://www.ipcc.ch/pdf/assessment-report/ar4/wg3/ar4-wg3-chapter6.pdf.

IPCC, Working Group III, Nebojsa Nakicenovic and Rob Swart, eds., *Special Report on Emissions Scenarios.* Cambridge: Cambridge University Press, March 2000. http://www.grida.no/climate/ipcc/emission/.

Jaffe, Judson, and Robert Stavins, *Linking Tradable Permit Systems for Greenhouse Gas Emissions: Opportunities, Implications and Challenges,* Report for the International Emissions Trading Association (Geneva Switzerland and Washington, DC: International Emissions Trading Association, November 2007). http://www.ieta.org/ieta/www/pages/getfile.php?docID=2733.

Jochem, Eberhard A. An Efficient Solution. *Scientific American*, September 2006, 64–67.

Johnson, Robbin S., and C. Ford Runge. Ethanol: The Train Wreck Ahead. *Issues in Science and Technology* (Fall 2007): 25–30. http://www.issues.org/24.1/p_johnson.html.

Joint Committee on Taxation. *Estimated Budget Effects of the Conference Agreement for Title XIII of HR 6, the Energy Tax Incentives Act of 2005 JCX 59–05*. July 27, 2005. http://www.house.gov/jct/x-59-05.pdf.

Jones, Charles I., and John C. Williams. Measuring the Social Return to R&D. *Quarterly Journal of Economics* 13, no. 114 (1998): 1119–1135.

Jorgenson, Dale. U.S. Economic Growth in the Information Age. *Issues in Science and Technology*, fall 2001. http://www.issues.org/18.1/jorgenson.html.

Kalicki, Jan, and David Goldwyn, eds. *Energy Security*. Baltimore: Woodrow Wilson Center/Johns Hopkins University Press, 2005.

Kammen, Daniel M. The Rise of Renewal Energy. *Scientific American* 295, no. 3 (September 2006): 86–89.

Kammen, Daniel M., and Gregory Nemet. Real Numbers: Reversing the Incredible Shrinking Energy R&D Budget. *Issues in Science and Technology*, fall 2005. http://rael.berkeley.edu/files/2005/Kammen-Nemet-ShrinkingRD-2005.pdf.

Kanan, Matthew W., and Daniel G. Nocera. In Situ Formation of an Oxygen-Evolving Catalyst in Neutral Water Containing Phosphate and Co^{2+}, *Science Online DOI*: 10.1126/science.1162018, July 31, 2008. http://www.sciencemag.org/cgi/content/abstract/1162018.

Karsner, Alexander. *Testimony of the Assistant Secretary for Energy Efficiency and Renewable Energy, before the Subcommittee on Energy and Water Development, Committee on Appropriations, United States Senate*, April 11, 2007. http://www.congressional.energy.gov/documents/April_12_-_EE_-_Karsner.pdf.

Katzer, James. *Testimony on Coal-Based Power Generation with CO_2 Capture and Sequestration, Senate Committee on Commerce, Science, and Transportation, Science, Energy, and Innovation Subcommittee*, 110th Cong., 1st sess., March 20, 2007.

Keasling, Jay D., and Howard Chou. Metabolic Engineering Delivers Next-Generation Biofuels. *Nature Biotechnology* 263 (March 26, 2008): 298–299.

Kenderdine, Melanie A., and Ernest J. Moniz. Technology Development and Energy Security. In David Goldwyn and Jan Kalicki, eds., *Energy Security in the 21st Century*. Baltimore: Woodrow Wilson Center, 2004: 429–459.

Kennedy, Donald. The Biofuels Conundrum. *Science* 316 (April 27, 2007): 515. http://physics.indiana.edu/~brabson/p310/kennedy.pdf.

Krauss, Clifford. Ethanol's Boom Stalling as Glut Depresses Prices. *New York Times*, September 30, 2007, Business section. http://www.nytimes.com/2007/09/30/business/30ethanol.html?_r=1&ref=business&oref=slogin.

Kreith, Frank, and Ron West. The Fallacies of a Hydrogen Economy. *Journal of Energy Resources Technology* 126, no. 4 (December 2004): 249–257.

Lazowska, Edward D., and David Paterson. An Endless Frontier Postponed. *Science* 308 (May 6, 2005): 757. http://www.sciencemag.org/cgi/content/summary/308/5723/757.

Lerner, Josh. The Design of Effective Public Venture Capital Programs. Paper in NIST, *Managing Technical Risk*, NIST GCR 00–787 (April 2000): 80–93.

Lester, Richard K. Universities, Innovation and the Competitiveness of Local Economies. Cambridge, MA: MIT Industrial Performance Center Working Paper 05-010 (Dec. 2005).

Lieberman, Joseph I. Global Warming Goes to Market. *The American Interest* 1, no. 1 (autumn 2005). http://www.the-american-interest.com/ai2/article.cfm?Id=63&MId=1 [portion of article].

Lipsey, Richard G. *Economic Transformations: General Purpose Technologies and Long-Term Economic Growth*. New York: Oxford University Press, 2005.

Lundvall, Bengt-Ake. *Innovation, Growth and Social Cohesion*. Cheltenham, UK: Edward Elgar, 2002.

Lundvall, Bengt-Ake. National Innovation Systems—Analytical Concept and Development Tool. 14 *Industry and Innovation 1*, (February 2007): 95–119.

Machiavelli, Niccolò. *The Prince and the Discourses.* New York: Modern Library, [1513] 1950. 21.

Markoff, John. Clouds over "Blue Sky" Research Agency. *New York Times,* May 4, 2005, 12.

Matthews, H. Damon, and Ken Caldeira. Stabilizing Climate Requires Near-Zero Emissions. *Geophysical Research Letters* 35, February 27, 2008. http://www.agu.org/pubs/crossref/2008/2007GL032388.shtml.

McCormick, David. *Undersecretary of the Treasury for International Affairs, Testimony before the Subcommittee on Monetary Policy of the House Financial Services Committee on $2b Proposed U.S. Contributions to the $10b Clean Technology Fund,* 110th Cong., 2nd sess., June 6, 2008.

McGee, Tim. Cut Solar Subsidies? Update with Vinod Khosla. *Los Angeles Times,* October 24, 2006. http://www.treehugger.com/files/2006/10/cut_solar_subsi_1.php.

McGuinness, Meghan, and A. Denny Ellerman. *The Effects of Interactions between Federal and State Climate Policies.* Report 08–004. Cambridge, MA: MIT Center for Energy and Environmental Policy Analysis, May 2008. http://web.mit.edu/ceepr/www/publications/workingpapers/2008–004.pdf.

MIT. *The Future of Coal.* Cambridge, MA: MIT, March 14, 2007. http://web.mit.edu/coal/The_Future_of_Coal.pdf.

MIT. *The Future of Geothermal Energy—Impact of Enhanced Geothermal Systems (EGS) on the U.S. in the 21st Century.* Cambridge, MA: MIT, February 2007. http://geothermal.inel.gov/publications/future_of_geothermal_energy.pdf.

MIT. *The Future of Nuclear Power.* Cambridge, MA: MIT, 2003. http://web.mit.edu/nuclearpower/.

MIT Energy Research Council. *Report of the Energy Research Council.* Cambridge, MA: MIT, May 3, 2006. http://web.mit.edu/mitei/about/erc-report-final.pdf.

MIT Joint Program on the Science and Policy of Global Climate Change. *The Environmental and Policy Issues Posed by New Concept Energy Technologies Operating at the Scale Required to Impact the Climate Problem.* Unpublished study proposal. February 21, 2007.

Mitchell, Donald. A Note on Rising Food Prices. World Bank Policy Working Paper 4682. Washington, D.C.: The World Bank

Development Prospects Group, July 2008. http://www.wds .worldbank.org/external/default/WDSContentServer/IW3P/1B/2008/ 07/28/000020439_20080728103002/Rendered/PDF/WP4682.pdf

Nadiri, M. Ishaq. *Innovations and Technological Spillovers.* NBER Working Paper No. 4423. Cambridge, MA: National Bureau of Economic Research, 1993.

National Academy of Sciences. *Rising above the Gathering Storm.* Washington, DC: National Academy of Sciences, 2007. http://www .nap.edu/openbook.php?record_id=11463&page=R1.

National Academy of Sciences. Board on Science, Technology, and Economic Policy. *Partnerships for Solid State Lighting.* Washington, DC: National Academy of Sciences, 2002.

National Academy of Sciences, Board on Energy and Environmental Systems, *Energy: What You Need to Know.* Washington, DC: National Academy of Sciences, 2008.

National Commission on Energy Policy, *Ending the Energy Stalemate: A Bipartisan Strategy to Meet America's Energy Challenges.* December 1, 2004. http://www.energycommission.org/ht/a/ GetDocumentAction/i/1088.

National Research Council, Board on Energy and Environmental Systems. *Energy: What You Need to Know.* Washington, DC: National Academy of Sciences, 2008. http://www7.nationalacademies.org/ energy/energy_booklet_pdf.pdf.

National Research Council. *Energy Research at DOE: Was It Worth It?* Washington, DC: National Academies of Science, 2001.

National Research Council, Board on Science, Technology and Economic Policy. *21st Century Innovation Systems for Japan and the United States: Lessons from a Decade of Change.* 2008. (in publication).

National Research Council, Board on Science, Technology, and Economic Policy *SBIR: Challenges and Opportunities.* Report. Washington, DC: National Academy Press, 1999.

National Research Council, Board on Science, Technology, and Economic Policy, *The Advanced Technology Program: Challenges and Opportunities.* Report. Washington, DC: National Academies Press, 1999.

National Research Council, Science and Telecommunications Board, Funding a Revolution: Government Support for Computing Research. Report. Washington, DC: National Academy Press, 1999.

Nelson, Richard R. *National Systems of Innovation*. New York: Oxford University Press, 1993.

Nelson, Richard R., and Sidney G. Winter. *An Evolutionary Theory of Economic Change*. Cambridge, MA: Harvard University Press, 1982.

Nemet, Gregory. *Policy and Innovation in Low Carbon Energy Technologies*. Unpublished doctoral dissertation, UC Berkeley, 2007.

Nemet, Gregory, and Daniel Kammen. U.S. Energy R&D: Declining Investment, Increasing Need, and the Feasibility of Expansion. *Energy Policy* 35 (2007): 747.

Newell, Richard G., and Nathan E. Wilson. *Technology Prizes for Climate Change Mitigation*. RFF Discussion Paper 05–33. Washington, DC: Resources for the Future, June 2005. http://www.rff.org/RFF/Documents/RFF-DP-05–33.pdf.

Nordhaus, Robert, and Kyle Danish. *Designing a Mandatory Greenhouse Gas Reduction Program for the U.S.* Executive Summary. Washington, DC: Pew Center for Global Climate Change, May 2003. http://www.pewclimate.org/docUploads/USGas.pdf.

William Nordhaus, *A Question of Balance: Weighing the Options for Global Warming Policies*. New Haven, CT: Yale Univ. Press, 2008.

Ogden, Joan. High Hopes for Hydrogen. *Scientific American* 295, no. 3 (September 2006): 94–101.

Ohmae, Kenichi. *The End of the Nation State*. New York: Simon & Schuster, 1995.

Ohmae, Kenichi. *The Next Global State—Challenges and Opportunities in Our Borderless World*. Philadelphia: Wharton 2005.

Pacala, Stephen W., and Robert H. Socolow. Stabilization Wedges: Solving the Climate Problem for the Next 50 Years with Current Technologies. *Science* 305 (August 13, 2004): 968. http://carbonsequestration.us/Papers-presentations/htm/Pacala-Socolow-ScienceMag-Aug2004.pdf.

Paltsev, S. J., J. Reilly, H. Jacoby, A. Gurgel, G. Metcalf, A. Sokolov, and J. Holak. *Assessment of U.S. Cap-and-Trade Proposals*. Report No. 146. Cambridge, MA: MIT Joint Program on the Science and Policy of Global Change, April 2007. http://web.mit.edu/globalchange/www/MITJPSPGC_Rpt146.pdf.

Perez, Carlota. *Technological Revolutions and Financial Capital*. Cheltenham, UK: Edward Elgar, 2002.

Pharmaceutical Research and Manufacturers of America (PhRMA). R&D Spending by Biopharmaceutical Reaches $58.8 Billion in 2007. March 24, 2008. http://www.phrma.org/news_room/press_releases/ us_biopharmaceutical_companies_r%26d_spending_reaches_record _%2458.8_billion_in_2007/.

Pizer, William A. *A U.S. Perspective on Future Climate Regimes.* RFF Discussion Paper 07–04. Washington, DC: Resources for the Future, February 2007.

Podesta, John, Todd Stern, and Kit Batten. *Capturing the Energy Opportunity: Creating a Low-Carbon Economy.* Washington, DC: Center for American Progress, November 27, 2007.

Pogue, Forest C. *George C. Marshall—Statesman 1945–1959.* New York: Viking Penguin, 1987.

Pontin, Jason. Vinod Khosla, Veteran VC's New Energy: Q and A. *Technology Review,* March/April 2007, 32. www.technologyreview .com/energy/18299/.

Popp, David. The Effect of New Technology on Energy Consumption. *Resource and Energy Economics* 23 (2001): 215–239.

Prather, Kristala Jones. *Testimony to the Senate Committee on Energy and Natural Resources, Conference on Accelerated Biofuels Diversity,* February 1, 2007, and accompanying *Comments Submitted to the Committee on Question 5 on Required R&D,* 110th Cong., 1st sess., January 26, 2007.

President's Council of Advisors on Science and Technology (PCAST). *Report to the President on Federal Energy R&D for the Challenges of the 21st Century.* Washington, DC: Executive Office of the President 7, November 1997. http://www.ostp.gov/cs/report_to _the_president_on_federal_energy_research_and_development_for _the_challenges_of_the_twentyfirst_century_table_of_contents.

President's Council of Advisors on Science and Technology (PCAST). *The Energy Imperative: Technology and the Role of Emerging Companies.* Washington, DC: OSTP, Executive Office of the President of the United States, November 2006. http://www.ostp.gov/pcast/ PCAST-EnergyImperative_FINAL.pdf.

President's Information Technology Advisory Committee (PITAC). *Cybersecurity: A Crisis of Prioritization.* Report to the President. February 2005. http://www.nitrd.gov/pitac/reports/20050301 _cybersecurity/cybersecurity.pdf.

Price, Harry B. *Marshall Plan and Its Meaning.* Ithaca, NY: Cornell University Press, 1955.

Public Law 96–480, *Stevenson-Wydler Technology Innovation Act of 1980* (1980), as amended by the *Federal Technology Transfer Act of 1986*, Public Law 99–502, (1986).

Public Law 99–272, *Termination of US SFC Act*, Title VII, Subtitle E, 100 stat. 143 (April 7, 1986).

Public Law 101–548, *Clean Air Act Amendments of 1990* (November 15, 1991).

Public Law 109–058, *Energy Policy Act of 2005* (July 29, 2005).

Rauch, Jonathan. Electro-Shock Therapy. *Atlantic,* July/August 2008, http://www.theatlantic.com/doc/200807/general-motors.

Reilly, John, and Sergey Palsev. *Biomass Energy and Competition for Land.* Report No. 145. Cambridge, MA: MIT Joint Program on the Science and Policy of Global Change, April 2007. http://web.mit.edu/globalchange/www/MITJPSPGC_Rpt145.pdf.

Reis, Victor. Nuclear Energy, Nuclear Weapons and Climate Change. Unpublished presentation, Washington, DC: Department of Energy, June 2008.

Romer, Paul M. Endogenous Technological Change. *Journal of Political Economy* 98, no. 5 (1990). http://www.nber.org/papers/w3210.pdf.

Romer, Paul M. Implementing a National Technology Strategy with Self-Organizing Investment Boards. In Martin N. Baily and Peter C. Reiss, eds., *Macronomics 1993.* Brookings Papers on Economic Activity. Washington, DC: Brookings Institution Press, 1993.

Romm, Joseph J. *Hell and High Water: Global Warming—the Solution and the Politics—and What We Should Do.* New York: Morrow, 2007.

Rosenthal, Elisabeth. China Leads the World in Emissions of Carbon Dioxide. *New York Times,* June 14, 2008. http://www.nytimes.com/2008/06/14/world/asia/14china.html.

Rotman, David. The Price of Biofuels. *Technology Review* 111, no. 1 (January–February 2008): 42. http://www.technologyreview.com/Energy/19842/.

Runge, C. Ford, and Benjamin Senauer. How Biofuels Could Starve the Poor. *Foreign Affairs* 86, no. 3 (May–June 2007): 41–53.

http://www.foreignaffairs.org/20070501faessay86305/c-ford-runge
-benjamin-senauer/how-biofuels-could-starve-the-poor.html.

Ruttan, Vernon W. *Is War Necessary for Economic Growth? Military Procurement and Technology Development.* New York: Oxford University Press, 2006.

Ruttan, Vernon W. *Technology Growth and Development: An Induced Innovation Perspective* (New York: Oxford University Press, 2001).

Ruttan, Vernon W. Will Government Programs Spur the Next Breakthrough? *Issues in Science and Technology,* winter 2006. http://www.issues.org/22.2/ruttan.html.

Ruttan, Vernon W., and Yujiro Hayami. *Agricultural Development: An International Perspective.* Baltimore, MD: Johns Hopkins University Press, 1985 ed.).

Ruttan, Vernon W., and Yujiro Hayami, "Induced Innovation Model of Agricultural Development," in Carl K. Eicher and John M. Staatz, eds., *International Agricultural Development.* Baltimore, MD: Johns Hopkins University Press 1998, 3rd ed., 163–178.

S. 761, *America COMPETES Act,* 110th Cong., 1st sess. (passed Senate April 25, 2007 as amended).

S. 932, *Energy Security Act, Public Law 96–294* (June 23, 1980).

S. 1151, *The McCain-Lieberman Climate Stewardship and Innovation Act of 2005,* 109th Cong., 1st sess. http://thomas.loc.gov/cgi-bin/bdquery/z?d109:s.01151.

S. 2191, *The Climate Security Act,* introduced October 18, 2007, 110th Cong., 1st sess. (debated on the Senate floor, as amended, as S. 3036), 110th Cong., 2nd sess. (June 6, 2008).

S. 2730, *Clean Energy Investment Bank Act,* 110th Cong., 2nd Sess. (introduced by Sen. Domenici, March 6, 2008).

S. 3036, *Boxer-Lieberman-Warner Substitute Amendment to S. 2191,* 110th Cong., 2nd sess. (introduced May 21, 2008), Title III, Subtitle B, Sec. 321–322.

S. 3233, *21st Century Energy Technology Deployment Act,* 110th Cong., 2nd Sess. (introduced by Sen. Bingaman, July 11, 2008).

Sachs, Jeffrey. Technological Keys to Climate Protection. *Scientific American* 297, March 2008. http://www.sciam.com/article.cfm?id=keys-to-climate-protection.

Sachs, Jeffrey. The Road to Clean Energy Starts Here. *Scientific American* 296, April 2007. http://www.sciam.com/article.cfm?id =the-road-to-clean-energy&SID=mail&sc=emailfriend.

Sanderson, Susan W., Kenneth L. Simons, Judith L. Walls, and Yin-Yi Lai. Lighting. In National Research Council, Board on Science, Technology, and Economic Policy, *Innovation in Global Industries*. Washington, DC: National Research Council, 2008.

Schelling, Thomas C. Climate Change: The Uncertainties, the Certainties and What They Imply about Action. *The Economists' Voice* 4, no. 3, article 3 (2007). http://www.bepress.com/ev/vol4/iss3/ art3.

Schilling, Melissa. *Strategic Management of Technological Innovation*. New York: McGraw-Hill, 2005.

Schock, Robert N. , William Fulkerson, Merwin Brown, Robert San Martin, David Greene, and Jae Edmonds. How Much Is Energy R&D Worth as Insurance? *Annual Review of Energy and the Environment* 24 (1999): 487–512.

Semiconductor Industry Association (SIA). Industry Facts and Figures. 2007. http://www.sia-online.org/ind_facts.cfm.

Senate Budget Committee. Hearing on the Long-Term Budget Outlook. *Testimony of GAO Comptroller General David Walker*. 110th Cong., 1st sess., January 11, 2007. http://www.senate.gov/~budget/ democratic/testimony/2007/Walkers%20Long-term%20Testimony .pdf. http://www.senate.gov/~budget/democratic/charts/2007/Hearings/ packet_LTBixby013107.pdf.

Senate Committee on Energy and Natural Resources. Hearing to Investigate Market Constraints on Large Investments in Advanced Energy Technologies. Senate Hearing 110–63, 110th Cong., 1st sess., March 7, 2007.

Senate Committee on Energy and Natural Resources. Hearings on the Global Nuclear Energy Partnership as It Relates to U.S. Policy on Nuclear Fuel Management. 110th Cong., 1st sess. (November 14, 2007). http://frwebgate.access.gpo.gov/cgi-bin/getdoc.cgi?dbname =110_senate_hearings&docid=f:41099.wais.

Senate Committee on Energy and Natural Resources. Hearings on Legislation to Improve the Availability of Financing for Deployment of Clean Energy and Energy Efficiency Technologies and to Enhance

United States' Competitiveness in this Market, S. 3233 and S. 2730, 110th Cong., 2nd sess. (July 15, 2008).

Shao-Horn, Yang. An Alternative Technology for Transportation: Fuel Cell Hybrid Vehicles. Presentation to CSIS Energy Technology Forum, Washington, DC, September 28, 2006.

Shapiro, Robert, Nan Phan, and Arun Malik. *Addressing Climate Change without Impairing the U.S. Economy—the Economics and Environmental Science of Combining a Carbon-Based Tax and Tax Relief*. Washington, DC: U.S. Climate Task Force, June 2008. http://www.climatetaskforce.org/pdf/CTF_CarbonTax_Earth_Spgs .pdf.

Shinnar, Reuel. The Hydrogen Economy. *Technology in Society* 25, no. 4 (2003): 455–476.

Sklar, Scott. The Solar Subsidy Crutch or an Uneven Playing Field? *Renewable Energy Access*, April 25, 2006. http://www .renewableenergyaccess.com/rea/news/story?id=44723.

Smil, Vaclaw. *Energy in Nature and Society: General Energetics of Complex Systems*. Cambridge, MA: MIT Press, 2008.

Sobel, Dava. *Longitude*. New York: Walker and Co., [1995] 2005.

Socolow, Robert H., and Stephen W. Pacala. A Plan to Keep Carbon in Check. *Scientific American* 295, no. 3 (September 2006): 50–57. http://www.princeton.edu/mae/people/faculty/socolow/socdoc/ carbonincheck.pdf.

Solar PV Set to Grow. *Oxford Analytica*, May 9, 2008.

Solow, Robert M. *Growth Theory: An Exposition*. 2nd ed. New York: Oxford University Press, 2000. (Nobel Prize Lecture, December 8, 1987.)

Stauffer, Nancy. Ethanol Study Show Biofuels Benefits. *MIT Tech Talk* 51, no. 15 (January 24, 2007). http://mit.edu/newsoffice/2007/ techtalk/51-15.pdf.

Stauffer, Nancy. *Research Spotlight: Algae System Transforms Greenhouse Emissions into Fuel*. Research of Isaac Berzin. Cambridge, MA: MIT ERC, 2006. http://web.mit.edu/erc/spotlights/ alg.html.

Stauffer, Nancy. *Research Spotlight: Engineering Viruses: Using Biology to Assemble Materials, Devices*. Research of Angela Belcher.

Cambridge, MA: MIT ERC, 2006. http://web.mit.edu/erc/spotlights/vir.html.

Stauffer, Nancy. *Research Spotlight: Giant Wind Turbines Floating Out of Sight*. Research of Paul D. Sclavounos. Cambridge, MA: MIT ERC, 2008. http://web.mit.edu/erc/spotlights/wind.html.

Stauffer, Nancy. *Research Spotlight: Making Solar Cells from Ribbons*. Research of Emanuel Sachs. Cambridge, MA: MIT ERC, 2006. http://web.mit.edu/erc/spotlights/solar_cells.html.

Steinfeld, Edward S. *Testimony to the House Committee on Energy and Commerce, Hearing on Climate Change—International Issues, Engaging Developing Countries*. 110th Cong., 1st sess., March 27, 2007. http://energycommerce.house.gov/cmte_mtgs/110-eaq-hrg.032707.Steinfeld-testimony.pdf.

Stephanopoulos, Gregory. Challenges in Engineering Microbes for Biofuels Production. *Science* 315 (February 9, 2007): 801–804.

Stern, Nicholas. *Stern Review on the Economics of Climate Change*. London: H. M. Treasury, 2006. http://www.hm-treasury.gov.uk/media/4/3/Executive_Summary.pdf.

Stokes, Donald E. *Pasteur's Quadrant: Basic Science and Technological Innovation*. Washington, DC: Brookings Institution Press, 1997.

Stolberg, Sheryl Gay. Richest Nations Pledge to Halve Greenhouse Gas—G8 Call for GHG Reductions beyond Stabilization. *New York Times*, July 9, 2008, Science/Environment section. http://www.nytimes.com/2008/07/09/science/earth/09climate.html.

Talbot, David. Emerging Technologies 2007—Nanocharging Solar. *Technology Review*, March/April 2007. http://www.technologyreview.com/Energy/18285.

Tester, Jefferson W., Elisabeth M. Drake, Michael J. Driscoll, Michael W. Golay, and William A. Peters. *Sustainable Energy: Choosing among Options*. Cambridge, MA: MIT Press, 2005.

Thompson, Elizabeth A. MIT Opens New "Window on Solar Energy. MIT News Office, July 10, 2008. http://web.mit.edu/newsoffice/2008/solarcells-0710.html.

Thorsteinsson, Hildigunnur, Chad Augustine, Brian Anderson, Michal Moore, P. von Rohr, T. Rothenfluh, and Jefferson Tester. Sustainable Energy Opportunities with the Geothermal Continuum. Paper, NSTI Nanotech 2008, June 1–5, 2008.

Thorsteinsson, Hildigunnur, Chad Augustine, Brian Anderson, Michal Moore, and Jefferson Tester. The Impacts of Drilling and Reservoir Technology Advances on EGS Exploitation. Paper, *Proceedings of the Thirty-Third Workshop on Geothermal Reservoir Engineering*, January 28–30, 2008.

Trafton, Anne. Major Discovery from MIT Primed to Unleash Solar Revolution. MIT News Office, July 31, 2008. http://web.mit.edu/newsoffice/2008/oxygen-0731.html.

UD Team Sets Solar Record. *Science Daily*, July 30, 2007. http://www.sciencedaily.com/releases/2007/07/070726210931.htm.

UD-Led Team Sets Solar Cell Record. *University of Delaware Daily*, July 23, 2007. http://www.udel.edu/PR/UDaily/2008/jul/solar072307.html.

Uranium Information Centre. *Nuclear Power in France*. Briefing Paper No. 28. April 2007. http://www.uic.com.au/nip28.htm.

Urge-Vorsatz, Diana, L. D. Harvey, Sevastianos Mirasgedis, and Mark D. Levine. Mitigating CO_2 Emissions from Energy Use in the World's Buildings. *Building and Research Information*, 2007. http://web.ceu.hu/envsci/publication/duv/BRImitiginbldgsppr2007.pdf.

Utterback, James M. *Mastering the Dynamics of Innovation*. Boston: Harvard Business School Press, 1996.

Van Atta, Richard H., Sidney G. Reed, and Seymour J. Deitchman. *DARPA Technical Accomplishments: An Historical Review of Selected DARPA Projects*. Vols. 1–5. Alexandria, VA: IDA, 1991.

Venture Capital Investment in Renewable Energy Soars to $3.4 Billion in 2007. Reuters, *Business Wire*, January 16, 2007. http://www.reuters.com/article/pressRelease/idUS153866+16-Jan-2008+BW20080116.

Vermerris, Wilfred, ed. *Genetic Improvement of Bioenergy Crops*. New York: Springer, 2008.

Waldrop, M. Mitchell. *Complexity*. New York: Simon & Schuster, 1992.

Waldrop, M. Mitchell. *The Dream Machine—JCR Licklider and the Revolution That Made Computing Personal*. New York: Viking, 2001.

Walker, David M. A Call for Stewardship. National Press Club speech by U.S. Comptroller General, December 17, 2007. http://www.gao.gov/cghome/d08371cg.pdf.

Weiss, Charles. *The Marshall Plan: Lessons for U.S. Assistance to Central and Eastern Europe and the Former Soviet Union.* Atlantic Council Occasional Paper. Washington, DC: Atlantic Council, 1995.

Wexler, Imanuel. *Marshall Plan Revisited.* Westport, CT: Greenwood Press, 1983.

Williams, Eric, Nora Greenglass, and Rebecca Ryals. *Carbon Capture, Pipeline, and Storage: A Viable Option for N.C. Utilities?* Report No. CC PP WP 07–01. Durham, NC: Nicholas Institute for Environmental Policy, Duke University, March 8, 2007. http://www.nicholas.duke.edu/institute/carboncapture.pdf.

Wilson, Theodore A. *The Marshall Plan: An Atlantic Venture of 1947–51 and How It Shaped the World.* New York: Foreign Policy Association, June 1977.

Wind Power Expands in Renewables Search. *Oxford Analytica,* November 15, 2007.

Wiser, Ryan H., and Galen Barbose. *Renewable Portfolio Standards in the U.S.: A Status Report with Data through 2007.* Berkeley, CA: Lawrence Berkeley National Laboratory, April 10, 2008. http://eetd.lbl.gov/ea/ems/reports/ibnl-154e-revised.pdf—or— http://eetd.lbl.gov/ea/ems/emp-ppt.html.

World Bank. *Proposal for a Clean Technology Fund.* Report on Design Meeting on Climate Investment Funds, Washington, DC: World Bank April 3, 2008. http://siteresources.worldbank.org/INTCC/Resources/Proposal_For_A_Clean_Technology_Fund_April_3_2008.pdf.

World Economic Forum. *Global Competitiveness Report 2007–08–National Competitiveness Rankings.* October 31, 2007. http://www.gcr.weforum.org/.

Wright, Tom. Indian Wind Turbine Firm Hits Turbulence, *Wall Street Journal,* June 30, 2008, 31.

WTRG Economics. *Oil Price History and Economics.* 2007. wtrg.com/prices.html.

Wulf, William A., and Thomas Leighton. Testimony to the House Science Committee Hearing on the Future of Computer Science Research in the U.S., 109th Cong., 1st sess., May 12, 2005; Joint Statement of the Computing Research Community; Letters in

Response to Committee Questions from W. Wulf and T. Leighton, July 2005; and DARPA responses to Committee Questions, House Science Committee Hearing, May 12, 2005 (DARPA Testimony, including Appendices A–D).

Yanuzzi, Rick E. In-Q-Tel: A New Partnership between the CIA and the Private Sector. *Defense Intelligence Journal* 9, no. 1 (2000). https://www.cia.gov/library/publications/additional-publications/in-q-tel/index.html#author.

Yokell, Michael D. The Role of the Government in Subsidizing Solar Energy. *American Economic Review* 69, no. 2, containing *Papers and Proceedings of the Ninety-First Annual Meeting of the American Economic Association*, May 1979.

Zittrain, Jonathan. *The Future of the Internet—And How to Stop It.* New Haven, CT: Yale University Press, 2008.

Zubrin, Robert. In Defense of Biofuels. *New Atlantis: A Journal of Technology and Society*, spring 2008. http://www.thenewatlantis.com/publications/in-defense-of-biofuels.

Index